THE GOLF FANATIC'S
GUIDE TO
HAWAII

Aloha!

THE GOLF FANATIC'S
GUIDE TO
HAWAII

BRYAN FRYKLUND

Photos by
JEN REEDER

HOT TUB
PUBLISHING

THE GOLF FANATIC'S GUIDE TO HAWAII
by Bryan Fryklund

Published by:
Hot Tub Publishing
P.O. Box 12227
Denver, CO 80212

The Golf Fanatic's Guide to Hawaii and Fanatic Guides™ are a trademark of Hot Tub Publishing.

Visit www.hottubpublishing.com for more titles, or www.fanaticguides.com for upcoming Fanatic Guide titles.

Interior design by Hot Tub Publishing.
Photographs by Jen Reeder, unless otherwise noted. See Acknowledgements.
Cover design by Christina Jackson.

Library of Congress Control Number: 2008929755

Publisher's Cataloging-in-Publication data

Fryklund, Bryan George.
  The golf fanatic's guide to Hawaii / Bryan Fryklund; photos by Jen Reeder.
  p. cm.
  Series: Fanatic Guides.
  Includes index.
  ISBN 978-1-935008-11-8
1. Golf courses--Hawaii--Guidebooks. 2. Golf courses--Hawaii--Maui. 3. Golf courses--Hawaii--Oahu. 4. Golf courses--Hawaii--Lanai. 5. Golf courses--Hawaii--Kauai. 6. Golf courses--Hawaii--Molokai. 7. Hawaii--Description and travel. 8. Hawaii--Guidebooks. I. Reeder, Jen. II. Series. III. Title.

GV975 .F79 2008
796.352/06/8969 20--dc22   2008929755

Production in the United States of America.
Printed in the United States of America by Lifetouch.

1% of the net sales of this book benefit Hawaii Literacy, www.hawaiiliteracy.org.

For the golfers in my life

But especially... for Jen

Early morning on the first at Coral Creek Golf Course

TABLE OF CONTENTS

Images of Hoakalei Country Club, opening late 2008

FOREWORD

I'm happy to have been given the opportunity to write this foreword for the Golf Fanatic's Guide to Hawaii. I'd certainly count myself a golf fanatic and I'm a big fan of Hawaii. I've been bringing my family here for many years and we've always loved our time in the islands. We've stayed in some lovely places, met a lot of great people and made some good friends, too.

I also have a lot of good memories of playing in the PGA Tour's twin curtain-raiser tournaments—the Mercedes Championship and the Sony Open. I've been fortunate enough to win them both and have always enjoyed the two courses that we play—the Plantation Course at Kapalua and Waialae Country Club in Honolulu. But at the same time, I know there are many other wonderful courses spread around these beautiful islands of Hawaii. I hope to someday have the opportunity to explore more of them.

Many of these courses are publicly accessible—open to all golfers, basically—and the top-50 are featured in this guide book. I hope the photos and course descriptions will inspire you to go and play as many of these golf courses as possible . . . in time, maybe even all of them. Now there's a lifetime goal worth shooting for!

As I said, I always look forward to my trips to Hawaii and am very excited about the opening of our own golf course here, Hoakalei Country Club. It is the first new golf course on the island of Oahu in over 10 years, and like so many Hawaii courses, the setting is beautiful. The course is located just 20 minutes from Honolulu and overlooks the stunning Ewa coastline. I do hope you get to play this course some day, too, because I know you'd enjoy it.

But that's one of the great things about Hawaii, there are so many courses to enjoy that Golf Fanatics are literally spoilt for choice. Hey, that's the kind of dilemma we'd all like to have.

Enjoy this guide book . . . and enjoy your golf!

—Ernie Els

Haleakala on Maui hovers over the 17th green at Hualalai on the Big Island.

INTRODUCTION

Hawaii is powerfully alluring. It is one of those modern rarities, where reality measures up to glossy ad campaigns. The beaches really are that powdery. The ocean really is that blue. Hawaii offers so many fantastic images for us to dream about when we slog off to another day at the office on a cold rainy day in November. Some want nothing more than a hammock under the palms. Others daydream of riding horses through lush green valleys on their way to a secret waterfall, or battling some of the largest waves in the world with only a piece of fiberglass between ultimate exhilaration or serious injury. Many want to view flowing lava, while others just want a pool to splash around in with their family. And then, for those of us with the fever, the illness, the addiction . . . for us, there's the golf.

Like the rest of these images of Hawaii, the reality is that Hawaiian golf courses are everything you've dreamed. They lie in the sun next to glistening bays offering over-the-water, do-or-die shots. They're cut through dense jungle, carved from precipitous mountain walls, laid out at the edge of cliffs. You'll need your 45 spf sunscreen, as well as your rain gear. You'll walk out the door of your hotel to find the first tee, but you'll also drive for miles up a lonely coast or take a ferry across a churning channel to make your tee time. There will be crowds. There will be moments of exquisite solitude. Lava, beach, ocean. Plains, mountains, volcanos. All of these images, these ideas of Hawaiian golf, they're all real. They're all waiting for you.

I've lived (and golfed) in Hawaii off and on since the mid-nineties. When it hasn't been my address I have visited regularly, and when I'm not there at all I'm still thinking about it, planning my next visit, fantasizing about my rounds. I will figure out how to play the trade winds, I will read enough break on the Bermuda greens, I won't forget to put sunscreen on my ears. This book is for folks like me, who just can't stop daydreaming about golf. Whether you're planning your first trip, your 20th return visit, or you're stuck in a frozen mainland winter and need something to pass the time until the local muny opens up in the spring, this book is for you. I hope you have as much fun discovering Hawaii and its golf as I have had over the years. Aloha!

Ko'olau Golf Club

GREENS FEES

Greens fees are expensive for a lot of people, but in the general grand scheme of resort golf, they're actually on the low end. If you shell out rack rate, with no discounts whatsoever, you're not going to pay much more than $300 for the most expensive course in the state: Hualalai. Now, compare that to Pebble Beach, which for the 2008 season has staked its course fee at $495, with a mandatory stay at the resort, where the bottom rate room begins at $580 per night. Or Shadow Creek, the most expensive public course in the country, at around $500 plus mandatory accommodation. Indeed, many of the Hawaiian courses should be considered a bargain by comparison.

GREENS FEE RATINGS	
$	< $50
$$	$50 - $100
$$$	$100 - $175
$$$$	$175 - $250
$$$$$	> $250

Most of the courses have, at the very least, a twilight rate, some of which can begin as early as 11 a.m. So be sure to ask when booking your tee times. Other courses break it down even further into morning rates (full), afternoon rates (discounted) and twilight rates (bargain). If you really want to meet the morning sun and get in your 18 before the spouse and kids finish at the breakfast buffet, then you are going to pay full price. On the other hand, if you're the kind of person who would rather join the family at the resort buffet, then sun for an hour by the pool before showing up in the early afternoon for some range time, finishing up your round just around cocktail hour— well, you're likely to play golf for less money.

THE COURSES

While there are numerous excellent private courses in the state, and more on the way, I decided that this book should focus only on the courses that are publicly accessible. And while some are more accessible than others (Hualalai, for instance, requires that players be hotel guests at the Four Seasons Resort, adding a hefty nightly charge to what is already the steepest greens fee in the book), they are all, technically, open. This also excluded the many military courses on O'ahu that limit play to current and retired military, and their guests.

WALKING

Few of the courses listed here encourage walking due to the slower pace of play and the sometimes great distances between holes, and most will require you to pay for the cart even if you decide to walk. Some allow walking only with their twilight rates. The municipals are the most tolerant of walkers.

GRASSES

The most common grass found on golf courses in Hawaii is Bermuda. This is a grass that generally thrives in warmer climates. It looks good, and plays nicely off of the fairway and well-trimmed rough. It's tougher to hit out of thick Bermuda rough, but fortunately most resort courses keep the rough in check. The biggest problem that most mainlanders have with Bermuda and its hybrids (Tifdwarf, 328, 419) is the amount of grain when putting the ball. Bermuda grasses creep toward light, and usually the biggest light source in the islands is the sunlight reflecting off of the ocean. That's why you'll usually hear, "play the break towards the ocean." That advice is sometimes sufficient, but it certainly doesn't work in every situation. You can usually tell which way the grain is running by looking at the cup: one side will be smooth and the other side rough. The grain grows smooth to rough. If that doesn't work, look for one direction to be a bit shiny and another direction to be dark: shiny is downgrain, dark is upgrain. When you are putting into the grain, the putt will be slower, and, vice-versa, when you are playing with the grain it can be alarmingly fast. At the same time, if you are putting across the grain, you may have to factor in some lateral movement due to the grain. The best advice I can give for putting on Bermuda grass, however, is to pick your line and stroke your putt firmly. This will work well, though if you are putting downgrain and you miss the hole you may just putt yourself straight off the green.

TifEagle Bermuda is a new strain of the grass that can be cut very low, allowing for quick greens with minimal grain implication. Many of the upper-tier courses are replanting their greens with this grass, including the courses at Ka'anapali, Kapalua, and Mauna Kea.

Seashore paspalum is a grass that is becoming increasingly common in the islands. It has several advantages, the primary one being that it can be irrigated with water with a high saline content. That means that courses don't need to tap the municipal water supply to irrigate their greens and fairways. Paspalum also has a bright green quality that is visually very appealing. The grass putts true on the greens, but can be quite grabby in the rough. Balls hit into paspalum rough also tend to sit way down in the grass, compounding the problem. It's best to use an iron out of the rough, with a steep angle of descent to pop the ball out. Open your clubface at address to allow for the face to close somewhat before impact.

Yardages/Ratings
In the statistic boxes for each course, the yardages from each tee are provided. However, the course rating and slope that is provided is the men's number from the back tees, which is the norm when reporting a course's vitals (it's just a space issue, ladies!).

Choke Holes
Each course has at least one hole where it's time to offer up guts for glory. Of course, this is usually the precise recipe for disaster for most golfers. But maybe this time will be different.

19th Pukas
The word for "hole" in the Hawaiian language is "puka," which is widely known throughout the state. Thus, 19th puka refers to the 19th hole, a.k.a. the bar. The cost ratings should be intuitive, but if there's any question, they progress from least expensive to most: Cheap! Cheap!; Par; Pricey; Stratospheric.

Things Change
Greens are aerated, ownership changes, houses are built along fairways. Some places even close (e.g., Kaluakoi on Moloka'i). Trust that my experiences were honestly reported, and if you find severe differences, please let me know and I will reevaluate the course for future editions of the book.
www.fanaticguides.com

The par-5 12th at the Waikoloa Beach Course

THE LISTS

- ▨ MAUI
- ▨ O'AHU
- ▨ MOLOKA'I
- ▨ KAUA'I
- ▨ BIG ISLAND
- ▨ LANA'I

TOP OCEAN HOLES

- ▨ #3 Mauna Kea Golf Course
- ▨ #12 The Challenge at Manele
- ▨ #11 Kauai Lagoons—Kiele Course
- ▨ #15 Mauna Lani—South Course
- ▨ #5 Kapalua—Bay Course
- ▨ #16 Poipu Bay Golf Course
- ▨ #7 Ocean, Princeville—Makai Course
- ▨ #17 Hualalai Golf Course
- ▨ #15 Waikoloa Beach Course
- ▨ #3 Kona Country Club—Ocean Course

#3 Mauna Kea Golf Course

THE CLASSICS

- ▨ Kapalua—Plantation Course
- ▨ Mauna Kea Golf Course
- ▨ Princeville—Prince Course
- ▨ The Challenge at Manele
- ▨ Wailea Gold Course
- ▨ Ko'olau Golf Club
- ▨ Poipu Bay Golf Course
- ▨ Turtle Bay—Palmer Course
- ▨ Ko Olina Golf Club
- ▨ Hualalai Golf Course

#8 Kapalua Plantation Course

TOP BARGAIN COURSES

- ▨ Waiehu Municipal Golf Course
- ▨ Makalei Golf Club
- ▨ The Dunes at Maui Lani
- ▨ Waikoloa Village Golf Club
- ▨ Kahili Golf Course
- ▨ Wailua Municipal Golf Course
- ▨ Waimea Country Club
- ▨ Puakea Golf Course
- ▨ Olomana Golf Links
- ▨ Volcano Golf and Country Club

#15 Waiehu Municipal Golf Course

| ▨ Maui | ▨ Moloka'i | ▨ Big Island |
| ▨ O'ahu | ▨ Kaua'i | ▨ Lana'i |

Top Beauties

- ▨ Kaua'i Lagoons—Kiele Course
- ▨ Wailea Emerald Course
- ▨ The Experience at Koele
- ▨ Princeville—Prince Course
- ▨ Mauna Lani—South Course
- ▨ Luana Hills Country Club
- ▨ Makena—North Course
- ▨ Hualalai Golf Course
- ▨ Poipu Bay Golf Course
- ▨ Makaha Resort Golf Club

#13 Kaua'i Lagoons Kiele Course

The Toughest

- ▨ Ko'olau Golf Club
- ▨ Kapalua—Plantation Course
- ▨ Wailea Gold Course
- ▨ Mauna Kea Golf Course
- ▨ Princeville—Prince Course
- ▨ Makalei Golf Club
- ▨ Luana Hills Country Club
- ▨ Big Island Country Club
- ▨ Poipu Bay Golf Course
- ▨ Hapuna Golf Course

#8 Ko'olau Golf Club

The Most Forgiving

- ▨ Ka'anapali—Kai Course
- ▨ Volcano Golf and Country Club
- ▨ Turtle Bay—Fazio Course
- ▨ Kona Country Club—Ocean Course
- ▨ Olomana Golf Links
- ▨ Kiahuna Golf Club
- ▨ Wailea Old Blue
- ▨ Makaha Valley Country Club
- ▨ Ko Olina Golf Club
- ▨ Waikoloa Village Golf Club

#11 Ka'anapali Kai Course

Maui   Moloka'i   Big Island
O'ahu   Kaua'i   Lana'i

Top Practice Facilities

- Princeville—Prince Course
- The Experience at Koele
- Waikoloa Kings' Course
- Kapalua—Plantation Course
- The Challenge at Manele
- Hualalai Golf Course
- Poipu Bay Golf Course
- Ko Olina Golf Club
- Kaua'i Lagoons
- Makena

#10 Princeville Prince Course

Author's Choice

- Big Island Country Club
- Kapalua—Plantation Course
- The Challenge at Manele
- Ko'olau Golf Club
- Makalei Golf Club
- Kahili Golf Course
- Mauna Lani—North Course
- The Experience at Koele
- Makena South Course
- Princeville—Prince Course

#17 Island green at Big Island Country Club

Top 19th Pukas

- Ko Olina Golf Club
- Hualalai Golf Course
- The Challenge at Manele
- Wailea Old Blue
- Kapalua—Plantation Course
- Kona Country Club
- Poipu Bay Golf Course
- Makena
- Kiahuna Golf Club
- Kapalua—Bay Course

19th Hole at Ko Olina

Hawaii

Area: 10,931 square miles
Highest Point: Mauna Kea 13,796 feet
Population: 1,211,537 (2000 census)
Admission to Union: August 21, 1959 (50th state)

KAUA'I

NI'IHAU

O'AHU

PACIFIC OCEAN

MOLOKA'I

MAUI

LANA'I

KAHO'OLAWE

HAWAI'I
(The Big Island)

The 5th at Kapalua's Bay Course is an over-the-water par-3

Maui

Like a half-submerged hourglass lying on its side on the ocean floor, Maui's two hulking volcanoes, and the fertile valley that bridges them, define the "Valley Isle." Tourists flock to Maui to sun on its powdery beaches, enjoy sunrise on Haleakala, sample its cutting-edge pan-Asian cuisine, and to golf. From the highest-end resort courses of Kapalua, to the off-the-beaten-track gems like Kahili, to the diamond-in-the-rough municipal of Waiehu, Maui's golf courses span all tastes and pocketbooks. The one thing they have in common? That special quality that leads locals and many visitors to proclaim "Maui no ka oi," or "Maui is the best."

THE DON'T MISS	THE BARGAIN	THE HIDDEN GEM
KAPALUA PLANTATION This is the Crenshaw/Coore design where the PGA kicks off the year with the Mercedes Championship.	**WAIEHU MUNICIPAL** You won't find more ocean-front golf for your money anywhere else in the state.	**KAHILI GOLF COURSE** This gently designed Robin Nelson layout is rarely crowded, cooler than the coastal courses, and easier on the wallet.
Page 42	Page 60	Page 38

Maui

Nickname: The Valley Isle
Area: 727.2 square miles
Highest Point: Haleakala, 10,023 feet
Population: 117,644 (2000 census)
Flower: Lokelani

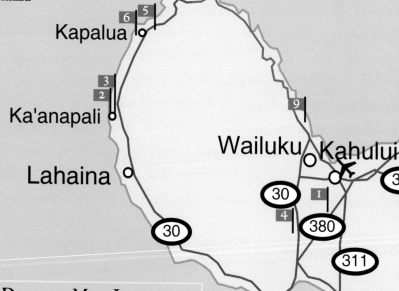

Kapalua

Ka'anapali

Wailuku Kahului

Lahaina

Kihei

Wailea

1 - The Dunes at Maui Lani

2 - Royal Ka'anapali Course

3 - Ka'anapali Kai Course

4 - Kahili Golf Club

5 - Kapalua Plantation Course

6 - Kapalua Bay Course

7 - **Makena South Course**

8 - **Makena North Course**

9 - **Waiehu Municipal Golf Course**

10 - **Wailea Gold Course**

11 - **Wailea Emerald Course**

12 - **Wailea "Old Blue" Course**

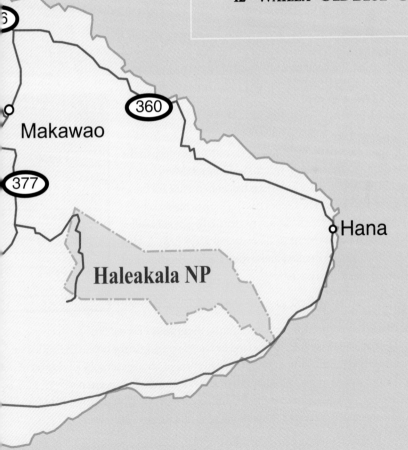

The par-3 third

THE DUNES AT MAUI LANI
~:Choke Hole: #6:~

While it may seem curious to find a links-style course this deep in the Pineapple Belt, it only takes a single visit to the Dunes at Maui Lani to discover that course architect Robin Nelson has crafted a fine tribute to the links of the British Isles. The Dunes has thick trees, high temperatures, and Bermuda grass greens, but it is the naturally occurring alluvial sand and the high winds that most affect the links style here. Add in nasty, diabolically placed pot bunkers and tartan-checked flagsticks and it's like Northern Ireland with palm trees.

THE COURSE
Though the course carves through thick *kiawe* forest, the architect moved little earth during construction and let the natural contours of the land dictate the routing of the holes. The carded yardage of the course is deceptively short as huge elevation changes, strategically placed clusters of pot bunkers, and either very narrow and long or extremely wide and shallow greens put a premium on accuracy and strategy. The ability to conquer long distances may still come in handy here, but wayward long balls are brutally penalized, while thoughtful, shorter shots are rewarded.

FANATIC Ratings
DESIGN INTRIGUE
★★★★
DIFFICULTY
★★★⯪
BEAUTY
★★★
MAINTENANCE
★★★★
SERVICE
★★★⯪
SWANK FACTOR
★★⯪

> *SWING EASY INTO THE WIND, AND STAY OUT OF THE TRAPS.*
> —DAVE GLEASON, HEAD PROFESSIONAL

The course lies at the edge of Kahului, only ten minutes from the airport, so expect a suburban setting, and don't be put off by the residential housing bordering many of the holes. Nelson has done an admirable job of framing most tees and approaches in such a way that your views are usually toward natural backgrounds, while houses are off to the side. That said, more development is in the works, and whether it eventually encroaches on the course views is unknown. Future development aside, the Dunes is an unexpected find in the largely non-touristed airport town.

17th from the tee.

WHAT IS A LINKS?

A LINKS COURSE IS THE TERM GIVEN TO THE TRADITIONAL COURSES OF SCOTLAND AND IRELAND WHERE GOLF EVOLVED. THE MOST COMMON FEATURES ARE POT BUNKERS, HIGH WINDS, DEEP ROUGH, FEW TREES, AND A SEASIDE SETTING. COURSES THAT BORROW SOME OF THESE FEATURES ARE KNOWN AS LINKS STYLE.

THE HOLES

#4

The par-5 fourth gives you your first real glimpse of the difficulty to come, with a cluster of deep pot bunkers discouraging you from getting all you can from your drive. The smart play is short and right, but that leaves a blind second shot.

#8

The par-3 eighth is the favorite of head pro Dave Gleason. With prevailing head winds and deep

The 4th: a wide-open driving hole.

pot bunkers protecting the front pin positions, you may be duped into over swinging, thereby decreasing the chances of finding refuge on this deep, skinny green.

#10

#10 is a hoot, with a high elevated tee dropping down to a tight fairway. A cut shot is your best bet at this par-4, as drives to the right side will catch the slope and roll the longest. Don't forget to listen for the bell from below before teeing off, and make sure you ring it yourself from the fairway when your group has cleared. A head contusion can ruin the best vacation.

THE DUNES AT MAUI LANI (LAH-nee)

ADDRESS		CONTACT	
1333 Maui Lani Parkway Kahului, HI 96732		808-873-0422 WWW.DUNESATMAUILANI.COM	
COURSE DETAILS		**SCORECARD**	
Architect	Robin Nelson	Par	72
Year Opened	1999	Slope	136
Renovated	No	Course Rating	73.5
Reservations	30 days out	**TEES/YARDAGES**	
Online Times	Yes	Black	6841
Greens Fees	$$$	Blue	6413
Discounts	Twilight/Replay	White	5833
Club Rentals	Yes	Red	4768
Premium	Yes		
Houses	Yes		
WATER		**DISTANCES**	
Types	Lakes	Well-marked	Yes
Water Holes	3	Yardage Book	Yes
Oceanfront	No	Sprinklers	Yes
		GPS	Sky Caddie
PRACTICE		**BUNKERS**	
Driving Range	Grass	How Many?	72
Practice Balls	Extra	Consistency	Thin, hardpack
Putting Green	Yes	**GRASS**	
Chip Green	Yes	Greens	Tifdwarf
Practice Bnkr.	Yes	Fairways	Bermuda

The Dunes at Maui Lani

#11

What makes #10 so much fun is exactly what makes #11 so difficult. The eleventh fairway rises nearly all the way back to the elevation of the tenth tee, meaning your approach needs plenty of club to reach this lofty green. Use two extra clubs and don't leave it short, as balls lacking in sufficient brawn will be rejected and sent rolling back down the hill.

19th Puka

Ambiance:	Modern plantation-style
Fully stocked:	Yes
Draft beer:	Yes
Menu:	Yes
Cost:	Par
Best bet:	Mac-nut Encrusted Chicken Sandwich
The Lowdown:	This clean place boasts a lovely terrace overlooking the course and the West Maui Mountains.

THE DUNES AT
MAUI LANI

✿

(FROM RIGHT)

RING THE BELL OR
GET CONKED ON
THE TENTH

RESIDENT NENE

#2 FROM THE TEE

SAGO PALMS

APPROACH AT #18
WITH THE SUGAR
CANE STACKS

Directions

From the airport, follow Hwy. 380 south and turn right into the Maui Lani subdivision about ¾-mile past the intersection of Hwy. 311 (to Kihei).

THE
DUNES AT
MAUI
LANI

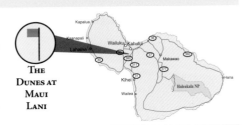

New bunkers along the 7t[

KA'ANAPALI—THE ROYAL KA'ANAPALI COURSE
~: Choke Hole: #18 :~
Site of Wendy's Champions Skins Game

THE RESORT

Bing Crosby hit the inaugural ball at Ka'anapali Resort way back when
JFK still occupied the Oval Office. There has been extreme growth
at the resort in the decades since, and in some ways it has become the
cautionary tale of over-exuberant development. However, it's safe to say
that the Ka'anapali Golf Resort is on the comeback trail. Back in the
mid-90s when I first lived on Maui, I often played these courses, but
that was more of an economic concession than anything else, as they
were cheaper alternatives to the more refined offerings at Kapalua and
Wailea. Unfortunately, the Ka'anapali courses were always a bit frayed around the edges. Beginning in late 2002, however, management of the courses changed hands and Ka'anapali begar
a resurgence, which has included the revitalization of both of these classic Hawaiian courses, a

FANATIC Ratings
DESIGN INTRIGUE
★★★⸲
DIFFICULTY
★★★
BEAUTY
★★★⸲
MAINTENANCE
★★★★
SERVICE
★★★★
SWANK FACTOR
★★★

> *THE ROYAL COURSE IS TRENT JONES, SR. AT HIS BEST! YOUR*
> *APPROACH SHOT IS PARAMOUNT—BE AWARE OF THE HOLE LOCA-*
> *TION AND MAKE SURE NOT TO SHORT SIDE YOURSELF WITH THESE*
> *GREENS. IF YOU DO, BE READY FOR A FUN PUTT OR CHIP!*
> *—SCOTT ASHWORTH, DIRECTOR OF GOLF*

major clubhouse renovation and a fresh image and brand makeover. The change is unmistakable and very impressive, and the staff is so friendly and enthusiastic about the revival that it's hard to believe it's the same place as a decade ago.

SENIOR SKINS GAME

THE ROYAL KA'ANAPALI COURSE BECAME THE NEW HOST OF THE WENDY'S CHAMPIONS SKINS GAME IN FEBRUARY 2008. THIS BROUGHT THE CHAMPIONS TOUR BACK TO KA'ANAPALI, WHERE THEY'D HOSTED THE KA'ANAPALI CLASSIC FROM 1987–2000.

THE COURSE

The renovation of the classic Royal Ka'anapali Course (formerly the Tournament North course), was completed in 2005. Management at Billy Casper Golf brought in architect Robin Nelson, who gathered a lot of input before making many significant changes. Nelson shied away from trying to stamp his own signature on the course and, instead, the characteristics of original designer Robert Trent Jones, Sr. live on. Many of the greens have been reworked (often to make them less complex), and bunkers have been modified, added, and removed. Jones' presence remains with difficult, penal bunkers on both sides of many fairways, demanding very long or very straight drives. Additionally, most of the greens tilt from front to back while many of the greenside bunkers surround the front portions of the greens. This creates interesting situations, where coming up short plays into the bunkers and going long results in slippery, downhill putts. Better to just play pin high on most holes!

Downhill drive on the 10th

The opening and finishing holes are laid out amidst the main resort area, with car-choked roads and people on power walks as moving targets. Beginning with the 7th hole the course crosses over the highway and heads up *mauka* (toward the mountain), where many of the most interesting holes are, and where certainly the finest views are to be had. The trade winds usually pick up in the afternoon, but as with many Hawaiian courses, this isn't something to fear; it's just another facet to the experience. The winds will help your play on certain holes as much as they hurt it on others.

The Holes

#5

The fifth is a brutally long (474 yards from the back tees) par-4 that plays right up to the edge of Ka'anapali Beach, and is widely considered one of the finest holes in Hawaii. When the trades are blowing, you will find some welcome help with your shots, but when it's calm or the Kona winds are blowing, this hole is a bear. Be aware on your approach that there are people just at the edge of the beach, so don't be shy about crying "Fore!" if your shot begins to leak right.

Beach at the 5th green

KA'ANAPALI—THE ROYAL KA'ANAPALI COURSE (kuh-AH-nuh-PAH-lee)			
ADDRESS		**CONTACT**	
2290 Kaanapali Pkwy. Lahaina, HI 96761		808-661-3691 WWW.KAANAPALIGOLFRESORT.COM	
COURSE DETAILS		**SCORECARD**	
Architect	Robert Trent Jones, Sr.	Par	71
Year Opened	1962	Slope	131
Renovated	2005 by Robin Nelson	Course Rating	74.2
Reservations	90 days out	**TEES/YARDAGES**	
Online Times	Yes	Blue	6700
Greens Fees	$$$$	White	6267
Discounts	Resort/Twilight	Gold	5839
Club Rentals	Yes	Burgundy	5016
Premium	Yes		
Houses	Yes		
WATER		**DISTANCES**	
Types	Lakes	Well-marked	Yes
Water Holes	3	Yardage Book	Yes
Oceanfront	Yes	Sprinklers	No
		GPS	In-cart
PRACTICE		**BUNKERS**	
Driving Range	Mats	How Many?	88
Practice Balls	Included	Consistency	Nice, fluffy
Putting Green	Yes	**GRASS**	
Chip Green	Yes	Greens	Tifeagle
Practice Bnkr.	No	Fairways	Bermuda 419

Royal Ka'anapali Course

#17

The par-3 17th is a classic Hawaiian one-shotter that plays over a small lake, with bunkers surrounding every other edge of the green. It's a shorty, but when the wind is blowing it changes everything, and that 150-yard shot may be negotiated with anything from a pitching wedge to a 4-iron.

19th Puka	
Ambiance:	Open-air clubhouse
Fully stocked:	Yes
Draft beer:	Yes
Menu:	Yes
Cost:	Par
Best bet:	Crab Benedict or Fried Chocolate Truffles with Papaya Syrup
The Lowdown:	Quench your thirst and watch 'em sink or swim as your fellow golfers approach on #18.

#18

You'll hear it said that Arnold Palmer has called the 18th one of the hardest finishing holes he's ever played, but keep in mind that he was quoted back in 1964 when he was paired with Jack Nicklaus in the Canada Cup (now the WGC—World Cup). Despite the antiquity of this quote, most players will agree that the finishing hole here is long and difficult, but also fun. The tee shot requires an unnerving short carry over water, while a massive fairway bunker straight out challenges you to try and carry it. Your other option is to play out to the right, but the lake rides up the entire right side of the hole, and if you play too much to the right a tree at the edge of the lake will be directly between you and a two-shot approach. The water dashes back to the left at the green, making your approach dicey. It's a classic finish to a classic Hawaiian course.

THE 2ND GREEN	RAINBOW OVER #17 (ABOVE) INFO ON MONUMENTS (BELOW)	MONKEYPOD BRANCHES

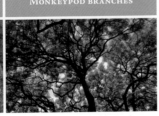

The par-3 14th

KA'ANAPALI—THE KA'ANAPALI KAI COURSE
~:Choke Hole: #18:~

THE COURSE

The Ka'anapali Kai Course (formerly the Resort South Course) was designed in 1971 by Arthur Jack Snyder, and is the more forgiving of the two courses at the resort. The sum of the wide fairways, near-perfect greens, and few serious challenges amounts to extremely pleasant resort golf. With the addition of some great views, you have a recipe for a near-perfect day of golf. Be sure to take some time to admire the panoramas, as well as the history that has taken place on and around the course (new yardage booklets detail some of the Hawaiian history that occurred along the course property, and a small "H" marks those areas on the course map). The tracks of the old Sugar Cane Train come right through the course, and a handsome trestle makes a charming backdrop to the 4th green. Expect trade winds in the afternoon to make things more challenging, but remember that a ball up in the wind can carry a long way, which makes some of the short par 4s even shorter and more receptive to birdies. With

FANATIC Ratings	
DESIGN INTRIGUE	★★↓
DIFFICULTY	★★↓
BEAUTY	★★★↓
MAINTENANCE	★★★★
SERVICE	★★★★
SWANK FACTOR	★★★↓

> " ON THE KAI COURSE, CLUB SELECTION IS VERY IMPORTANT ON THE TEE SHOT AND ON YOUR APPROACH SHOT AS THE MANY BUNKERS ARE STRATEGICALLY PLACED IN COMMON LANDING AREAS. "
> —KENDRIC KIMIZUKA, HEAD GOLF PROFESSIONAL

vide fairways stretching like a friendly green living room carpet, this course provides a relaxed Hawaiian resort experience.

THE HOLES

1

The first hole begins along the highway, but be patient as the second is across the road and you will soon be well away from the sound of cars. #1 is a straightaway par-4 that will allow you to find your swing a bit before moving on to the holes with sidehill lies and elevation changes that wait across the road.

7

The seventh is a fun par-4 with a forced carry over a vegetated area and a big gully to the right. It will be quite clear from the tee that the ideal shot is to the left toward

The 2nd flag

the barber pole. From there, the green is close, but your target is long and narrow with bunkers on both sides.

16

The par-4 16th returns to the main resort flat, but has an approach shot over a lake that is the first water hole on the course. Long drives aren't in any danger of finding the water, so let it rip and come over the hazard with the highest-lofted club you can.

The 11th green

#18

The 18th is a great finishing hole. Your ideal tee shot would draw left, starting toward the fairway bunker on the right and curving around the trees on the left side of the fairway. That shot leaves a short- to mid-iron approach into a water-fronted green. If your draw hangs on you off the tee, though, and you end up in the fairway bunker (guilty!), then a daring 150-yard approach from the beach has a much less certain outcome.

The 18th green

KA'ANAPALI—THE KA'ANAPALI KAI COURSE (kuh-AH-nuh-PAH-lee KYE)			
ADDRESS		**CONTACT**	
2290 Kaanapali Pkwy. Lahaina, HI 96761		808-661-3691 WWW.KAANAPALIGOLFRESORT.COM	
COURSE DETAILS		**SCORECARD**	
Architect	Arthur Jack Snyder	Par	70
Year Opened	1971	Slope	135
Renovated	2006 by Robin Nelson	Course Rating	70.7
Reservations	90 days out	**TEES/YARDAGES**	
Online Times	Yes	Lava	6388
Greens Fees	$$$$	Sand	6010
Discounts	Resort/Twilight	Fern	5563
Club Rentals	Yes	Hibiscus	4522
Premium	Yes		
Houses	Yes		
WATER		**DISTANCES**	
Types	Lakes	Well-marked	Yes
Water Holes	3	Yardage Book	Yes
Oceanfront	No	Sprinklers	No
		GPS	In-cart
PRACTICE		**BUNKERS**	
Driving Range	Mats	How Many?	88
Practice Balls	Included	Consistency	Nice, fluffy
Putting Green	Yes	**GRASS**	
Chip Green	Yes	Greens	Tifeagle
Practice Bnkr.	No	Fairways	Bermuda 419

Ka'anapali Kai Course

FOR THE WAHINE

THE KA'ANAPALI KAI COURSE HAS BEEN NAMED AS ONE OF THE TOP 100 "WOMEN FRIENDLY" COURSES IN AMERICA BY READERS OF GOLF FOR WOMEN MAGAZINE. SO, ACCORDING TO THE MAGAZINE, WHAT MAKES A COURSE FRIENDLY TO THE FAIRER SEX? FIRST, A FACILITY THAT IS AMIABLE AND WELCOMING TO WOMEN, AND EMPLOYS WOMEN, IS THE BASIS FOR A FEMALE-FRIENDLY ENVIRONMENT. SECOND, MANY WOMEN LIKE TO SEE TWO SETS OF FORWARD TEES TO CHOOSE FROM, WITH AT LEAST ONE THAT IS UNDER 5,000 YARDS. AS FAR AS LAYOUT GOES, MOST LADIES PREFER FEW FORCED CARRIES OFF THE TEE, FEW APPROACH SHOTS THAT REQUIRE LONG, SOFT LANDINGS, AND HOLES THAT PLAY AS THE ARCHITECT INTENDED, RATHER THAN CONVEYING THE SENSE THAT THE FORWARD TEES WERE ADDED AS AN AFTERTHOUGHT. THE PRO SHOP SHOULD CARRY PLENTY OF GEAR FOR WOMEN, AND THERE SHOULD BE AN ABUNDANCE OF REST ROOMS ON THE COURSE. ALL OF THESE THINGS ARE WELL REPRESENTED AT THE KA'ANAPALI KAI COURSE, AND IT DESERVES ITS DESIGNATION AS ONE OF THE TOP 100 "WOMEN FRIENDLY" COURSES IN THE COUNTRY.

The 7th green with Lana'i in the background

Directions

From the airport, follow Hwy. 380 south, and turn left on Hwy. 30 toward Lahaina. From South Maui, proceed west on Hwy. 31 and turn left on Hwy. 30. Continue on Hwy. 30 through the town of Lahaina. After about a mile, turn left into the first Ka'anapali Resort turnoff, and take an immediate right into the clubhouse parking lot.

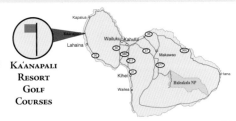

KA'ANAPALI
RESORT
GOLF
COURSES

2nd green backed by the West Maui Mountain

Kahili Golf Course
~:Choke Hole: #12:~

FANATIC
Ratings

DESIGN INTRIGUE	★★★★
DIFFICULTY	★★★
BEAUTY	★★★★
MAINTENANCE	★★★★
SERVICE	★★★
SWANK FACTOR	★★★

Kahili may be a little off the beaten resort track, but those who find their way here can enjoy a beautiful, well-designed layout that won't dent the wallet like the Waileas and Kapaluas. The course changed ownership in 2004, and has since been treated to an excellent renovation and renewed investment. The property is lushly planted, and the staff pays great attention to the landscaping, with bright, chromatic splashes around many corners. The course winds through the foothills of the West Maui Mountains, allowing peeks into alluring green valleys, but also boasts incredible views of both the north and south coasts, and of the massive hulk of Haleakala across the valley. A final cherry: there are no houses on the course, a refreshing change from most other courses in the state.

The Course
The original architect, Robin Nelson, returned in 2004 to update the course and ease some of its harshest edges. With new putting surfaces, softer landing areas and fresh sand, the resulting

> *PLAY THE ANGLES. SHY AWAY FROM SUCKER PINS AND DON'T SHORT SIDE YOURSELF.*
>
> —Brad Bowen, Head Professional

ayout strikes a balance between challenge and playabil-ty. When the trade winds are blowing, though, they can nake even the short holes arduous. At the same time, the orilliance of the routing is in its orientation to the wind. Three of the four par-5s on the course play with the wind at the golfer's back, which gives players of even average ength the tantalizing possibility of eagle. Imagine decid-ng whether or not you should hit your second shot into a par-5 green with either your 5- iron or 6-iron. What a concept! Players will need the wherewithal to know when to club up or down, or play to one side of a fairway if the wind is whipping across it. Often, however, even these decisions are eased by friendly contours that gently redi-ect a blown ball, or the fairway opens up in the direction of the prevailing wind.

#11 from the tees

The course plays a bit kinder since its renovation, but it is no pushover. There are enough ight tee shots, penal bunkers, and risk-reward propositions to keep things interesting. There are also a number of blind tee shots, and gentle elevation changes that cause holes to play a lot longer than the carded yardages. The course maintenance is excellent, and when you find yourself in the sand, take some time to appreciate its fluffy consistency from bunker to bunker, as this is an area where many Hawaiian courses fall short. Not so at Kahili.

THE HOLES

PAR-5S

Without a doubt, each of the par-5s that play with the prevailing trades (#3, #9, #12) are choice holes. The dogleg left #3 is especially fun, as a shot over the fairway bunkers at the corner makes for an adventurous tee shot. If you can carry them, then you're looking at nothing more than a

The approach at #18

mid-iron into the green. The ninth plays straight away, but fairway bunkers lurk on both sides, daring you to clear them. A long second-shot approach is a possibility, but be wary of the massive mound housing two big bunkers that protects the green front right. #12 is a blind tee shot, but plays straight out and up a mild rise. A tee shot up into the wind will ensure

5th green with views of Haleakala

Kahili Golf Course (kuh-HEE-lee)

ADDRESS		CONTACT	
2500 Honoapiilani Highway Wailuku, HI 96793		808-242-4653 WWW.KAHILIGOLF.COM	
COURSE DETAILS		**SCORECARD**	
Architect	Robin Nelson	Par	72
Year Opened	1991	Slope	135
Renovated	2004	Course Rating	72.3
Reservations	7 days out	**TEES/YARDAGES**	
Online Times	Yes	Blue	6554
Greens Fees	$$$	White	6029
Discounts	Resort/Twilight	Red	4948
Club Rentals	Yes		
Premium	Yes		
Houses	No		
WATER		**DISTANCES**	
Types	Lakes/Creek	Well-marked	Yes
Water Holes	4	Yardage Book	No
Oceanfront	No	Sprinklers	Yes
		GPS	In-cart
PRACTICE		**BUNKERS**	
Driving Range	Grass	How Many?	56
Practice Balls	Extra	Consistency	Nice, fluffy
Putting Green	Yes	**GRASS**	
Chip Green	Yes	Greens	Tifeagle
Practice Bnkr.	No	Fairways	Bermuda 419

Kahili Golf Course

your ball is in for a long ride, leaving you to decide whether to go for the green in two with a narrow lake guarding the left side, or simply lay up safely.

#6

The par-3 6th may be the most beautiful hole on the course, with a crooked creek bed winding down to the tee box from the green above. Big flower beds adorn the area behind the green, which is backed by the steep valleys of the West Maui Mountains. Don't forget to take at least two clubs longer into this elevated green, and if the wind is howling, take even more club!

19th Puka

Ambiance:	Clean and Casual
Fully stocked:	Yes
Draft beer:	Yes
Menu:	Yes
Cost:	Pricey
Best bet:	Ali'i Platter: Coconut shrimp, beer-battered fish, egg rolls & fries
The Lowdown:	The lanai boasts a wide angle of the north and south shores with Haleakala towering in between.

SUMPTUOUS LANDSCAPING	THE TRICKY 6TH (ABOVE) GAGGLE OF NENE (BELOW)	GOOD LUCK ROCK

Directions

From the airport, follow Hwy. 380 south, then turn right at the intersection with Hwy. 30. The entrance is a ½-mile down on the left.

KAHILI
GOLF
COURSE

A rain curtain approaches the epic par-5 18th

Kapalua—The Plantation Course
~: Choke Hole: #18 :~
Site of PGA Tour Mercedes-Benz Championship

FANATIC Ratings	
DESIGN INTRIGUE	★★★★✦
DIFFICULTY	★★★★★
BEAUTY	★★★★★
MAINTENANCE	★★★★✦
SERVICE	★★★★
SWANK FACTOR	★★★★✦

The Resort

Spread across 23,000 acres of former pineapple fields, Kapalua represents the pinnacle of luxury resorts on Maui. With two championship golf courses (the Village Course closed in 2007), three white sandy beaches, an array of casual and fine-dining restaurants, shops, and loads of lodging, this is where the "haves" come to play. Positioned at the northwest side of the island, just across the Palilolo Channel from Moloka'i, Kapalua receives varied weather and a unique light. Colors seem more vivid here, as if the hues are a bit more saturated than usual, and the landscape is often bathed in a gentle golden glow.

Despite all of its natural beauty, Kapalua is not afraid of development. The Kapalua Bay Hotel has been recently deconstructed (no, not demolished—most of its materials were reused) to make way for new luxury residences. A development called Kapalua Mauka is underway and

> *Be ready to do some lag putting. With the huge greens here, you need to be prepared to face long putts. And the grain works toward the left end of Moloka'i.*
> —Gary Planos, Senior VP/Resort Operations

will include 2,200 units, along with a new private golf course designed by Tom Fazio (replacing the former Village Course). The Bay Course weaves its way through countless condos, homes, and the Ritz-Carlton, and even the lauded Plantation Course has some homes along it, though most are set back from the course and designed to fit rather discreetly into the setting.

THE COURSE

The Plantation Course at Kapalua is golf on its grandest scale. With its wide, sweeping fairways, immense greens, blistering trade winds, giant bunkers, and vast distances tee to green, playing here as an amateur is a bit like trying on your father's shoes as a kid. You've seen the big boys play this course at the Mercedes-Benz Championship, which kicks off the PGA Tour every year. Watching them from the comfort of the couch, the course seems playable, but when you try it yourself you feel small, humble and like you're a lot further from coming of age than you thought you were.

That said, this course is a must-play. The immensity of each hole affects you, as do the stunning views of the Pacific, of Honoloa Bay (the legendary surf spot), and of the islands of Moloka'i and Lana'i. Ben Crenshaw and Bill Coore have made their reputation as golf course architects by adapting their courses to the natural terrain and letting the land dictate the layout. This is evident while playing the course, as the bunkers feather naturally into the high grass, and the downhill doglegs seem to follow the logical direction of the hole, rather than being arbitrarily cut through the trees. The level of service here is high as well, and the excitement that golfers feel milling around waiting for their chance to tee off is electrifying and contagious.

Wide open fairway at the par-4 10th

THE HOLES

#1

The first lets you know immediately what's in store for you, with great views and a long distance to get home with a par four. It may play downhill, but even with a good roll your second shot is still going to be sizeable. Your approach is over a deep gully into a huge green with a grabby patch of long grass and vegetation on the right. Your tee shot is better off to the left, which will open up the green a little more.

#2

The second is the toughest par-3 on the PGA Tour, with a scoring average in 2006 of 3.42. I once saw Glenn Frey from the Eagles tee off during the Pro-Am here, and he lurched it 30 yards left into the 3-foot-high grass. None of this bodes well for the average amateur, but at least you won't be on national TV when it's time for your own personal struggle. But really, the green is huge, the sand is all on the right side and there's plenty of room to the left. So, what's the problem?

1st flag with West Maui Mountains

KAPALUA—THE PLANTATION COURSE (CAP-uh-LOO-uh)			
ADDRESS		**CONTACT**	
2000 Plantation Club Dr. Lahaina, Hi 96761		1-877-KAPALUA (527-2582) WWW.KAPALUA.COM	
COURSE DETAILS		**SCORECARD**	
Architect	Ben Crenshaw/Bill Coore	Par	73
Year Opened	1991	Slope	138
Renovated	No	Course Rating	74.9
Reservations	25 days out	**TEES/YARDAGES**	
Online Times	Yes	Blue	7263
Greens Fees	$$$$$	White	6547
Discounts	Resort/Twilight	Red	5627
Club Rentals	Yes		
Premium	Yes		
Houses	Yes		
WATER		**DISTANCES**	
Types	N/A	Well-marked	Yes
Water Holes	0	Yardage Book	Yes
Oceanfront	No	Sprinklers	Yes
		GPS	In-cart
PRACTICE		**BUNKERS**	
Driving Range	Grass	How Many?	90
Practice Balls	Included	Consistency	Super fluffy
Putting Green	Yes	**GRASS**	
Chip Green	Yes	Greens	TifEagle
Practice Bnkr.	No	Fairways	Bermuda 328

Kapalua Plantation Course

#6

The par-4 6th has a massive bunker in the middle of the fairway to consider. A heroic drive that rides the quartering crosswind and bounces just past the bunker could roll all the way to the green. At least, that's how they do it on TV. For most of us mortals, the steep hill on the back side of the bunker should help our second shots funnel down toward the green for one of the rare birdie chances here.

19th Puka	
Ambiance:	Hawaiian plantation-style
Fully stocked:	Yes
Draft beer:	Yes
Menu:	Yes
Cost:	Stratospheric
Best bet:	Cajun Sashimi Ahi Benedict with Wasabi Hollandaise
The Lowdown:	The Plantation House bar offers upscale breakfast and lunch over-looking the legendary 18th green.

#18

Eighteen is a legendary finishing hole, an endless par-5 that plays downhill and with the trades, but requires a daring second shot over a deep gully to two-shot your way in. Then, even if you do, hold-ing the huge green is a tricky proposition. The green is set only slightly back to front, but the grain grows straight away from incoming balls, and shots that look good when landing at the front of the green often roll right to the back or into the cavernous bunker on the left side. Stuart Appleby nearly holed out from that bunker during the 2006 Mercedes Championship, leaving two feet for a tap-in birdie that beat Vijay Singh in a playoff. Have fun on this hole and imagine the stadium seats packed with cheering fans as you approach the green. Today, you're one of the big boys.

THE BIG BOYS

THE COURSE RECORD HERE IS 62 BY K.J. CHOI, AND THE TOURNAMENT RECORD IS 31-UNDER BY ERNIE ELS, BOTH OCCURRING IN 2003. HOW DOES ANYONE GET THAT LOW ON THIS COURSE?!?

Back side of the par-4 6th | Knee-buckling carry on the 8th

Directions

From the airport, follow Hwy. 380 south, and turn left on Hwy. 30 toward Lahaina. From South Maui, proceed west on Hwy. 31 and turn left on Hwy. 30. Continue on Hwy. 30 through the town of Lahaina. In about 10 miles, turn right on Plantation Dr., then take a quick left and follow to the clubhouse.

KAPALUA
THE
PLANTATION
COURSE

The tee at the par-5 10th

KAPALUA—THE BAY COURSE
~:Choke Hole: #5:~
Site of the Kapalua LPGA Classic

FANATIC
Ratings

DESIGN INTRIGUE	★★★✓
DIFFICULTY	★★★✓
BEAUTY	★★★★
MAINTENANCE	★★★★✓
SERVICE	★★★★
SWANK FACTOR	★★★★

THE COURSE

With one of the most dramatic ocean holes in the state, The Bay Course has been an island favorite since it became the first of the Kapalua courses to open in 1975. Arnold Palmer and Francis Duane partnered up to design a track that winds through the Kapalua Resort complex, with stately Cook pines lining fairways that plunge and heave through old pineapple fields. While much of the development that is visible along the course didn't exist back in the mid '70s, at today's Kapalua you will find yourself playing a course stacked from fairway to fairway with condos, private homes, and the Ritz-Carlton. The development doesn't rob too much from the golf experience, however, which remains a challenging and satisfying test, especially when the trade winds are ripping around the northwest tip of Maui, as they often do in the afternoon. A few holes play along the road, but a massive netting complex is in place to keep you from jerking a ball into the windshield of a passing Mercedes or Porsche. It's a good idea to book early tee times

> " AT THE BAY COURSE, DON'T BE AFRAID TO LAY UP OFF THE TEE. THINK TWICE BEFORE AUTOMATICALLY PULLING OUT YOUR DRIVER ON EVERY HOLE. "
> —GARY PLANOS, SENIOR VICE PRESIDENT/RESORT OPERATIONS

avoid the full brunt of the afternoon rains and trades, if quasi-Scottish weather isn't what you're
oking for on your Hawaiian vacation. Slicers get the worst of it here, as there are large fairway
unkers on the right side off of ten tees. If you swing that way, so to speak, give yourself a little
1ore room to the left and try to avoid an otherwise long day at the beach.

HE HOLES

4

he short, par-4 4th is a beauty, with a sharp dogleg left that heads right for the ocean. Don't
verclub your tee shot unless you're trying to cut the corner. Be aware that there are exposed lava
ocks at the corner for those who attempt the cut but don't have enough muscle to get it all the
ay through. You may find a decent lie there, or your ball may come to rest right up against the
ocks. Hard luck. The green is backed by ironwood trees that should keep long balls from tum-
ling into the Pacific.

5

he 5th is the only over-the-ocean par-3 on the island of Maui, and it is a beauty. It's a mid-length
1ot over angry waves to a large green with bunkers short, long, and right. No mercy on this one:
rab it, stab it, and hope for the best.

15

he fifteenth is a downhill, downwind par-5 with a narrow landing area off the tee that is
queezed by fairway bunkers left and right. The bunker on the left has a beautiful African tulip
ee growing right in the middle of it. You'll surely agree that it is lovely too—that is, unless you
ave driven your ball into that bunker and are not only in the sand, but also behind a very large
ee. Two small bunkers protect the green, but leave it fairly wide open for those who have the
ngth to get home in two.

Out of the bunker on the 5th

#16

The par-4 16th is a sinister construct, seemingly designed to torture those who lack the skill or good fortune to navigate its myriad pitfalls. The scene from the tee features a foreground filled with a thirsty lake that must be carried off the tee. Even worse, what would normally be the comfy middle of the fairway is cut by a jagged creek that

16th te

KAPALUA—THE Bay COURSE (CAP-uh-LOO-uh)

ADDRESS	CONTACT
300 Kapalua Drive	1-877-KAPALUA (527-2582)
Lahaina, Hi 96761	WWW.KAPALUA.COM

COURSE DETAILS		SCORECARD	
Architect	Arnold Palmer/F. Duane	Par	72
Year Opened	1975	Slope	136
Renovated	2007–2008	Course Rating	72.1
Reservations	25 days out	**TEES/YARDAGES**	
Online Times	Yes	Blue	6600
Greens Fees	$$$$$	White	6051
Discounts	Resort/Twilight	Silver	5676
Club Rentals	Yes	Red	5124
Premium	Yes		
Houses	Yes		

WATER		DISTANCES	
Types	Lakes/Creeks	Well-marked	Yes
Water Holes	4	Yardage Book	Yes
Oceanfront	Yes	Sprinklers	No
		GPS	In-cart

PRACTICE		BUNKERS	
Driving Range	Grass	How Many?	68
Practice Balls	Included	Consistency	Super fluffy
Putting Green	Yes	**GRASS**	
Chip Green	No	Greens	Tifeagle
Practice Bnkr.	No	Fairways	Bermuda 328

Kapalua Bay Course

ooks like someone took a dull knife to lovely Ansel Adams landscape, leaving he hapless golfer with a choice of the left or right remnants of a fairway. The left airway will open up the green better, but t requires a longer water carry shot to each that fairway—no small feat when he trades are howling in your face. Most players will probably be pretty happy just staying dry and taking a bogey. Good luck on this one.

19th Puka

Ambiance:	Aquarium chic
Fully stocked:	Yes
Draft beer:	Yes
Menu:	Yes
Cost:	Pricey
Best bet:	Jawaiian Spiced Grilled Chicken Sandwich
The Lowdown:	With views of the course, the Pineapple Grill embodies the "resort casual" style of Kapalua.

KAPALUA
THE BAY COURSE

(From right)

The 18th

Red-Crested
Cardinal

Approach on #4

Tee monument

Kapalua's trademark
Cook Pines

One

Championship 504
Regular 472
Ladies 406

Directions

From the airport in Kahului, follow Hwy. 380 south, and turn left on Hwy. 30 toward Lahaina. From South Maui, proceed west on Hwy. 31 and turn left on Hwy. 30. From both areas, proceed through the town of Lahaina. After about 9 miles, turn left on Office Rd., then turn left on Kapalua Dr. after a ½ mile. The entrance to the Bay Course is on the left in about a ¼ mile.

KAPALUA
THE
BAY
COURSE

KAPALUA GOLF ACADEMY

808-669-6500
www.kapaluagolfacademy.com

Designer: Hale Irwin Design Company
Opened: January 2000
Practice Facility: 23 acres
Facilities: Pro shop, classroom, golf fitness room, multiple practice greens, 85,000-square-foot grass teeing area, greenside and fairway practice bunkers, 2,500-square-foot learning center, 18-hole putting course, short game area, 600-square-foot indoor hitting bay with digital video analysis, wedge area with multiple target greens

The Kapalua Golf Academy is one of those places golfers dream about, somewhere to finally get their game in order. Believe it: spending some time in a controlled practice environment with quality instructors may finally make that dream come true. The facilities are like a wonderland of practice golf stations, from the 18-hole practice putting course, to the funky short game green loaded with toys, to the driving range fitted with multiple targets.

Take whacks out of the digital hitting ba

The centerpiece of the academy, however, is the digital hitting bay. While you whack balls onto th range from something like a super clean, high-tech garage, the same instructors who advise PGA pro record your swing and break it down for you on a computer screen. The video analysis can be a revela tion. Are you jerking the ball to the left off the tee? Or do you know that something is just not quite righ with your hip turn? Well, the videos don't lie and your eagle-eyed (pun intended) instructors will spy you problem immediately. They'll also match your swing type with a well-known pro (I was paired wit Ernie Els) and point out key elements of the swing that the pro is doing that you, most likely, are not.

With everything on the menu from half-hour digital video analysis and two-hour tune up clinics t comprehensive three-day schools, there's something here for everyone. Just think, a few days or hours a this place may save you handfuls of strokes—and gray hairs—on the course.

One testimonial: I personally sunk into the 70s following my video swing analysis. What's tha worth to you?

Directions

From the airport, follow Hwy. 380 south, and turn left on Hwy. 30 toward Lahaina. From South Maui, proceed west on Hwy. 31 and turn left on Hwy. 30. Continue through the town of Lahaina. After about 9 miles, turn left on Office Rd. The entrance to the golf academy is immediately on the right.

KAPALUA
GOLF
ACADEMY

2nd pin at the Kapalua Plantation Course

The fantastic 10th from the t

MAKENA—SOUTH COURSE
~:Choke Hole: #10:~

FANATIC
Ratings

DESIGN INTRIGUE		
★★★★		
DIFFICULTY		
★★★✦		
BEAUTY		
★★★★		
MAINTENANCE		
★★★★✦		
SERVICE		
★★★★		
SWANK FACTOR		
★★★★		

THE RESORT

It may only be a couple of solid 3-woods away from the trendy hustle of Wailea, but somehow Makena Resort feels like another world. There is a sense of isolation at Makena that is uncommon on Hawaiian courses, and it is something to be relished while you're here. As the architect, Robert Trent Jones, Jr., explained after the original eighteen holes were expanded to thirty-six in 1991, "By very careful planning and careful attention to some technical engineering principles, we have been able to present many of these new holes separately and apart from all the others. Often no other hole is even visible beyond the one you are playing. This creates a very special feeling for the golfer, almost like this tiny little part of the world wa created just for you . . . For me, it is still that same little old place at the end of the road, and it sti retains that marvelous feeling of isolation from all the cares and troubles of the world."

> " *MAKENA HAS SOME OF THE FASTEST GREENS IN THE STATE OF HAWAII, SO YOU MUST FOCUS MORE ON THE SPEED OF YOUR PUTTS AND LESS ON YOUR LINE. AND OF COURSE YOU MUST BE AWARE OF THE GRAIN, WHICH RUNS TOWARDS THE ISLAND OF KAHO'OLAWE.* "
> —SCOTT BRIDGES, GOLF OPERATIONS MANAGER

While there's only one large hotel in Makena at present, widespread development of the area may be about to begin. The resort and golf property are in sales negotiations that may bring many new private residences, as well as the possible closing of one of the courses to the public. This is in line with the recent trend in the islands toward the development of more private golf courses for the

7th from the fairway

exclusive use of property owners. Whatever happens, you'll want to get to Makena to enjoy both of the courses before one of them is forever closed to public access.

THE COURSE

With a fairly flat layout and some generous fairways, the South Course is the kinder of the two tracks at Makena. However, there are a few tremendously difficult aspects to the course, such as an abundance of rolling undulations and mounding along the impeccably maintained fairways. Quintessential RTJ II bunkering will also keep your interest. Jones utilizes the natural lava formations well, positions several lakes in which to drown your balls, and features two holes along the Pacific—the only holes on the ocean in South Maui.

THE HOLES

4

The par-4 4th is the first demanding hole on the course. A lake on the right is in play off the tee, and runs all the way up to the front of the green. In true Trent Jones, Jr. fashion, however, the hole dogs right, tight to the hazard, while a series of seven small bunkers along the left side of the fairway keep you from bailing out away from the water. Anything that's not fairly straight off the tee or on approach will be punished.

The par-3 13th

#7

The seventh is an epic par-5, long from whichever tees you're playing. Your tee shot is over an old lava rock wall, and must clear a series of deep bunkers on the inside corner of a dogleg right. The perfect shot is a long fade over the bunkers, while a shot out to the left further lengthens the hole. The fairway narrows dramatically at the landing area for your second shot, and fingers of lava hide below undulations in the fairway, waiting for an uninformed ball. The volcanic crescent island of Molokini sits in the ocean directly above the green, creating a lovely distraction (and, incidentally, a fantastic dive site for

7th gree

MAKENA—SOUTH COURSE (muh-KEN-uh)			
ADDRESS		**CONTACT**	
5415 Makena Alanui		808-879-3344	
Makena, HI 96753		WWW.MAKENAGOLF.COM	
COURSE DETAILS		**SCORECARD**	
Architect	Robert Trent Jones, Jr.	Par	72
Year Opened	1981	Slope	137
Renovated	1991	Course Rating	73.8
Reservations	1 month out	**TEES/YARDAGES**	
Online Times	Yes	Black	7014
Greens Fees	$$$$	Blue	6630
Discounts	Resort/Twilight	Orange	6112
Club Rentals	Yes	White	5489
Premium	Yes		
Houses	No		
WATER		**DISTANCES**	
Types	Lakes/Ocean	Well-marked	Yes
Water Holes	4	Yardage Book	Yes
Oceanfront	Yes	Sprinklers	Yes
		GPS	Sky Caddie
PRACTICE		**BUNKERS**	
Driving Range	Grass	How Many?	85
Practice Balls	Included	Consistency	Nice, playable
Putting Green	Yes	**GRASS**	
Chip Green	Yes	Greens	Bermuda 328
Practice Bnkr.	No	Fairways	Bermuda 328

Makena South Course

hose of you who are also SCUBA fanatics). Bunkers in front of the green will catch second shots that don't quite make it, while the back is unprotected.

#10

The tenth is not only one of the most picturesque holes on the island, but also demands shots with a high degree of difficulty. The huge volcanic cinder cone of Pu'u Olai is the point that you aim toward, but a lake on the right is in play off the tee and a second lake on the left is in play on your second, and possibly third, shots. With a perfectly long and straight drive, it may be possible to fly the lake on approach and make a quick landing on the wide, shallow green. The more sensible move is a second shot out to the right side of the fairway that will take the lake out of play for a short-iron approach into the green.

19th Puka	
Ambiance:	Casual clubhouse patio
Fully stocked:	Yes
Draft beer:	Yes
Menu:	Yes
Cost:	Par
Best bet:	Volcano Spiced Ahi sandwich
The Lowdown:	Watch players drop $3 golf balls into the lakes on #10 while relaxing on the lanai with a cold beer and a sandwich.

#16

The par-4 16th plays right along the Pacific, and if you aren't careful it is easy to transform your ball into shark bait. Your tee shot is semi-blind, so you can't see that the fairway ends straight out as the hole doglegs right into the green. Hit a fairway wood straight out, or fade a long driver directly over the palm trees on the right side of the fairway. This is a fair hole with no fairway bunkers, but two greenside traps guard a green that falls away to the left. Beware: the grain grows out to sea, and between that and the slope, shots that wind up right of the pin may be hard to stop at the hole when putting.

COOTS AND A STILT | 5TH FLAG (ABOVE) TEE MARKER (BELOW) | GREY FRANCOLIN

On approach at #1

MAKENA—NORTH COURSE
~:Choke Hole: #14:~

THE COURSE

Just as at the South Course, the chief defenses used by Robert Trent Jones, Jr. are the thick *kiawe* forest, natural lava rock, mounding, undulations, and an abundance of sand. Unlike its sister course, however, the North Course slowly climbs the slopes of Haleakala as it tacks away from the clubhouse. This means that the majority of the first ten holes play longer than the printed yardages suggest, especially the par-5 5th and 10th. After your tee shot on the par-4 11th, you've arrived at the apex of the course, and the views over the next four holes are some of the best you'll find anywhere in Hawaii. The North Course also has many forced carries over deep gullies and stream beds that make it a more demanding course than the one to the south.

FANATIC Ratings
DESIGN INTRIGUE
★★★★
DIFFICULTY
★★★★
BEAUTY
★★★★⯪
MAINTENANCE
★★★★⯪
SERVICE
★★★★
SWANK FACTOR
★★★★

> *ON THE NORTH COURSE, DO NOT HIT THE BALL WHERE YOU CAN'T SEE IT LAND. IF IT IS A DOGLEG RIGHT, DO NOT ATTEMPT TO CUT IT OVER THE TREES, FOR THERE ARE MORE TREES, AND YOU'RE NOT THAT LONG. (SORRY, MOST GOLFERS, INCLUDING MYSELF, ALWAYS THINK THEY HIT IT 150 YARDS FARTHER THAN REALITY).*
> —KIRK NELSON, HEAD GOLF PROFESSIONAL

The Legend of Molokini and Puʻu Olai

Hawaiian legends abound about Molokini, the crescent-shaped islet off Maui's south shore, and Puʻu Olai, the scenic cinder cone that towers above Makena. One of these legends holds that Pele, the goddess of fire, became jealous of the love between a warrior and a moʻo, a giant female lizard. Pele turned the lizard to stone, cut her in half and threw her tail out to sea where it became Molokini. The head of the lizard was left behind on the beach, becoming Puʻu Olai.

The 6th with views of Puʻu Olai, Kahoʻolawe, and Molokini

The Holes

#3

The short par-4 3rd is an easily recognizable Robert Trent Jones, Jr. hole, with an abrupt dogleg right and a massive bunker straight out to catch those drives that don't quite cut around the corner. It's a wise move to reach for a fairway wood off the tee to come up short of the bunker, though a faded drive around the trees at right will get you closer to the elevated green.

#6

The sixth features a fairway split by a rocky black creek bed that makes the hole look like it's been gashed in half by a frustrated giant. The fairway to the left requires a carry off the tee and opens up the green for a short approach, while the right fairway is worm-burner friendly from the tee box. However, players who opt for the right side will have to come over the gash at some point, so the closer you play to it off the tee, the shorter carry you'll have on your second shot.

#11

The final uphill tee shot on the course is at #11, which dogs slightly right with bunkers at the inside corner. When you arrive at the green, take a look around. You're at 1,000 feet and can see the islands of Kahoʻolawe, Molokini, Lanaʻi, the west Maui volcano, and even Molokaʻi on clear days. In winter you'll likely see the carousing humpback whales, looking like splashes in a pond from this elevation.

A hefty carry approaching #1

MAKENA—NORTH COURSE (muh-KEN-uh)				
ADDRESS		**CONTACT**		
5415 Makena Alanui		808-879-3344		
Makena, HI 96753		WWW.MAKENAGOLF.COM		
COURSE DETAILS		**SCORECARD**		
Architect	Robert Trent Jones, Jr.	Par		72
Year Opened	1981	Slope		138
Renovated	1991	Course Rating		73.8
Reservations	1 month out	**TEES/YARDAGES**		
Online Times	Yes	Black		6914
Greens Fees	$$$$	Blue		6567
Discounts	Resort/Twilight	Orange		6151
Club Rentals	Yes	White		5303
Premium	Yes			
Houses	No			
WATER		**DISTANCES**		
Types	Lakes/Creek	Well-marked		Yes
Water Holes	3	Yardage Book		Yes
Oceanfront	No	Sprinklers		Yes
		GPS		Sky Caddie
PRACTICE		**BUNKERS**		
Driving Range	Grass	How Many?		79
Practice Balls	Included	Consistency		Nice, playable
Putting Green	Yes	**GRASS**		
Chip Green	Yes	Greens		Bermuda 328
Practice Bnkr.	No	Fairways		Bermuda 328

Makena North Course

#14

With the par-5 14th, the course begins its descent back to the clubhouse with a 200-foot drop from tee to green. From the tee, the fairway sweeps down and left; only a trail of large bunkers in the fairway points the way to the green. A tee shot that remains close to those bunkers is best, as shots out to the right have to carry over trees on the second shots. It's possible to bite off too much on your second shot and fly this one, so take careful note of the drop to the green and the direction of the wind. A huge fairway bunker short and right looks to gobble up conservative second shots, though, so maybe you're better off trying to slam it all the way home.

| 16TH GREEN | TOP OF THE 14TH (ABOVE) 10TH FLAG (BELOW) | 13TH FROM THE TEE |

Directions

From the airport, follow Hwy. 380 south for about a mile, then turn left on Hwy. 311 toward Kihei. At the intersection with Hwy. 31, turn left toward Wailea and follow that road until it enters Wailea Resort. Turn left at intersection with Wailea Alanui Dr. and continue for about 3 miles until the entrance on your left.

MAKENA
GOLF
COURSES

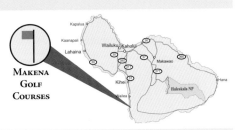

15th green and Maui's north shore

WAIEHU MUNICIPAL GOLF COURSE
~:Choke Hole: #7:~

FANATIC
Ratings

DESIGN INTRIGUE	★★✦
DIFFICULTY	★★★
BEAUTY	★★★★✦
MAINTENANCE	★★✦
SERVICE	★
SWANK FACTOR	★

With the countless investment dollars that the major resorts on Maui have shelled out for golf development, it seems unlikely that the most oceanfront golf on the island would be found at its only municipal. But it is. Tucked away in a slow-paced town northwest of the airport, worlds away from the spas and boutiques of the resorts, you will find Waiehu. The original nine, constructed in 1929, sit on the wind-battered flats of Maui's north shore, and feature three holes that run right along a white-sand beach for a total of 1,000 yards of oceanfront. While that much primo real estate might not have amounted to too much in the early years of the last century, on today's Maui, the value of this land can be conservatively estimated at just north of a kajillion dollars. So naturally, one would expect to pay greens fees through the roof. Wrong again. Welcome to the cheapest golf on the island. Welcome to Waiehu. From the creaky golf carts to the views of the Pacific Ocean, Haleakala, and the West Maui Mountains, this place is another gem on the jewel-studded crown of Maui golf courses.

> "ON THE BACK NINE, LEAVE EVERYTHING LEFT, BECAUSE EVERYTHING RUNS TO THE OUT OF BOUNDS."
> —ARTHUR REGO, DIRECTOR OF GOLF

> ### REMEMBER
> NO HASSLE DA LOCALS. THEY WERE NOT ONLY HERE FIRST, BUT IT'S THEIR TAX DOLLARS
> THAT KEEP THE GREENS FEES AFFORDABLE.

THE COURSE

With wide fairways and moderate yardages, this course could be played as effortlessly as a player piano if it weren't for the trade winds, which reliably keep things challenging. Many of the holes can be approached with a bump and run, however, so even when your ball is blowing off the tee it's still possible to keep it under the wind and score reasonably well. The condition of the greens and fairways can range from very good to downright crusty, so be prepared to deal with some funky lies and putts. If you find yourself getting frustrated with the conditions, remember to stop, admire your surroundings, count the extra money in your wallet, and you should feel much better. Tall palms and ironwood trees line many of the fairways, but if you really jerk one, it will usually run onto an adjacent fairway where you should have a decent chance of putting it back into play. There isn't a load of strategy here, just keep the ball in play and enjoy the views.

At the beach along #7

THE HOLES

#5

The par-3 fifth is the first of the holes that really make the front nine special, and that is mostly because of the sublime view from the elevated tee. The shot, however, is a demanding 234-yard blast to a distant green that's flanked by a hill of vegetation on the right and a large greenside bunker on the left. The prevailing winds are directly at your back, though, which makes this a tough one to club correctly. I couldn't talk my playing partner out of his driver, despite the sharp wind at our backs, and his perfectly struck ball caught high in the wind and was never seen again.

6th green

#6

#6 is the first to play at the edge of the Pacific (you'll want to take pictures of it from the elevated tee at #5—it's breathtaking). Your mission on this par-4 seems clear: don't hit it right. This simple rationale is challenged

Waiehu Municipal Golf Course (why-ay-hoo)				
Address			**Contact**	
200 Halewaiu Road Wailuku, HI 96793			808-270-7400—Tee Times 808-244-5934—Pro Shop	
Course Details			**Scorecard**	
Architect			Par	72
Year Opened	1929 (front nine)		Slope	120
Renovated	1966 (back nine added)		Course Rating	70.1
Reservations	2 days out/Singles standby		**Tees/Yardages**	
Online Times	No		White	6330
Greens Fees	$		Red	5478
Discounts	None			
Club Rentals	Yes			
Premium	No			
Houses	No			
Water			**Distances**	
Types	Lakes/Ocean		Well-marked	Yes
Water Holes	3		Yardage Book	No
Oceanfront	Yes		Sprinklers	Yes
			GPS	Sky Caddie
Practice			**Bunkers**	
Driving Range	Mats		How Many?	47
Practice Balls	Extra		Consistency	Decent
Putting Green	Yes		**Grass**	
Chip Green	No		Greens	Tifdwarf
Practice Bnkr.	No		Fairways	Bermuda

Waiehu Municipal Golf Course

y the fact that a shot that is dumped safely
ut to the left leaves a blind approach over
mound into a narrow green guarded by
unkers left and right.

7

he seventh is a par-5 that can play differ-
ntly depending on where the tee box is
laced. Shots to the right are in danger of
nding the beach (not a sand trap, the actual
each), but balls on this side open up the
ossibility of a run-up approach between the
unkers that front the green. Two-shotting your way into this one requires two strong shots into
ie prevailing trades.

19th Puka	
Ambiance:	Cinder block muny
Fully stocked:	Yes
Draft beer:	No
Menu:	Yes
Cost:	Cheap! Cheap!
Best bet:	Pancake sandwich at breakfast and Chicken Katsu for lunch
The Lowdown:	Simple gathering place for folks to gather for a cold one and some good local grinds.

MAUI "NO KA OI" (IS THE BEST) | THE 14TH GREEN (ABOVE) WIND-BATTERED TREES (BELOW) | CARDINAL

Directions

rom South and West Maui, follow Hwy. 30 into Wailuku
nd turn left on Hwy. 330. From the airport, turn right on
Hwy. 36, and follow it as it becomes Hwy. 32 into Wailuku.
Turn right on Hwy. 330. Proceed along Hwy. 330 for about
4 miles and turn right just past the baseball diamond at
Waihee Park onto Halewaiu Rd. and follow it to its end.

WAIEHU
MUNICIPAL
GOLF
COURSE

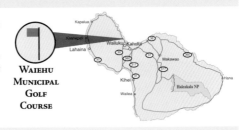

The par-3 8th with Molokini and Kaho'ola[w]

WAILEA GOLF CLUB—GOLD COURSE
~:Choke Hole: #6:~

Former site of Champions Tour Wendy's Skins Game

FANATIC Ratings

DESIGN INTRIGUE	★★★★
DIFFICULTY	★★★★
BEAUTY	★★★★
MAINTENANCE	★★★★✓
SERVICE	★★★★
SWANK FACTOR	★★★★✓

THE RESORT

The renowned Wailea Resort encompasses an idyllic community spread along the peaceful waters of Maui's southern coast. This area receives more sun and less wind than the resorts of West Maui—pretty sweet golf conditions—and is lushly planted with tropical trees and plants. There is a more relaxed feel here than at Lahaina and Ka'anapali. The three golf courses at Wailea are some of the finest courses in the state, and you can't go wrong with any of them. All three climb the slopes of Haleakala to afford incredible vistas of the sparkling waters around Molokini and Kaho'olawe. Accordingly, some of the finest accommodations and restau[rants] on the island can be found in Wailea, too.

> *TAKE MORE CLUB THAN YOU INITIALLY THINK. A LOT OF AMATEURS COME UP SHORT, AND THE COURSE IS SET UP TO PUNISH SHORT APPROACH SHOTS. LONGER IS BETTER.*
> —RUSTY HATHAWAY, HEAD GOLF PROFESSIONAL

THE COURSE

As I approached the first tee of the Wailea Gold course, the starter gave me a preview of what lay ahead. "I hope you brought a pail and shovel, 'cause there's ninety-three bunkers out there," he said with a laugh. My playing partner for the day had this take: "Whoever designed this course has a sand fetish." Well, you'll have to ask Robert Trent Jones, Jr. about that, but it's hard to think otherwise after a day spent playing the Gold. There may be ninety-three bunkers, but there are several that look like three or four separate traps that are actually one large, intricately shaped bunker complex. On some of the par-3s, it appears that there is more sand than green, which may actually be the case.

And so, we arrive at the definition of target golf: this course. On many holes, you must check your yardages on your GPS or yardage booklet and hit from one green spot to another over all that fluffy white stuff that sits in your way. It's fun, though, and the maintenance crews do an excellent job of keeping the sand consistent and playable.

The tee at #4

The Gold Course is not as user-friendly as the Old Blue, and not as scenic as the Emerald, but it is the most hard-core of the courses at Wailea. You'll still enjoy some fine views and a few wide fairways on the Gold, but by and large, you are going to have to put the ball in the air and land it where you intend if you are going to score well here.

THE HOLES

#1

Just like its neighbor, the Emerald, the Gold Course has a fantastic starting hole. The first is a downhill par-4 that sweeps left, with fairway bunkers in play and some room out to the right for those who haven't quite gotten their swing together by the first tee. The views of Molokini, the small crescent-shaped islet straight out to sea, are impressive and the hole gets your blood pumping for things to come.

The first gree

#6

The sixth is a diabolical construct. It's a short par-4 of a drivable distance for those with a

WAILEA GOLF CLUB—GOLD COURSE (why-lay-uh)

ADDRESS		CONTACT	
100 Wailea Club Drive Wailea, HI 96753		808-875-7450 WWW.WAILEAGOLF.COM	
COURSE DETAILS		**SCORECARD**	
Architect	Robert Trent Jones, Jr.	Par	72
Year Opened	1994	Slope	137
Renovated	No	Course Rating	73.4
Reservations	30 days out	**TEES/YARDAGES**	
Online Times	Yes	Gold	7078
Greens Fees	$$$$	Blue	6653
Discounts	Resort/Twilight	White	6152
Club Rentals	Yes	Red	5317
Premium	Yes		
Houses	No		
WATER		**DISTANCES**	
Types	Lake	Well-marked	Yes
Water Holes	1	Yardage Book	Yes
Oceanfront	No	Sprinklers	Yes
		GPS	In-cart
PRACTICE		**BUNKERS**	
Driving Range	Grass	How Many?	93
Practice Balls	Included	Consistency	Good, dense
Putting Green	Yes	**GRASS**	
Chip Green	Yes	Greens	Tifdwarf
Practice Bnkr.	Yes	Fairways	Bermuda 328

Wailea Gold Course

easonable gift for length, but the bunkers that surround the green demand precision as well as distance. If you catch a bit too much of the ball, which is certainly possible on days with the wind t your back, there's a bunker directly behind the green that melts into a black lava rock wall that makes for some exciting and unpredictable bounces. This hole amounts to great, fiendish fun.

7

The seventh is a station-to-station, double-dog-legged monstrosity that requires even further precision. The initial dogleg right is protected by bunkers at the corner. Beat those and you have a good shot of laying a nice one up over the third fairway bunker on the left, but short of the green-side traps. An undulating green makes for dramatic holds. Is it sand heaven or sand hell? I predict he answer to that question will depend on your score.

8

f there was a signature hole at the Gold, #8 would probably be it. This gorgeous par-3 plays out to the best view of Molokini on any of the Wailea courses. With the winds blowing, this can be really difficult to club correctly. On this trip, I hit a sweet-spot 4-iron from 180 yards out toward he center of the green but didn't see it land. It wasn't on the green when I came up, so I assumed it had gone over but couldn't find it there. I almost gave up until my playing partner pointed out the ball sitting in the front bunker twenty-five yards short of the pin. My advice, and the advice of the head pro: take enough club!

WAILEA GOLF CLUB
GOLD COURSE
♣
(FROM RIGHT)
••••••
DIABOLICAL
BUNKERING
••••••
5TH GREEN WITH WEST
MAUI BEHIND
••••••
PLUMERIA
••••••
6TH GREEN
••••••
9TH GREEN WITH PU'U
OLAI

A gorgeous opener: the first at Wailea Emerald

WAILEA GOLF CLUB—EMERALD COURSE
~:Choke Hole: #10:~

The Wailea Gold and Emerald courses are centered around a different, more upscale clubhouse than the Blue. It's like a fine Hawaiian hotel, with an elegant lobby, posh lounge, chic restaurant, and fantastic pro shop stuffed full of Wailea-branded apparel. What the Old Blue lacks in warm-up facilities, this area more than makes up for, with a large driving range, pitching green with practice bunkers, and a putting green. Players take specially labeled range carts up to the practice area, rather than their playing carts. This place has some snob appeal, but the staff keeps it real and everyone seems to be having too much fun to be annoying.

FANATIC Ratings

DESIGN INTRIGUE	★★★★
DIFFICULTY	★★★✦
BEAUTY	★★★★✦
MAINTENANCE	★★★★✦
SERVICE	★★★★
SWANK FACTOR	★★★★✦

THE COURSE

With sweeping views and terrific golf, the Emerald Course is special. The landscaping and maintenance is superb, and while the layout isn't seriously demanding, players are still faced with many

> " PUTTS BREAK TOWARD THE OCEAN, SO CLUB SELECTION
> IS IMPORTANT IN POSITIONING THE BALL ON THE COR-
> RECT SIDE OF THE HOLE FOR AN EASIER PUTT. "
> —RUSTY HATHAWAY, HEAD GOLF PROFESSIONAL

nteresting problems and choices. The fairways are wide and there are plenty of safe landing areas, but Trent Jones, Jr. has jammed most holes so full of shaped bunkers that they dictate the shots that you must play off the tee. There are a few forced carries and one lake comes into play on both #10 and #17, but mostly your adversaries on the course are the sand and the wind. Take note: the local rule on a ball that goes into one of the landscaped areas is a free drop. How many courses give you that?

The Holes

#1

The first hole is a perfect opener: par-4 that plays straight downhill to a medium-sized green framed right above the ocean. The view is so pretty the starter will likely offer to take your picture on the tee. Anything straight will roll well down the fairway, providing that warm feeling we all enjoy when we blast one off of the first tee.

#4

The fourth is a short par-4 that looks narrow from the tee, but widens out in the landing area. A unique string of bunkers crosses the hole diagonally, beginning short on the left side and stretching all the way to a greenside bunker on the right. This makes driving the ball long and safe a difficult task; though the fairway tips slightly to the right, the prevailing trade winds push the ball toward bunkers on the left. The sensible shot is a fairway-wood short of the bunkers on the right side, then a short-iron in.

#6

The sixth is a tough-to-gauge par-4 that plays downhill and doglegs left. A bunker on the short left corner and another long on the right side of the fairway are actually far enough apart to drop a drive in between, but from the tee the landing area looks small. Use the GPS to figure out your shot, as you may be able to clear the first bunker, cut the corner and roll your drive way down

The double green at #10 and #17

the hill. The green has no sand protection, only grass bunkers and collection areas that make for fun pitching. Crack out a grabby Pro VI for this one.

#10
The tenth is a par-4 with a blind tee shot and a reachable lake on the left side. Play either right or short to avoid the water.

A big drive will serve you well on #

WAILEA GOLF CLUB—EMERALD COURSE (why-LAY-uh)			
ADDRESS		**CONTACT**	
100 Wailea Club Drive Wailea, HI 96753		808-875-7450 WWW.WAILEAGOLF.COM	
COURSE DETAILS		**SCORECARD**	
Architect	Robert Trent Jones, Jr.	Par	72
Year Opened	1994	Slope	126
Renovated	No	Course Rating	72.8
Reservations	30 days out	**TEES/YARDAGES**	
Online Times	Yes	Green	6825
Greens Fees	$$$$	Blue	6407
Discounts	Resort/Twilight	White	5873
Club Rentals	Yes	Red	5268
Premium	Yes		
Houses	No		
WATER		**DISTANCES**	
Types	Lakes	Well-marked	Yes
Water Holes	3	Yardage Book	Yes
Oceanfront	No	Sprinklers	Yes
		GPS	In-cart
PRACTICE		**BUNKERS**	
Driving Range	Grass	How Many?	72
Practice Balls	Included	Consistency	Good, dense
Putting Green	Yes	**GRASS**	
Chip Green	Yes	Greens	Tifdwarf
Practice Bnkr.	Yes	Fairways	Bermuda 328

Wailea Emerald Course

Your approach will likely have the lake in play unless you play way right. The green is double, shared with the 17th, and the view from the green and the fairway is wonderful.

17

The seventeenth is a lot like the tenth, but the water is visible off the tee. It's even more reachable, however, so it may be a good idea to lay up short. At the same time, long hitters may be able to drive this green, which slopes away from the water, increasing your chances of staying dry. What would a Golf Fanatic do?

19th Puka

Ambiance:	Posh
Fully stocked:	Yes
Draft beer:	Yes
Menu:	Yes
Cost:	Stratospheric
Best bet:	Mac-nut Encrusted Brie
The Lowdown:	A Wailea institution, The Seawatch features high-end Pacific Rim cuisine served with ocean and golf course views.

BUNKERS AT THE 9TH

GREAT DRIVING ON #18 (ABOVE)
APPROACHING ON #5 (BELOW)

#15 FROM THE TEE

Directions

From the airport, follow Hwy. 380 south for about a mile, then turn left on Hwy. 311 toward Kihei. At the intersection with Hwy. 31, turn left toward Wailea and continue until it enters Wailea Resort. Turn left at the intersection with Wailea Alanui Dr. and follow for about a mile. The entrance is on the left on Wailea Club Dr.

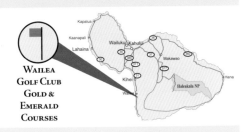
WAILEA GOLF CLUB GOLD & EMERALD COURSES

The lovely par-3 12t

WAILEA GOLF CLUB—OLD BLUE COURSE
~:Choke Hole: #9:~

The Course

After his success on the South course at Ka'anapali, Arthur Jack Snyder returned to Hawaii to begin work on a layout for the new planned resort of Wailea in South Maui. His efforts on the Old Blue are more expansive here, with huge greens and massive greenside bunkers as the course's most conspicuous traits. Most of the greens are gently sloped, and don't break as much as they appear to, while the bunkers are oval and lack intricate fingering and big lips. Coupled with coarse and consistent sand, this makes exiting the bunkers a relative snap.

Opened in 1972, The Old Blue was the first of the Wailea courses to go in, and as such it plays through the resort areas a little more than the other two. However, th

FANATIC Ratings
DESIGN INTRIGUE
★★★
DIFFICULTY
★★★
BEAUTY
★★★✦
MAINTENANCE
★★★★
SERVICE
★★★★
SWANK FACTOR
★★★★

> *BEWARE OF THE VISUAL HAZARDS. TYPICALLY COURSES HAVE BUNKERS, WATER AND OTHER THINGS LIKE WASTE AREAS AS HAZARDS, BUT AT WAILEA THE BEAUTIFUL SCENERY CAN BE QUITE DISTRACTING. GET INTO A RHYTHM OF TAKING IN THE BEAUTY AND THEN FOCUS ON YOUR SHOT. AND IF THE GROUP IN FRONT PAUSES FOR A MOMENT TO OBSERVE A BREACHING WHALE, ENJOY THE MOMENT WITH THEM.*
> —BARRY HELLE, GENERAL MANAGER

ndscaping is well done and features many fully-grown trees and plants that obscure views of the
oads, so it seems more isolated than it actually is. You can still hear traffic moving through, but it
s less a roar than a soft hiss, the rumble of cars somehow absorbed and softened by the bountiful
plant life.

There are no oceanfront holes on the course, but several feature great views of West Maui,
nd across the channel to Molokini and Kaho'olawe. There has been a recent flurry of new home
onstruction along several fairways, which, unfortunately, robs the course of some its traditional
iews, but when you gain a nice vista the panorama is still awe-inspiring. The many mature trees
nd lush plantings lend a nice, aged (like a wine, not a liver) feel to the course. Ultimately, the Old
Blue plays gently, with wide fairways and few difficult carries. It is the least demanding of the
hree courses at Wailea, but it's a very pleasant way to spend an afternoon. And if you find your-
elf in doubt on a putt, aim straight at or inside the hole, as there generally isn't as much break as
here appears to be. Employees will advise you that putts break toward the ocean, but the ocean
tretches far and wide so it can be a little difficult to judge exactly which way the grain grows.

The Holes

The Old Blue isn't the kind of course that features just a few exceptional holes with the rest merely
ounding out the track. Rather, the holes are very cohesive and uniform, and together amount to
n excellent course. That said, there are a few holes that exemplify the course experience.

6

The par-4 6th is a great driving hole that swoops down from the tee and back up to the green.
Fairway bunkers short right and long left keep you on your toes, and big greenside bunkers nar-
ow your focus.

Artful bunkering at #4

#9

Number nine is a gorgeous, short par-3 with two small lakes guarding short, and big bunkers sitting left and right. The tee and green are pretty much level, so it is a straightforward mid- to short-iron shot that requires a straight, high pop off the tee. The only elements that can beat you on this hole are the light trades and the magnetic attraction of water. What really makes this hole, though, are the palms, the thick vegetation behind the green highlighted by fluorescent bougainvillea and the chartreuse slopes of Haleakala beyond.

A rainbow eucalyptu

WAILEA GOLF CLUB—OLD BLUE COURSE (why-LAY-uh)

ADDRESS		CONTACT	
120 Kaukahi Street		808-879-2530	
Wailea, HI 96753		WWW.WAILEAGOLF.COM	
COURSE DETAILS		**SCORECARD**	
Architect	Arthur Jack Snyder	Par	72
Year Opened	1972	Slope	129
Renovated	No	Course Rating	72.2
Reservations	30 days out	**TEES/YARDAGES**	
Online Times	Yes	Blue	6765
Greens Fees	$$$$	White	6397
Discounts	Resort/Twilight	Red	5208
Club Rentals	Yes		
Premium	Yes		
Houses	Yes		
WATER		**DISTANCES**	
Types	Lakes	Well-marked	Yes
Water Holes	3	Yardage Book	Yes
Oceanfront	No	Sprinklers	Yes
		GPS	In-cart
PRACTICE		**BUNKERS**	
Driving Range	Mats into nets	How Many?	68
Practice Balls	Included	Consistency	Consistent
Putting Green	Yes	**GRASS**	
Chip Green	Yes	Greens	Tifdwarf
Practice Bnkr.	Yes	Fairways	Bermuda 328

Wailea Old Blue Course

12

The par-3 12th is another short one-shot-er, but this one plays from an elevated tee with great views of Molokini and Kahoʻolawe out to sea. The green is a bungee-jump plunge below, and along with the prevailing trade winds, this is a tough one to club correctly. Bunkers short, long, left, and right punish your miscalculation. Enjoy the view before aiming for the center of the green.

19th Puka

Ambiance:	Irish country club
Fully stocked:	Yes
Draft beer:	Oh, yes
Menu:	Yes
Cost:	Pricey
Best bet:	Irish Potato Boxty followed by the Bangers and Mash
The Lowdown:	Mulligan's on the Blue is as close as Hawaii ever gets to Ireland. Cheers, mate!

WAILEA GOLF CLUB OLD BLUE COURSE
❀
(FROM RIGHT)
•••••••
OVER THE WATER ON #2
•••••••
CATTLE EGRET
•••••••
GOLF CART
•••••••
LAVA ROCK FOUNTAIN
•••••••
THE FLAG AT #3

Wailea
Wailea Golf Club

Directions

From the airport, follow Hwy. 380 south for about a mile, then turn left on Hwy. 311 toward Kihei. At the intersection with Hwy. 31, turn left toward Wailea and continue until it enters Wailea Resort. Turn left at the intersection with Wailea Alanui Dr. and follow for about a ½ mile. The entrance to the Old Blue is on the left on Kaukahi St.

WAILEA GOLF CLUB OLD BLUE COURSE

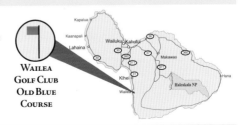

The 17th hole at the Palmer Course at Turtle Ba

O'ahu

As it has been since long before Western contact, O'ahu remains the "Gathering Place," where people and cultures blend to create a human landscape unlike anywhere else. O'ahu's physical features are as diverse as its people. Waikiki, the ultimate symbol of the high-rise Hawaiian vacation, exists on the same mass of land as the laid-back North Shore, where some of the world's fiercest waves beckon to surfers, and the Wai'anae Coast, an outpost of local culture and isolation. The varied experience translates to golf, as well. The rural courses at Turtle Bay coexist with the dense, jungly tracks at Ko'olau and Luana Hills as well as the suburban layouts in the Ewa Plain, including Coral Creek and Kapolei, and resorts like Ko Olina.

THE CHALLENGE	THE PALMER	THE GETAWAY
KO'OLAU GOLF CLUB	TURTLE BAY PALMER	MAKAHA RESORT
Architect Dick Nugent's raw, twisted design can be brutal, but is worth it for its beauty and sheer golf exhilaration.	The King has stamped his mark on the remote North Shore, where the Seniors and LPGA gather to pay respect.	It's not Waikiki, which is exactly what makes the Wai-anae Coast so nice: it's a real retreat from civilization.
Page 97	Page 125	Page 110

O'ahu

Nickname: The Gathering Place
Area: 596.7 square miles
Highest Point: Mt. Ka'ala, 4,003 feet
Population: 876,151 (2000 census)
Flower: Ilima

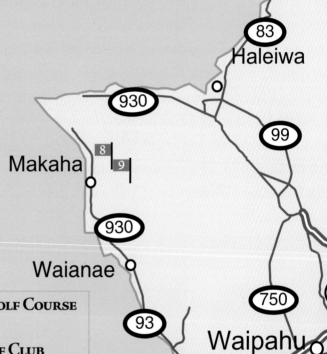

83

Haleiwa

930

99

8
9

Makaha

930

Waianae

750

F

93

Waipahu

H1

6

I   3   E

4

2

Kapolei

H

1 - **Coral Creek Golf Course**

2 - **Ewa Beach Golf Club**

3 - **Hawaii Prince Golf Club**

4 - **Kapolei Golf Course**

5 - **Ko'olau Golf Club**

6 - **Ko Olina Golf Club**

13
12

7 - LUANA HILLS COUNTRY CLUB

8 - MAKAHA RESORT GOLF CLUB

9 - MAKAHA VALLEY COUNTRY CLUB

10 - OLOMANA GOLF LINKS

11 - PEARL COUNTRY CLUB

12 - TURTLE BAY PALMER COURSE

13 - TURTLE BAY FAZIO COURSE

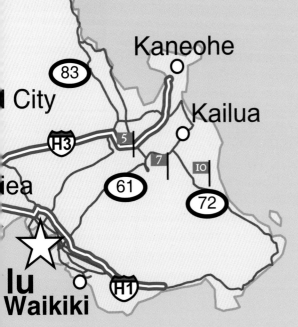

The signature 10

Coral Creek Golf Course
~:Choke Hole: #10:~

FANATIC Ratings

DESIGN INTRIGUE	★★★
DIFFICULTY	★★★★⯪
BEAUTY	★★★
MAINTENANCE	★★★★
SERVICE	★★★
SWANK FACTOR	★★★⯪

Located right in the thick of O'ahu's booming new suburbia, Coral Creek is one of several quality courses on the Ewa Plain. The design utilizes ancient coral beds for an intriguing effect—they're the blanched, dry walls on several lakes on the course. The course's namesake Coral Creek, which is a dry coral bed that runs through the front nine, thrives with bougainvillea and hides the hazard that lies beneath. More than anything, the porous coral that underlies the turf provides fantastic drainage, so when heavy rains roll through Ewa, they don't flood the course, and it dries quickly. As with the other layouts in the Ewa area, Coral Creek is under the landing pattern for Honolulu International Airport and Hickam Air Force Base. Don't let the thought of jets overhead put you off, just consider passing on that third cup of coffee in the morning to keep your nerves from flinching at the sound of a pair of F-18s streaking by while you're standing over a birdie putt.

> " Visitors to Hawaii get used to putting the Bermuda grass greens that are prevalent at most courses on the islands, but Coral Creek has seashore paspalum greens, which have very little grain. Just read the slope and you'll putt well. "
> —Derek Claveran, Head Professional

THE COURSE

The course is very well maintained, and features seashore paspalum on the greens and along the fairways, so the landscape boasts that iridescent emerald glow that paspalum provides. The aspect of the course that will most affect your play is the bunkering, which has some steep backs and faces that are difficult to escape. Unfortunately, they are removing a number of these bunkers because of the maintenance demands of such elaborate bunkering. (They also removed a trap in the middle of the 4th fairway because players were driving away from it, and into the houses along the left side of the fairway.) In addition to all that sand, there are many grass bunkers and collection areas that set up some challenging short game situations. It's a good idea to spend some time warming up in the short game area before beginning your round.

One practice that sets Coral Creek apart from any other course in the state is the measurement of stimp readings every morning. Signs are located next to each green so that you know how fast each is putting. On the first couple of holes this isn't that helpful (how many people instinctively know how fast a stimped "8" is putting?), but after a while you get a relative feel for the readings from green to green.

THE HOLES

2

The diminutive 2nd employs an unusual technique that is rarely seen in Hawaii. The teeing area spreads across a wide "L" that takes up two sides of a deep gulch. The tees can be arranged on either side, essentially creating a hole that plays totally differently depending on where the tees are set each day. One side plays into the trades to a shallow green, while the other side presents you with a crosswind that brings a triplet of bunkers into play and narrows the putting surface considerably. Of course, if there's no wind it's pretty much a pitch-and-putt from either side.

Coral Creek crosses the 14th fairway

#3

The third is a short par-4 that doglegs right and invites longer hitters to make a play across the waste toward the green. Fairway bunkers on the far side punish hitters who have plenty of power but don't want to risk the shot over the waste.

#10

The signature 10th is a tricked-up beauty. A wide waterfall is the centerpiece of a tropical garden backdrop that is stuffed with flowering plumeria trees and bougainvillea. A second waterfall bubbles off to the right side of the green, emptying into the large, coral-lined lake that fronts the green.

CORAL CREEK GOLF COURSE			
ADDRESS		**CONTACT**	
91-1111 Geiger Road		808-441-4653	
Ewa Beach, HI 96706		WWW.CORALCREEKGOLFHAWAII.COM	
COURSE DETAILS		**SCORECARD**	
Architect	Nelson & Haworth	Par	72
Year Opened	1999	Slope	135
Renovated	No	Course Rating	72.2
Reservations	30 days out	**TEES/YARDAGES**	
Online Times	Yes	Black	6808
Greens Fees	$$$	Blue	6347
Discounts	Twilight	White	5912
Club Rentals	Yes	Yellow	4935
Premium	Yes		
Houses	Yes		
WATER		**DISTANCES**	
Types	Creeks/Lakes	Well-marked	Yes
Water Holes	13	Yardage Book	Yes
Oceanfront	No	Sprinklers	Yes
		GPS	Sky Caddie
PRACTICE		**BUNKERS**	
Driving Range	Mats	How Many?	76
Practice Balls	Extra	Consistency	Good, coarse
Putting Green	Yes	**GRASS**	
Chip Green	Yes	Greens	Paspalum
Practice Bnkr.	Yes	Fairways	Paspalum

Coral Creek Golf Course

he hole has some teeth, too, as it's straight to the trades, and anything short is likely to t wet. The green is wide and forgiving on f-center shots, however. Before the round, u may want to sign up for a hole-in-one omotion that offers a free round-trip flight Asia for those who can one-shot this hole.

19th Puka

Ambiance:	Comfy grillroom
Fully stocked:	Yes
Draft beer:	Yes
Menu:	Yes
Cost:	Par
Best bet:	The burgers
The Lowdown:	The North Shore Cattle Company raises grass-fed, hormone-free beef on their ranch on the North Shore. Tip: try the beef.

I

t 636 yards, playing the par-5 11th can
e a painfully drawn out experience. The
ole dogs left and has some uncooperative
ounding that pushes tee shots right through the bend. Bunkers and swales the rest of the way
emand that you carefully place your second (or third, or fourth . . .) shot, and a shallow green
ecessitates exacting distance control on approach.

GREENS STIMPED DAILY	APPROACH ON #18 (ABOVE) CARRY ON THE 2ND (BELOW)	HIBISCUS

Directions

From Waikiki, follow the H-1 West towards Waianae for about 8 miles and get off on exit #5a, Ewa. Continue straight ff of the off ramp for about 2.5 miles along Kunia Rd./Ft. Weaver Rd. Turn right at the light on Geiger Rd., and find he entrance a half-mile down on the left.

CORAL CREEK GOLF COURSE

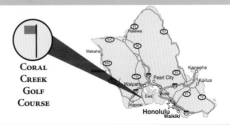

The par-3 13

Ewa Beach Golf Club
~:Choke Hole: #8:~

This excellent Robin Nelson design is fun, well-maintained, and a great value. The course receives fairly light play during the week, so it can be a great option for getting away from the sometimes uncomfortable swell of people on Oʻahu golf courses. It's at the end of the road in Ewa Beach, and, well, it's directly under the landing pattern for planes coming into Honolulu International and massive military jets landing at Hickam Air Force Base. It reminds me of the exchange between Jake and Elwood in "The Blues Brothers": "How often does the train come by?" "So often you won't even notice."

The clubhouse is a clean, modern affair with a well-equipped pro shop, locker room, and restaurant. The lack of a driving range is a drag, and you shouldn't show u expecting the VIP treatment. However, several of the holes have particularly fancy ball washer so the club is not without its charms.

FANATIC Ratings	
DESIGN INTRIGUE	★★★⯪
DIFFICULTY	★★★⯪
BEAUTY	★★★
MAINTENANCE	★★★★
SERVICE	★★
SWANK FACTOR	★★★

> " WHEN PLAYING AT EWA BEACH, KEEP THE BALL UNDER THE WIND FOR BEST CONTROL. ALSO, OUR SEASHORE PASPALUM GRASS CAN BE A LITTLE STICKY BOTH IN THE ROUGH AND THE FAIRWAY, SO BE SURE TO PICK YOUR BALL CLEAN. "
> —AILEEN YAMAUCHI, PRO SHOP MANAGER

The Course

While I'd like to say that the course is cut through a *kiawe* forest, they didn't actually cut down many trees, and the result is a very tight layout. The fairways are narrow, but if you hit one off line will probably just hit one of the trees, eliciting a resonant thunk, and drop into the nearby rough. All of the grass on the course is seashore paspalum, which is great for the environment (can be watered with high saline water, requires few chemicals), greens (no grain, putts are fast and true), and fairways (nice roll), but paspalum is infamous for being tough to play out of the rough. The grass is extremely grabby and balls tend to sit down, making it unlikely you'll get a good lie. The course would be quite difficult if it were any longer, but at 6,676 yards from the tips, distances on most holes are manageable.

As mentioned, there's no driving range for warm up, so be sure to take some hacks onto the chipping green. Get the feel for the kind of stroke required to escape from the grabby paspalum.

Before Waikiki

There are a number of archaeological ruins scattered around the golf course at Ewa Beach Golf Club, including the kauhale (residential complex) located right by the first hole. The sites date back as far as 1000 a.d. and were occupied until nearly 1700, just prior to Western contact.

The Holes

8

The 8th is one of those short par-3s that looks so easy. Sure, there's water in front and to the right, but it's only a 9-iron or so away! Well, this is Hawaii, and that means trade winds. They generally pull right to left on this one, so when the pin is cut on the left side (or the trades are really screaming) you have to hang your ball over the water on the left and trust that it'll come back in order to have any chance to get it close. Hoo-ha! Also, the winds may swirl while you're in your back swing and suddenly that high fade stops short over the lake. Hope you hit enough club!

The 18th green

#10

The par-5 10th opens the back nine with a bang. The water on the right isn't in play off the tee, but it will work into your second shot. If you want to blast it into the green in two, don't leave it too far out to the left or you'll find one of the cluster bunkers on that side.

#11 & #12

The 11th and 12th are a rare duet of drivable par-4s. These holes just beg for birdies, but they're tricky! The 11th requires a short water carry off

Hawaiian St

EWA BEACH GOLF CLUB (AY-vuh)			
ADDRESS		**CONTACT**	
91-050 Fort Weaver Road Ewa Beach, HI 96706		808-689-6565 WWW.EWABEACHGC.COM	
COURSE DETAILS		**SCORECARD**	
Architect	Robin Nelson	Par	72
Year Opened	1992	Slope	134
Renovated	No	Course Rating	72.5
Reservations	30 days out	**TEES/YARDAGES**	
Online Times	Yes	Black	6676
Greens Fees	$$	Blue	6306
Discounts	Twilight	White	5839
Club Rentals	Yes	Red	4894
Premium	Yes		
Houses	Yes		
WATER		**DISTANCES**	
Types	Lakes	Well-marked	Yes
Water Holes	8	Yardage Book	No
Oceanfront	No	Sprinklers	Yes
		GPS	Sky Caddie
PRACTICE		**BUNKERS**	
Driving Range	None	How Many?	68
Practice Balls	N/A	Consistency	Good, playable
Putting Green	Yes	**GRASS**	
Chip Green	Yes	Greens	Paspalum
Practice Bnkr.	Yes	Fairways	Paspalum

Ewa Beach Golf Club

he tee, but you'll be more interested in getting your drive as close to the pin as possible. The winds blow left to right, which, inconveniently enough, is precisely where all of the bunkers are. The green is long and narrow, so while distance off the tee is nice, accuracy is really the key. The 12th is even shorter at only 235 yards from the resort tees. The bunkers are all in the front, so come in high with plenty of club. Of course, too long is a possibility, and Nelson didn't add any back bunkers to bail out those who let their adrenaline get the best of them.

19th Puka	
Ambiance:	Modern clubhouse
Fully stocked:	Yes
Draft beer:	No
Menu:	Yes
Cost:	Par
Best bet:	Touch of the Orient selections
The Lowdown:	With air-conditioning, comfy chairs, widescreen TVs, and views of the course, this is a nice spot to take the edge off.

EWA BEACH GOLF
CLUB

(FROM RIGHT)
......
SHAPED BUNKERS
ON #12
......
HAWAIIAN RUINS AT
THE FIRST GREEN
......
GOLF CART LOGO
......
TIGHT DRIVING ON #4
......
THE 9TH PIN

ewa beach
GOLF CLUB

Directions

From Waikiki, follow the H-1 West towards Waianae for about 8 miles and get off on exit #5a, Ewa. Continue straight off the offramp as Kunia Road becomes Ft. Weaver Road and follow it for about 6.5 miles. The entrance is on your left just before the end of the road.

EWA
BEACH
GOLF
CLUB

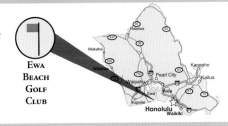

The par-4 B5t

HAWAII PRINCE GOLF CLUB
~:Choke Hole: #B9:~

Attention Golf Fanatics: You know that feeling you get when you finish 18 holes and it just wasn't enough? You're in luck. The Hawaii Prince Course boasts three sets of nines that should scratch that itch and leave you satisfied. Along with Ed Seay, Arnold Palmer has laid out three distinct nines on some varied terrain. (I know, first The King gives us an amazing playing career, then famously adds lemonade to his iced tea, and now this!) The course is owned and operated by the Prince group, and it's associated with the Hawaii Prince Hotel Waikiki, which sits amid the other towers along Waikiki Beach. Meanwhile, the course is located miles away on the dry Ewa Plain (along with several other courses), surrounded by a booming residential area and under the landing pattern for the airport. So don't expect to be playing along Waikiki Beach. One advantage to staying at the hotel is that you receive a small discount to play here. Free transportation is provided from all major Waikiki hotels, which is a nice feature that the other courses out here don't offer.

FANATIC Ratings	
DESIGN INTRIGUE	★★★↲
DIFFICULTY	★★★↲
BEAUTY	★★★
MAINTENANCE	★★★↲
SERVICE	★★★
SWANK FACTOR	★★★

> " COURSE DESIGNER ARNOLD PALMER PLAYED A NICE LITTLE DRAW, AND THAT'S THE BEST SHOT SHAPE TO PLAY HERE. THERE ARE LESS BUNKERS ON THE LEFT SIDE AND THAT SHOT CAN HOLD THE BALL IN THE TRADE WINDS. "
> —TIM HEREK, HEAD PROFESSIONAL

The Course

As with most Palmer courses, you'll do better if you put on your thinking cap and cogitate your way around the course. There are plenty of pitfalls on each hole and the ability to shape your shots (intentionally) is a huge bonus here. However, it's best to look at the course map and decide while you're on the tee which side of the fairway you want to play. The overall effect of the course is kinksy, in that there are plenty of rolls and mounding that leave you with awkward lies, and most of the greens are open in front and amenable to run-up shots that take the wind out of the equation. They've recently debunkered the course a bit; now there are 27 fewer traps to get in your way. They like to talk about the closing holes of the "B" nine and the opening duo of the "C" nine

The pin at A1

as "the longest mile of Hawaiian golf." In my experience, that's more than marketing—that's the truth. There are four par-4s, each over 400 yards, each playing directly into the prevailing trades, each with water in play. This ferocious combination plays to 1,826 yards from the tips, and that's without factoring in anything from a brisk breeze to an eye-drying gale.

The wind howls on B4

My Only Beef

I'M A LITTLE BEWILDERED AT THE NAMING OF THE NINES, A, B AND C, WHICH LEADS TO THIS TYPE OF POST-ROUND BANTER:

"AWW, MAN, I CAN'T BELIEVE THAT PUTT DIDN'T SINK ON C6."

"YEAH, BUT YOUR CHIP SHOT ON A9 WAS MICKELSON-STYLE."

"WELL, SURE, BUT YOUR DRIVE ON B8 WAS THE SHOT OF THE DAY…OR WAS THAT C8…?"

COULDN'T THEY HAVE BEEN A LITTLE MORE INVENTIVE? YOU KNOW, THE IRONWOOD NINE, THE GINGER NINE, HELL, EVEN THE PIÑA COLADA NINE WOULD STICK IN YOUR MIND BETTER.

The starter keeps tabs on how many folks are on each nine and will direct you toward the loop that is moving the quickest at the onset and mid-point of your round. That keeps play moving, but you may prefer to request a certain combination. The "A" nine is fun from a golf perspective, but it is now lined with houses along the fairways. The "B" loop is lined with lovely ironwood and Norfolk pines, cutting down on some of the wind and lending more of a sense of solitude that series of holes. The "C" nine is the longest from the tips, and features what may be my favorite hole on the course, C2. If you want to play all 27 holes, you'll need to buck out a little bit more, but the restaurant serves an excellent lunch to fuel you up before your final nine.

My favorite combination of loops is B-C, so if you find that your tastes are in line with

Hawaii Prince Golf Club

HAWAII PRINCE GOLF CLUB			
ADDRESS		**CONTACT**	
91-1200 Fort Weaver Road Ewa Beach, HI 96706		808-944-4567 WWW.PRINCERESORTSHAWAII.COM	
COURSE DETAILS		**SCORECARD**	
Architect	Arnold Palmer/Ed Seay	Par	See
Year Opened	1992	Slope	Box
Renovated	No	Course Rating	
Reservations	2 weeks out	**TEES/YARDAGES**	
Online Times	No	Black	
Greens Fees	$$$	Blue	See
Discounts	Twilight/Resort	White	Box
Club Rentals	Yes	Yellow	
Premium	Yes		
Houses	Yes		
WATER		**DISTANCES**	
Types	Lakes	Well-marked	Yes
Water Holes	16/27 holes	Yardage Book	Yes
Oceanfront	No	Sprinklers	Yes
		GPS	Sky Caddie
PRACTICE		**BUNKERS**	
Driving Range	Grass	How Many?	91/27 holes
Practice Balls	Included	Consistency	Decent
Putting Green	Yes	**GRASS**	
Chip Green	Yes	Greens	Tifdwarf
Practice Bnkr.	Yes	Fairways	Bermuda 328

ny own, you may want to specifically request hose nines.

THE HOLES

A7

The par-4 A7th is a perfect example of how The King likes to torture slicers. Shots that draw out to the left open up the green and take the punitive bunker on the short right side out of the equation. Meanwhile, anything that bends right off the tee will usually bite into the trades, go hard right, and find a watery end in the lake that runs the entire length of the hole. Just think hooky thoughts.

B9

The long par-4 B9 is a bruiser. The fairway snakes between lakes with water left off the tee and right on approach (finally, some equality!). The wind will usually blast into your face, so low-running shots are ideal. The medium-small green is open at the front for such an approach.

HAWAII PRINCE GOLF CLUB			
A Nine			
Black		3514	
Blue		3352	
Orange		3138	
White		2685	
B Nine			
Black		3603	
Blue		3407	
Orange		3099	
White		2590	
C Nine			
Black		3652	
Blue		3394	
Orange		3076	
White		2615	
18 Hole Combos	Par	Slope	Rating
A/B	72	137	73.8
A/C	72	137	74.1
B/C	72	136	74.8

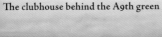
The clubhouse behind the A9th green

C2

The second along the C nine is one of those "tough but fun" holes. The par-4 dogs to the left so, again, a draw is ideal. Fortunately (for me, anyway) a nice hook is facilitated by the trade winds that usually blow right to left and will help most shots carry around the corner. Still, one has to decide off the tee how much of the lake to bite off on the drive. The more the better, of course, but if the wind blows your ball too much then you'll wet your egg. And for those who just play straight out, two happy bunkers are placed on the far side of the corner to ruin the hole for you.

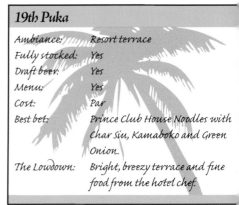

19th Puka

Ambiance:	Resort terrace
Fully stocked:	Yes
Draft beer:	Yes
Menu:	Yes
Cost:	Par
Best bet:	Prince Club House Noodles with Char Siu, Kamaboko and Green Onion.
The Lowdown:	Bright, breezy terrace and fine food from the hotel chef.

Hawaii Prince Golf Club

(FROM RIGHT)
......
Pin at A8
......
Green C1
......
Hawaiian Coot
......
Over the lake on A7
......
The B8th green

Directions

From Waikiki, follow the H-1 West towards Waianae for about 8 miles and get off on exit #5a, Ewa. Continue straight off the off ramp for about 2.5 miles along Kunia Rd./Ft. Weaver Rd. Turn left at the light on Iroquois Rd./Geiger Rd., then take a quick right onto Keaunui Rd. The entrance is on the left just before the road reconnects with Ft. Weaver Rd.

HAWAII PRINCE GOLF CLUB

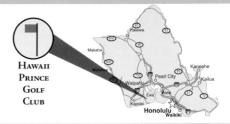

Tee shot on #16

KAPOLEI GOLF COURSE
~:Choke Hole: #18 :~
Pro Site: Formerly the Cup Noodles Hawaiian Ladies Open

One of the island's most highly regarded courses is situated amidst the boom and bustle of the Ewa Plain along O'ahu's southwestern coast in the nouveau settlement of Kapolei. Dubbed "The Second City," Kapolei has exactly the kind of familiar landscape that Americans have grown accustomed to everywhere, with extensive cookie-cutter subdivisions and strip malls full of megastores and chain restaurants. Luckily, the golf experience at Kapolei Golf Course is less generic than its immediate surroundings.

A $10 million dollar renovation of the clubhouse was completed in late 2007, giving it a stylish, post-modern look, almost more like a fashionable art gallery or bistro than a golf clubhouse.

FANATIC Ratings	
DESIGN INTRIGUE	★★★★
DIFFICULTY	★★★★
BEAUTY	★★★★
MAINTENANCE	★★★★✦
SERVICE	★★★★
SWANK FACTOR	★★★★

> *REMEMBER THAT THE GREENS ARE PASPALUM, SO WHAT YOU SEE IS WHAT YOU GET. THERE'S NO GRAIN HIDDEN THERE, JUST READ THE SLOPE. MOST OF OUR GREENS ARE ELEVATED, SO YOUR APPROACH SHOTS ARE KEY. SHORT SHOTS CAN ROLL WELL BACK.*
> —KEN TERAO, GOLF OPERATIONS MANAGER

THE COURSE

The first thing you'll notice about Kapolei Golf Course is that it has that fuzzy, emerald carpet look that makes golfers salivate. Water hazards seem to be everywhere, too, and are, along with a pair of Ted Robinson's signature waterfalls at the 9th and 18th. Robinson has infused the track with loads of interesting bunker designs, including flash and strip bunkers, as well as pot bunkers located at the bottom of larger grass collection areas. There's a fine collection of tropical trees, including fragrant plumeria, shady monkeypod, and statuesque palms, as well as the yellow flowering golden shower tree. The course plays through a dense subdivision, but its quality is that of a fine resort. It's well-designed, visually appealing, and flawlessly main-

14th green

tained. The layout is challenging, especially with the frequent trade winds, and features holes that tend to stand out in your memory more than some of the other local offerings.

Approach on #18

THE HOLES

#6

The short par-4 6th is an interesting test, as full drives that hit a downslope straight out will bounce through the fairway and into an area of light rough stuffed with randomly arranged mounds. With the trades at your back off the tee, long hitters will certainly be tempted to have a go at the blind green, but it would take exceptional luck to skip the ball through this area and past five little pot bunkers to the green. A long iron off the tee will get most hitters to the edge of the fairway for a short shot to the green.

he ninth is a dogleg left par-4 with a lake on the left side and bunkers off the tee to the right.
he Robinson waterfall to the left of the green creates a placid finish to the front nine - unless
ie trades push your ball into it on approach, in which case you may have the impulse to fill in the
vely waterscape with high-density concrete.

he tenth is a long par-4 with a unique island tee. Drives must be long and straight to do well
i this hole. If you slice one off toward the water, there's a long bunker built out into the water

Kapolei Golf Course (KAH-poh-lay)

ADDRESS		CONTACT	
91-701 Farrington Highway Kapolei, HI 96707		808-674-2227 WWW.KAPOLEIGOLF.COM	
COURSE DETAILS		**SCORECARD**	
Architect	Ted Robinson	Par	72
Year Opened	1994	Slope	135.6
Renovated	No	Course Rating	74.3
Reservations	1 month out	**TEES/YARDAGES**	
Online Times	No	Gold	7001
Greens Fees	$$$	Black	6586
Discounts	Weekday/Twilight	White	6136
Club Rentals	Yes	Red	5490
Premium	Yes		
Houses	Yes		
WATER		**DISTANCES**	
Types	Lakes/Creeks	Well-marked	Yes
Water Holes	10	Yardage Book	Yes
Oceanfront	No	Sprinklers	No
		GPS	In-cart
PRACTICE		**BUNKERS**	
Driving Range	Mats	How Many?	80
Practice Balls	Extra	Consistency	Fluffy, nice
Putting Green	Yes	**GRASS**	
Chip Green	Yes	Greens	Paspalum
Practice Bnkr.	Yes	Fairways	Paspalum

Kapolei Golf Course

that may mercifully keep your drive dry. Of course, you're still in the sand, but better there than the bottom of the lake.

#18

The signature 18th plays tough when the trade winds are in your face, but a decent drive can get a good bounce down the hill, leaving you with a short iron into a two-tiered green. A lake juts into the fairway just before the green to make your approach shot interesting, and another beautiful waterfall sits next to the green, providing the kind of extra touch that makes shelling out for a round he seem worth it.

19th Puka

Ambiance:	Modern Japanese
Fully stocked:	Yes
Draft beer:	No
Menu:	Yes
Cost:	Par
Best bet:	Kalbi Plate (marinated Korean short ribs)
The Lowdown:	A new retractable awning on the terrace makes this a sweet spot to chill out after a round.

NIGHT HERON	APPROACH ON #15 (ABOVE) GOLF CART (BELOW)	DRIVING RANGE

Directions

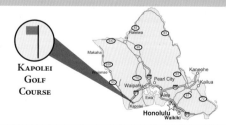

From Waikiki, follow the H-1 West toward Waianae for about 30 minutes and get off on exit #2, Makakilo/Kapolei. Turn left at the top of the ramp onto Makakilo Dr. and turn left at next intersection onto Farrington Highway. Enter the course a mile down the road, the 4th street on the right.

KAPOLEI GOLF COURSE

The par-4 tenth from the drop area

O'OLAU GOLF CLUB
~:Choke Hole: #18:~

FANATIC Ratings	
DESIGN INTRIGUE	★★★★✦
DIFFICULTY	★★★★★
BEAUTY	★★★★✦
MAINTENANCE	★★★
SERVICE	★★✦
SWANK FACTOR	★★★✦

ade winds as reliable as the rising sun blow in off the Pacific from the rtheast, bringing warm moisture onto the island of O'ahu, where it eets a wall. The Ko'olau Mountains, which are the interior wall of a assive, collapsed volcano, consist of over 3,000 feet of ribbed rock and eer ridges. The wind and moisture that have shaped this massive formation have also bred dense life across its cliffs like velvet green stubble. Vaterfalls cascade down verdant chutes. Impossibly beautiful tropical wers burst open on vertical bluffs. And at the base of this physical aprobability lies a golf course.

THE COURSE

Vhat a spot. Hawaii's toughest track may also be its most beautiful. Architect Dick Nugent has rved a living, breathing course out of this strange and wonderful place. Deep, twisted gullies d sudden ravines begin the golfers' difficulties. An impenetrable jungle ensures that bags will home many balls lighter. A relentless design means these holes will stick with golfers forever.

> *PLAY IT TWICE. IT CAN BE HELPFUL TO PLAY WITH SOMEONE WHO KNOWS THE COURSE, BUT HAVING PLAYED IT YOURSELF IS THE MOST BENEFICIAL.*
> —MONICA DAVIS, GENERAL MANAGER

Forced carries are everywhere, as are deep pockets of sand and collection areas. The greens, in classic Nugent style, are like long, thin torpedoes that punish anything off-center or, conversely, wide shallow affairs that demand pinpoint distance control. Don't look for big, friendly resort greens here, as they simply don't belong here in golf's heart of darkness.

"Jeez," you might say, "is it really that hard?" Well, maybe not anymore. There used to be a sign at the entrance that welcomed golfers to "the toughest course in the country," but management got tired of seeing people lose their nerve at the gate, turning around and seeking better scores elsewhere. They pulled down the sign and softened the course, removing scads of punishing, overkill bunkers. Today the course remains challenging, but very playable.

Without a housing development in sight, it's just you, the jungle, and misty mountain views. With over 100 inches of rain a year, you'll be wise to bring your rain gear, but don't chicken out at the last minute: this course will not only give you bragging rights with the foursome back home, but will also be a wonderful, unique experience. Just, you know—bring enough balls.

NIGHT MARCHERS

ONE OF HAWAII'S MOST WIDELY BELIEVED LEGENDS HOLDS THAT, ON MOONLESS NIGHTS, THE GHOSTS OF HAWAIIAN WARRIORS RISE FROM OLD BATTLEFIELDS AND HEAD IN PROCESSION TO SACRED SPOTS AND ENTRANCES TO THE UNDERWORLD. ANY LIVING PEOPLE IN THE AREA ARE APT TO HEAR CHANTING AND DRUMS, AND SEE THE PALE GLOW OF GHOSTLY TORCHES. WITNESSES TO THIS SIGHT WILL BE KILLED BY THE NIGHT MARCHERS AS THEY PASS, UNLESS THEY FACE THE GROUND AND RESIST THE URGE TO LOOK AT THE GRIM PROCESSION.

NU'UANU PALI IN THE KO'OLAU MOUNTAINS JUST HAPPENS TO BE THE SCENE OF A PARTICULARLY BLOODY BATTLE WHERE KAMEHAMEHA I FINALLY SECURED VICTORY OVER O'AHU BY DRIVING THE RESISTING WARRIORS OVER THE CLIFFS TO THEIR DEATHS, WHERE KO'OLAU GOLF CLUB SITS TODAY. AS SUCH, STORIES ABOUND THAT NIGHT MARCHERS FREQUENT THE FAIRWAYS OF THE GOLF COURSE. YOU'D THINK THE SETTING AND LAYOUT OF THIS COURSE WAS SCARY ENOUGH, BUT NO, IT'S ACTUALLY HAUNTED AS WELL. SO, YOU MAY WANT TO THINK TWICE BEFORE BEING CAUGHT IN THE DARK ALONG THE 14TH FAIRWAY. JUST REMEMBER: DON'T LOOK UP!

Approaching on #1

: HOLES

par-4 6th is challenging, to say the least. A deep, vegetated ravine
:rates the fairway from the approach and looks about a mile across,
igh the trees obscure the fact that even a shot of 80 yards will find
:y on the other side. The green, however, is about 160 yards from the
: of the ravine, so players looking to score will need to play something
than a driver off the tee, then play a mid-iron into the green, which
otected by deep bunkers left and right. The green is two-tiered and

15th green

Ko'olau Golf Club (KOH-oh-lau)

ADDRESS		CONTACT	
45-550 Kionaole Road		808-236-4653	
Kaneohe, HI 96744		WWW.KOOLAUGOLFCLUB.COM	
COURSE DETAILS		**SCORECARD**	
Architect	Dick Nugent	Par	72
Year Opened	1992	Slope	152
Renovated	2007	Course Rating	75.7
Reservations	30 days out	**TEES/YARDAGES**	
Online Times	Yes	Black	7310
Greens Fees	$$$	Gold	6797
Discounts	Twilight	Blue	6406
Club Rentals	Yes	White	5102
Premium	Yes		
Houses	No		
WATER		**DISTANCES**	
Types	Pond	Well-marked	OK
Water Holes	1	Yardage Book	Yes
Oceanfront	No	Sprinklers	Yes
		GPS	Sky Caddie
PRACTICE		**BUNKERS**	
Driving Range	Grass and Mats	How Many?	92
Practice Balls	Included	Consistency	Good, playable
Putting Green	Yes	**GRASS**	
Chip Green	Yes	Greens	Paspalum
Practice Bnkr.	Yes	Fairways	Paspalum

long from front to back, so three-putting is possible for those who pay more attention to just making it to the green rather than the correct position on the green. You'll need your game clicking on all points to conquer this one.

#11

Two carries are required to manage the par-5 11th, one modest pop off the tee to an uphill fairway and another on approach. The green is wide and genial in the front, then elbows right to a shallow area in the back. Pin positions on the fat part of the putting surface are easy enough to handle,

16th pi

but a deep, sinister bunker in the bosom of the green means that cups cut in the back right portion of the green are the definition of a sucker pin.

#15

Even if you don't plan to play from it, be sure to drive up to the back tees of #15 and soak in the view. There is also a little trail off to the left of the tee that leads to some ancient Hawaiian birthing stones. So, you have views, culture, history . . . what about the golf? Well, since you're up here you might as well crank off a drive on this short par-4 and see how it goes. The back tees are much loftier than any of the forward tees, so you'll probably get more distance from here anyway.

With a right-to-left sloped fairway you may be tempted to bite off a whole lot on the drive but a series of grass bunkers along the right side, acres of room left, and a modest distance from te to green means it's wise to just play it safe and take a short-iron or wedge into the green. The thick jade ribs of the Ko'olau Mountains come right down to the green on this hole, which will leave you pondering whether the view is better from the tee or the green.

#18

The 18th is a doozy, with twenty-four bunkers, two tough forced carries, and a chance for a moon shot at the green off the tee. Welcome to the toughest hole on the (3rd) toughest course in the country. For sane folks, you must carry a ravine off the tee while splitting the middle of a fairway that runs quickly away to the right. Anything left may miss a couple of bunkers and be okay while shots to the right will either find one of the nine bunkers or miss the beach and be lost in the jungle. Assuming you do find the fairway, however, you are then faced with a tricky mid- to long

18th from behind the green

on into a long, narrow green surrounded by more bunkers. Sound like too much? Well, there is another option for the truly unhinged Golf Fanatic.

The 18th features a second fairway on the far side of the woods that runs all the way up to the green. With a huge wallop and plenty of luck, you just might make it. You'll need at least 260 yards of high carry to have any chance. If you make it, you'll be looking at a little wedge in. Ask in the pro shop for current info on where to aim off the tee.

19th Puka

Ambiance:	Hawaiian lounge
Fully stocked:	Yes
Draft beer:	No
Menu:	Yes
Cost:	Par
Best bet:	Honey's Wrap with Kalua Pig
The Lowdown:	An unofficial Hawaiian music hall of fame, Honey's features pictures of legendary crooners on the walls.

KO'OLAU GOLF CLUB

♣

(FROM RIGHT)

•••••••

15TH FROM THE BACK TEES

•••••••

18TH ON APPROACH

•••••••

GOT REVENGE?

•••••••

8TH GREEN

•••••••

THE 3RD FROM THE FAIRWAY

WANT REVENGE ON YOUR PARTNER PLAY ANOTHER ROUND FOR ONLY A CART FEE

Directions

From Waikiki, follow the H-1 West, exiting at #1D/1E onto the H-3 East toward Kaneohe. Remain on the H-3 for 10 miles and take exit #11 toward Kaneohe. Turn left at bottom of ramp onto Hwy. 83 (Kamehameha Hwy.), then take your first left onto Kahiko St. and turn immediately left onto Kionaele Rd. Follow signs to entrance.

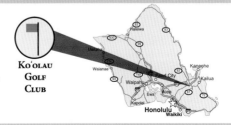

KO'OLAU GOLF CLUB

Signature 8th from behind the gree

KO OLINA GOLF CLUB
~: Choke Hole: #18 :~
Site of LPGA Fields Open

FANATIC
Ratings

DESIGN INTRIGUE
★★★★
DIFFICULTY
★★★
BEAUTY
★★★★
MAINTENANCE
★★★★
SERVICE
★★★★
SWANK FACTOR
★★★★

This quintessential resort course sits in the southeast corner of O'ahu in an area that is being developed like the next Waikiki. The course plays through a lot of resort development, but is laden with enough swanky touches by architect Ted Robinson (including a drive-through waterfall) to make it a fun course to seek out and play. The clubhouse is modern and fully equipped, with a particularly nice pro shop, and locker rooms that feature Jacuzzis and steam rooms. Then there's the clubhouse restaurant: Roy's, one in the line of Roy Yamaguchi's chain of upscale eateries, which consistently plates up some of the most inventive Pacific Rim Cuisine to be found. Even if you're not staying at the resort, Ko Olina is a great plac to plan for a full day, with a morning of practice on their range and short game area, followed by leisurely round, then a soak, steam, a change of clothes, and an early dinner at Roy's. That's a per fect Hawaiian day.

> " TAKE MORE CLUB THAN YOU THINK, AS A SHORT APPROACH
> SHOT WILL BE DEFLECTED AWAY FROM YOUR TARGET.
> REMEMBER YOU ARE HITTING INTO ELEVATED GREENS. "
> —DAVE KOWALCZYK, HEAD PROFESSIONAL

THE COURSE

While most of the course is fairly straightforward, water comes into play on half of the holes, and plenty of bunkering means that this isn't a complete cupcake. When the trade winds blow it can be quite difficult, but when the winds lie low it's a friendly track, amenable to scoring well. There's a certain Disney quality to all of the Ted Robinson "waterscapes," topped off with the undeniably fun drive-through waterfall between the eleventh green and twelfth tee. The twelfth hole isn't particularly compelling itself, simply a straightforward par-3, but the waterfall is an attraction that seems to give quite a bit of "wow" factor and helps justify the steep greens fees. One of my playing partners was so excited he drove through the waterfall while filming with his video camera and ended up driving right up onto the back tees of #12. Despite the gaffe, he kept up the narration for the camera, exclaiming "Hawaii . . . amazing," over and over.

WHAT'S WITH THE CUPS?

Ko Olina is "famous" for their 24-oz. logo cups that come gratis with a round of golf. They're great (especially if you're headed to a keg party straight after your round), but their value to your golf game remains a bit of a mystery.

THE HOLES

5

When the trades are howling, you'll have them at your back on the par-5 5th, giving you an exciting opportunity for an eagle or birdie. There's a lake off the tee to the right, with one of Robinson's signature savior bunkers along the shore that will rescue a wayward drive from the depths, but still force you to play your second shot from the sand. A long high shot down the middle will place you in a good position to take the green in two shots, but a second lake guards the front left of the green. Unless you're REALLY long and can fly a high approach in from well over 200 yards, you'll probably want to try to sneak it onto the green on the right side, taking the water out of play. But then, when there's water anywhere on a hole, is it ever really out of play?

The other signature hole: #12 from the tee

#8

The eighth is a short par-3 with a lovely waterfall running along the left side. This signature hol isn't just pretty to look at, but also features a large shaped bunker on the right side of the green fo all those chickens playing away from the water on the left.

#12

The 12th is the second signature hole, and features the aforementioned drive-through waterfall Beautiful cascades along the left side are just ornamental, and your tee shot is unlikely to splash down there. However, a prevailing headwind will cut down shots that lack ample brawn, so pla

Ko Olina Golf Club (koh-oh-LEE-nuh)				
Address		**Contact**		
92-1220 Aliinui Drive		808-676-5300		
Kapolei, HI 96707		WWW.KOOLINAGOLF.COM		
Course Details		**Scorecard**		
Architect	Ted Robinson	Par		72
Year Opened	1990	Slope		135
Renovated	No	Course Rating		72.3
Reservations	30 days out	**Tees/Yardages**		
Online Times	Yes	Blue		6867
Greens Fees	$$$$	White		6450
Discounts	Twilight/Resort	Golf		6022
Club Rentals	Yes	Red		5361
Premium	Yes			
Houses	Yes			
Water		**Distances**		
Types	Lakes	Well-marked		Yes
Water Holes	9	Yardage Book		Yes
Oceanfront	No	Sprinklers		No
		GPS		In-cart
Practice		**Bunkers**		
Driving Range	Grass	How Many?		70
Practice Balls	Included	Consistency		Variable
Putting Green	Yes	**Grass**		
Chip Green	Yes	Greens		Bermuda 328
Practice Bnkr.	Yes	Fairways		Bermuda

Ko Olina Golf Club

nough club to keep it out of the nasty bunker on the short right side.

18

he 18th is a fantastic finisher, and another gnature hole (not one, not two, but THREE f them!). The wind will probably be behind ou, helping you drive it up to the edge of the ke straight out. If you lose it right, a waterape is there to moisten your Titleist. Your pproach is over water too, to a multi-tiered reen with a large bunker in the back. Just member, everyone in the outdoor bar across the pond is watching your approach.

19th Puka	
Ambiance:	swanky gazebo
Fully stocked:	Yes
Draft beer:	No
Menu:	Yes
Cost:	Pricey
Best bet:	Anything. Plus, try your Bloody Mary with wasabi.
The Lowdown:	Roy's bar sits in an open-air gazebo perched up across the lake from the 18th green.

KO OLINA
GOLF CLUB

(FROM RIGHT)

• • • • • •

SWAN AT 18TH GREEN
ACROSS FROM ROY'S

• • • • • •

#13 FROM THE TEE

• • • • • •

BILINGUAL SIGNAGE

• • • • • •

WATERFALL BEHIND
THE 12TH TEE

• • • • • •

5TH PIN

LOCKER ROOMS
御手洗い

Directions

From Waikiki, follow the H-1 West towards Waianae for about 16 miles as the H-1 becomes Farrington Hwy. Proceed for another 2 miles and exit at the sign for Ko Olina and enter the resort.

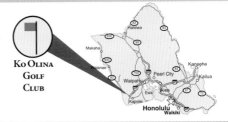

KO OLINA
GOLF
CLUB

A challenging drive awaits you at the firs

LUANA HILLS COUNTRY CLUB
~:Choke Hole: The Pond Hole:~

Laid out amidst some of the densest vegetation in the state, with Mount Olomana on one side and the verdant sweep of the Koʻolau Mountains on the other, Luana Hills is a luau for the senses. Some of the earliest signs of Hawaiian civilization have been found in this valley, and later the area was frequently visited by *aliʻi* (Hawaiian royalty) including King Kalakaua and Queen Liliʻuokalani, the last monarch of the Hawaiian Kingdom. The Queen often came to the valley to relax, and even wrote the classic song "Aloha ʻOe" while visiting.

The club began life as one in a string of doomed private clubs for Japanese investors; when the financial bubble burst in Asia in the mid-'90s, the owner went bankrupt. At the time, two 18-hole courses were under construction, th private jungle King's Course and the public mountain Queen's Course. However, all constructio ceased with the bankruptcy, with nine holes completed in the mountain "front" side and ten hole completed on the jungle "back" side. When a new investor was found, the operation was rechri: tened Luana Hills Country Club with 19 holes, including a pair of alternating par-3's on the back.

FANATIC Ratings

DESIGN INTRIGUE	★★★★⯪
DIFFICULTY	★★★★⯪
BEAUTY	★★★★⯪
MAINTENANCE	★★⯪
SERVICE	★★★
SWANK FACTOR	★★★

> " *LEAVE YOUR DRIVER IN THE BAG. THE COURSE IS SHORT, AND TARGET-STYLE WITH TROUBLE EVERYWHERE YOU WANT TO HIT IT.*
> —DARIN SUMIMOTO, GENERAL MANAGER

HISTORICAL INTEREST

THE VERY FIRST MEMBER OF LUANA HILLS COUNTRY CLUB WAS JOHN ALLEN, A MILITARY PILOT BASED ON O'AHU DURING WORLD WAR II WHO LOST CONTROL OF HIS PLANE AND DITCHED INTO THE THICK JUNGLE OF WHAT IS NOW LUANA HILLS. DECADES LATER, HE WAS THE FIRST TO SEEK MEMBERSHIP IN THE NEW GOLF CLUB AND BECAME MEMBER #0001.

THE COURSE

The course is short, but don't assume that will translate to a low score. This is quintessential target golf. The ability to whack your driver 300 yards in the general direction of your target, while a killer weapon on most of Hawaii's forgiving resort courses, is potentially your biggest liability here (hubris is going to force you to use it at some point, right?). There are chances for glory with such a shot, but the likelihood of irreversible damage to your round is much more likely. While the front side is difficult and intriguing, it's the back side that makes this course. The back nine is cut through dense jungle, the kind that seems more likely in the Amazon basin than a patch of land less than eight miles from downtown Honolulu (as the *nene* flies). Playing the back is like embarking on a backcountry expedition. Often you may feel like a machete would be more useful than that old 2-iron you still carry around for some reason. Many of these holes are short, but a slightly misplaced ball will be stymied by a perfectly placed obstacle. This is Dye golf, Hawaiian-style!

THE HOLES

1

The first is a fun opener that amply sets the pace for what's in store for you. A very inconvenient wedge of jungle juts into the fairway right where most drives will want to land. Do you go with that fairway wood off the first tee, like you know you should, or are you going to try and fly it? Get used to asking yourself that question on the first: it will keep coming up.

#13: The shortest, toughest par-5 in the state

#11

If you're lucky, you'll be playing the Pond Hole as your 11th, which alternates with another par-3 to keep the greens from getting too beat up. This par-3 is a classic Dye island-style one-shotter (like the 17th at the TPC at Sawgrass), though it's actually a peninsula rather than an island. However, the pond oozes around nearly every side of the green, even behind the putting surface, which arcs in from the back right. The tee is elevated, so the shot plays very short—just a wedge for many. This one *should* be a no-brainer for golfers of all levels. But there's all that water, and only so much green . . .

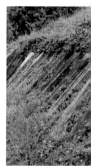

Dye-style railroad ti

Luana Hills Country Club (loo-ah-nuh)			
Address		**Contact**	
770 Auloa Rd. Kailua, HI 96734		808-262-2139 WWW.LUANAHILLS.COM	
Course Details		**Scorecard**	
Architect	Dye Designs	Par	72
Year Opened	1993	Slope	135
Renovated	No	Course Rating	73.3
Reservations	Open	**Tees/Yardages**	
Online Times	Yes	Black	6595
Greens Fees	$$$	Blue	6164
Discounts	Twilight	White	5522
Club Rentals	Yes	Yellow	4654
Premium	Yes		
Houses	No		
Water		**Distances**	
Types	Creeks/Ponds	Well-marked	No
Water Holes	3	Yardage Book	Yes
Oceanfront	No	Sprinklers	Yes
		GPS	Sky Caddie
Practice		**Bunkers**	
Driving Range	Mats	How Many?	79
Practice Balls	Extra	Consistency	Variable
Putting Green	Yes	**Grass**	
Chip Green	Yes	Greens	Bent
Practice Bnkr.	Yes	Fairways	Bermuda 419

Luana Hills Country Club

3

t 401 yards from the back tee, the 13th is an most laughably short par-5. To get under r, you'll need a big drive over a nasty jungle aste area off the tee to get into short-iron nge. Optionally, you can just plunk down iron to an intermediate landing area, but get home in two from there will take a ood or long iron into an extremely elevated een with a limited landing area long, short, d left. Two punishing bunkers at the green ill make you pay for approaches that lack

e proper precision. Predictably, it makes the most sense to just 3-shot your way through what is e toughest short par-5 most of us will ever play.

LUANA HILLS COUNTRY CLUB

(FROM RIGHT)

••••••

PAR-3 16TH

••••••

THE 5TH GREEN

••••••

JUNGLE EVERYWHERE

••••••

APPROACH ON #18

••••••

THE POND HOLE

Directions

From Waikiki, follow the H-1 West, exiting shortly at #21B onto the Pali Highway. After about 9 miles, proceed past the ight at Kapaa Quarry Rd. and take your next right onto Auloa Rd. Turn immediately left onto the frontage road hat parallels the highway. Turn right into the entrance after about 100 yards.

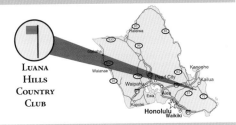

LUANA HILLS COUNTRY CLUB

The lovely par-3 9

MAKAHA RESORT GOLF CLUB
~:Choke Hole: #9:~

FANATIC Ratings
DESIGN INTRIGUE
★★★☆
DIFFICULTY
★★★☆
BEAUTY
★★★★
MAINTENANCE
★★★☆
SERVICE
★★★☆
SWANK FACTOR
★★★

THE RESORT

Far, far away from the bling and zazz of Waikiki, the Makaha Valley sits as it has since it was a private recreational enclave for Hawaiian royalty. This has to be considered one of the most beautiful valleys in all of Hawaii (despite an adjacent eyesore—my nominee for the state's ugliest apartment building).

Legendary Chinese-Hawaiian developer Chinn Ho built two golf courses and the Makaha Resort here with the intention of introducing gambling to the state, an effort that ultimately failed to pass into legality. Originally, the two Makaha courses, termed the "East" (Country Club) and "West" (Resort) courses by locals, were part of the same facility, though now they are split in

> " MAKAHA VALLEY TILTS DOWNHILL, SO THERE IS AN OPTICAL ILLUSION WHEN HOLES APPEAR TO BE PLAYING UPHILL WHEN THEY'RE NOT, AND FOLKS FLY THE GREEN. ON APPROACH, LEAVE THE BALL BELOW THE HOLE WHEN PLAYING TOWARD THE MOUNTAINS AND PLAY OVER THE HOLE WHEN PLAYING TOWARD THE OCEAN, AS THAT WILL LEAVE YOU WITH PUTTS UP THE GRAIN. "
> —RON KIA'AINA, JR., DIRECTOR OF GOLF

vo operations. However, they are very similar courses, as they occupy adjacent real estate, are the
me vintage, and are both designed by William Bell. Both of these courses, while not at the high-
st echelon of Hawaiian golf, offer unique layouts, low prices, and solitude—a rare commodity on
ιe hyper-populated island of O'ahu.

HE COURSE

ating from the late 1960s, this mature course feels a little worn in places but, like a broken-in
aιr of jeans, the course is comfortable and easy to love. Short hitters may get the worst of it here,
; the yardages from the three sets of tees range from over 7,000 yards from the tips to a sizeable
800 yards from the forward tees. This can make for some long days when the winds are really
lowing, but the fairways are wide, and there isn't an excess of bunkers or hazards to punish poor
ιots. Most holes play fairly straightforward with little in the way of deception, but the course is
ot without its pleasant surprises. The front plays down toward the ocean while the back explores
·gions farther up the valley, but both nines have plenty of views of mountains and the ocean. You
ιn expect plenty of "Kodak Moments."

HE HOLES

he first is a fine opener, a par-5 that can be reached in two as it plays downhill and downwind of
ιe trades. The hole retains a quirk, however, in the form of a large *kiawe* tree right in the middle
f the fairway just about a good drive's distance out. The director of golf says that they've long con-
dered axing the tree because some people think it is unfairly punishes quality drives. But until
ιey fire up the chain saws, most golfers should decide on the tee to play to the left or right of the
ffending timber. Long hitters can probably roll it past the tree and take it out of the equation, and
laying it to the left leads to a more open look at the green.

The approach on #12

#9

The signature 9th is a par-3 with a large, undulating green that sits right in front of the clubhouse. There's a slice of lake to get over, and small bunkers at each point of the compass keep you honest. Finding the putting surface here shouldn't be too difficult (unless the cluster of people watching you while enjoying lunch on the veranda is the kind of thing that

Teeing off on #

MAKAHA RESORT GOLF CLUB (muh-KAH-hah)

ADDRESS		CONTACT	
84-626 Makaha Valley Road Waianae, HI 96792		808-695-9544 WWW.MAKAHARESORT.NET	
COURSE DETAILS		**SCORECARD**	
Architect	William Bell	Par	72
Year Opened	1969	Slope	137
Renovated	No	Course Rating	74.3
Reservations	30 days out	**TEES/YARDAGES**	
Online Times	Yes	Blue	7040
Greens Fees	$$$	White	6414
Discounts	Resort/Twilight	Red	5856
Club Rentals	Yes		
Premium	Yes		
Houses	No		
WATER		**DISTANCES**	
Types	Lakes	Well-marked	OK
Water Holes	6	Yardage Book	No
Oceanfront	No	Sprinklers	No
		GPS	Sky Caddie
PRACTICE		**BUNKERS**	
Driving Range	Mats	How Many?	68
Practice Balls	Extra	Consistency	Decent
Putting Green	Yes	**GRASS**	
Chip Green	Yes	Greens	Tifdwarf mix
Practice Bnkr.	Yes	Fairways	Mix

Makaha Resort Golf Club

rs your nerves). Even if you drop one into he drink, be sure to savor the views up the alley.

18

The par-4 finisher is probably the finest hole n the course. Bunkers are in play straight ut off the tee, while a lake long left keeps ou from trying to cut the corner. A lake ong right shouldn't really be in play, but if ou try and play a safe shot off to that side, be ware that shots hit too squarely may get you

19th Puka	
Ambiance:	'70s-style golf chic
Fully stocked:	Yes
Draft beer:	Yes
Menu:	Yes
Cost:	Par
Best bet:	Go with the classic—Club Sandwich with fries
The Lowdown:	The lanai looks out over the 9th green and the ocean beyond.

vet on that side, too. There's sand on every side of the green to keep things interesting. You'll enjoy our post-round Mai Tai even more after surviving #18.

2ND GREEN	THE 17TH (ABOVE) CART LOGO (BELOW)	FIRST TEE

Directions

From Waikiki, follow the H-1 West towards Waianae for about 16 miles as the H-1 becomes Farrington Hwy., and proceed up the Waianae coast for 12.5 miles. Take a right onto Makaha Valley Rd., proceed for a mile and turn right into the resort.

MAKAHA RESORT GOLF CLUB

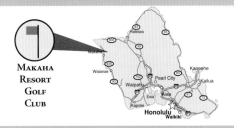

The 17th from the tee

Makaha Valley Country Club
~:Choke Hole: #17:~

FANATIC
Ratings

DESIGN INTRIGUE
★★★✦
DIFFICULTY
★★★
BEAUTY
★★★✦
MAINTENANCE
★★★✦
SERVICE
★★
SWANK FACTOR
★★

The Course
This sister course to Makaha Resort Golf Club is similar in that it has the touch of the same architect and an identical setting, but the "East Course," as it's known, is shorter and has fewer bunkers. While this should make it play a bit easier, the holes are narrower, with leaner fairways and more rough. Several of the holes sweep, swoop, and dip for some fun elevation changes and tough blind shots—qualities that are absent across the street. The East also has the best view of any of the 36 holes in the Makaha Valley: from the 17th tee there's a high, sweeping vista of the sparkling Pacific.

The Holes
#3
The par-5 3rd drops to a blind landing area and dogs hard right at the bottom of the drop. A small pond sits at the elbow to discourage big hitters from trying to cut too much off the hole. The green

> " THE GRAIN ON THE GREENS GROWS OUT TOWARD THE OCEAN, SO PUTTS THAT GO IN THAT DIRECTION WILL BE A LOT FASTER. "
> —RUSSELL HIRATA, CLUB MANAGER

top an ample rise, making it fairly difficult to get home in two,
...le a prevailing crosswind will try to dump your approach into
...of the four bunkers positioned at each corner of the green.

...eight is a par-4 with a semi-blind tee shot that comes back in
...opposite direction as #3, and utilizes the same big dip. A decent
...ve should hit the downslope and leave you with a short-iron
...roach. Again, anything that gets away to the right will probably

The 6th green

Makaha Valley Country Club (muh-KAH-hah)

ADDRESS		CONTACT	
784-627 Makaha Valley Road Waianae, HI 96792		808-695-9578 WWW.MAKAHAVALLEYCC.COM	
COURSE DETAILS		**SCORECARD**	
Architect	William Bell	Par	72
Year Opened	1971	Slope	123
Renovated	No	Course Rating	70.8
Reservations	30 days out	**TEES/YARDAGES**	
Online Times	Yes	Blue	6399
Greens Fees	$$	White	6091
Discounts	Twilight	Red	5720
Club Rentals	Yes		
Premium	No		
Houses	No		
WATER		**DISTANCES**	
Types	Lakes	Well-marked	OK
Water Holes	9	Yardage Book	No
Oceanfront	No	Sprinklers	No
		GPS	Sky Caddie
PRACTICE		**BUNKERS**	
Driving Range	Grass	How Many?	48
Practice Balls	Extra	Consistency	Powdery
Putting Green	Yes	**GRASS**	
Chip Green	Yes	Greens	Tifdwarf
Practice Bnkr.	Yes	Fairways	Bermuda

find the small but well-placed pond on the right side.

#17

Then, of course, there's the lovely 17th. The green sits at least two club lengths below the tee, depending on the wind, which will usually be at your back. A lake on the right will swallow poor tee shots, but the toughest aspect of the hole is guessing the correct club off the tee. It's better to be short than long, as balls that fall short may bounce down onto the front portion of the green, while balls over the back might just end up on the 10th green.

19th Puka	
Ambiance:	'80s-style lounge
Fully stocked:	Yes
Draft beer:	Yes
Menu:	Yes
Cost:	Par
Best bet:	Teriyaki Beef Burger or Croquette Curry Rice
The Lowdown:	Not much in the way of a view here, but a wide-screen TV keeps the locals up on the PGA Tour.

HEADS UP

BE SURE TO BRING DRINKS WITH YOU, AS THERE ARE FEW WATER STATIONS AND NO CART SERVICE ON THE COURSE. THERE IS A SNACK WINDOW AT THE TURN WHERE YOU CAN FILL UP ON NECESSITIES, BUT THERE ARE NO COOLERS ON THE CARTS TO KEEP YOUR BEVIES COOL.

#18

The 18th is a dramatic finisher that plays downhill with the trades at your back, and sweeps out of sight to the right. Tee it up high and try to bounce it around the corner. Keep well left of the fairway bunkers at the right corner, as a shot down the left side of the fairway will leave an open green. Shots that end up on the right side will have to come over one of the large *kiawe* trees. Fairly long hitters should be able to get home in two and finish up under par.

| 14TH GREEN | UNIQUE DRIVING RANGE | THE SWOOPING 8TH |

Directions

From Waikiki, follow the H-1 West toward Waianae for about 16 miles as the H-1 becomes Farrington Hwy., and head up the Waianae Coast for 12.5 miles. Take a right onto Makaha Valley Rd. and continue for just over a mile past the resort and into the country club.

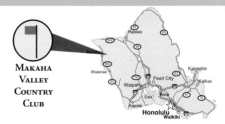

MAKAHA VALLEY COUNTRY CLUB

The 14th fairway with the Ko'olau range

OLOMANA GOLF LINKS
~:Choke Hole: #8:~

Spread along the base of the Ko'olau Mountains on the windward side of O'ahu, Olomana is a locals' favorite that is both a satisfying golf experience and a solid bargain for visitors. The views of the mountains are expansive, more so than the other, more high-profile courses in the area, even if the golf has a slightly more "lived in" feel. It's also a wide open track, which may come as welcome relief to those who have just battled neighboring courses Ko'olau and Luana Hills. Mount Olomana towers solemnly above the course, lending even more view value to the experience.

This is also the course where youth-phenom Michelle Wie honed her game as a kid. According to the staff, Michelle and her parents came "every day" for years, with her mom, Bo, carrying her bag and her father, B.J., directing her game. She was also a student of Casey Nakama, who runs his own golf development school on the lower tier of the Olomana

FANATIC Ratings	
DESIGN INTRIGUE	★★⯨
DIFFICULTY	★★★
BEAUTY	★★★⯨
MAINTENANCE	★★★
SERVICE	★★
SWANK FACTOR	★★

> NUMBER 12 IS SLIGHT DOGLEG LEFT, BUT WITH THE SLOPE OF THE FAIRWAY, MOST PEOPLE END UP WAY DOWN ON THE RIGHT SIDE. PLAY TO THE LEFT SIDE OF THE FAIRWAY OFF THE TEE, AND THE BALL WILL FIND THE MIDDLE OF THE FAIRWAY, WHICH IS THE DIRECTION THAT THE GREEN IS OPEN.
> —PETER YAMASHITA, GENERAL MANAGER

driving range. Michelle still holds the unof-
ficial course record, a 64 from the middle tees,
which she set when she was only 13!

THE COURSE

From two sets of tees, the layout is very short
by modern standards, measuring only 6,306
yards from the tips. The forward tees, however, weigh in at over 5,400 yards, so it is still a
significant test of distance for those who play

13th p

from those tees. The front nine contends with water on all but the 5th hole; trouble lurks in t
form of lovely lotus ponds, filled with colorful flowers and, undoubtedly, decades worth of go
balls. The back nine contains fewer hazards, but rolls and tumbles a bit more, and is the mo
compelling nine. Bunkering is sparse and concentrated at the greens, but I can attest that they a
large and wisely placed.

The course isn't overly maintained or irrigated, but the greens look good and putt true, an
the fairways are generally closely mown. The rough is . . . well, rough, but isn't that the way
should be? And, in a throwback move, pins are anchored in genuine tin cups. There is a distin
pleasure in rolling in a birdie putt that clanks home, one of the lost sounds of the game.

THE HOLES

#5

The fifth is a super-short par-4 that is drivable for many golfers. However, two mammoth bunke
with big lips front the green, meaning it's all carry to get back to the pin for a shot at eagle. It's

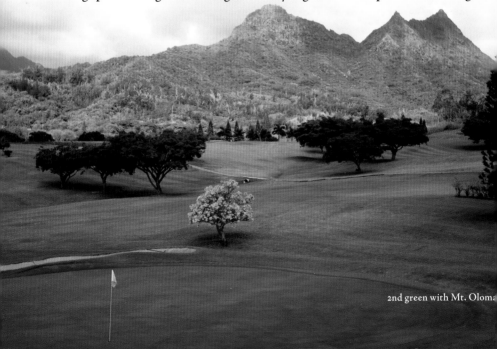

2nd green with Mt. Oloma

un hole that should yield its fair share of low
numbers. And for those who come up short,
t probably sees plenty of doubles and triples.

8

The signature par-3 8th is a short one, over a
pond, with bunkers on all sides. It's a pretty
hole and should be the easiest on the course.
But what is it about teeing up a wedge that is

3rd from the tees

Olomana Golf Links (oh-lo-MAH-nuh)

ADDRESS		CONTACT	
41-1801 Kalanianaole Highway Waimanalo, HI 96795		808-259-7926 WWW.OLOMANAGOLFLINKS.COM	
COURSE DETAILS		SCORECARD	
Architect	Bob Baldock	Par	72
Year Opened	1967	Slope	126
Renovated	No	Course Rating	69.8
Reservations	60 days out	TEES/YARDAGES	
Online Times	Yes	Blue	6306
Greens Fees	$$	White	5907
Discounts	Twilight	Red	5473
Club Rentals	Yes		
Premium	Yes		
Houses	No		
WATER		DISTANCES	
Types	Creeks/Ponds	Well-marked	OK
Water Holes	10	Yardage Book	No
Oceanfront	No	Sprinklers	No
		GPS	Sky Caddie
PRACTICE		BUNKERS	
Driving Range	Mats	How Many?	38
Practice Balls	Extra	Consistency	Variable
Putting Green	Yes	GRASS	
Chip Green	No	Greens	Tifdwarf
Practice Bnkr.	No	Fairways	Bermuda

Olomana Golf Links

so often a recipe for disaster? Add that to the over-the-water factor and multiply it by the likelihood of some light trade winds and this gimme one-shotter suddenly grows some hair.

#14

The 14th is another looker, a short par-4 with an open green, but bunkers on both sides and behind. The putting surface is backed by the kind of mountain views you could stare at forever, and has bright, multi-colored bougainvillea accenting the view. A big, straight drive could lead to an eagle putt clanking down to the bottom of the tin cup.

19th Puka

Ambiance:	Funky Asian
Fully stocked:	Yes
Draft beer:	Yes
Menu:	Yes
Cost:	Par
Best bet:	Chicken Katsu Curry
The Lowdown:	Airy space with wide views of the driving range and spectacular Japanese food.

OLOMANA GOLF LINKS

(FROM RIGHT)

•••••
APPROACH ON #4
•••••
BLOSSOMING LOTUS
•••••
THE 11TH FROM THE TEES
•••••
NO PARTYING IN DA LOT
•••••
4TH TEES

KAPU

NO OUTSIDE FOOD OR BEVERAGES

NO TAILGATE PARTIES OR PICNICS ON PREMISES

Directions

From Waikiki, follow the H-1 East. As it merges into Hwy. 72 (Kalanianaole Hwy.) continue for about 10 miles into the town of Waimanalo. The course is on your right side.

OLOMANA GOLF LINKS

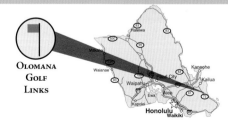

The par-3 16th

EARL COUNTRY CLUB
~:Choke Hole: #7:~

his urban course is set high above Pearl Harbor, where the clubhouse d several holes open up stirring views of the USS *Arizona* Memorial d the USS *Missouri*. There are a few subdivisions that run throughout e course, and, well, the holes that run by H-1, the main freeway through onolulu, don't exactly create get-away-from-it-all Hawaiian resort golf. hat said, this remains a solid value and a distinctive golf experience.

THE COURSE
here's an old-school Honolulu vibe to Pearl Country Club that is ry appealing. With mature coconut palms, shady monkeypods and atuesque Norfolk pines lining the fairways, it's easy to envision the heyday of Hawaiian golf of the os and early '80s. The course rolls up hills and down dales that at one time were fairly rural. Now, u're in the thick of urban-suburban Aiea, which is east of Honolulu's airport, close to Aloha Sta- um and the modern bustle of Pearl City.

> *IF YOU'RE IN DOUBT ON A PUTT, PLAY IT TO BREAK TOWARDS*
> *PEARL HARBOR. THE GRAIN ON ALL OF OUR BERMUDA*
> *GREENS TENDS TO GROW IN THAT DIRECTION.*
> —GUY YAMAMOTO, GOLF OPERATIONS MANAGER

The fairways are wide, with almost no fairway bunkers, and the distances are friendly, even from the back tees. The large greens are pretty easy to find, but most of the sparse thirty-four bunkers on the course are massive and deep. They're filled with coarse sand scattered over hard pack, which makes one of those fluffy sand saves you watch the PGA tour guys pull off just a pipe dream. This is urban Hawaii: no such fluff here.

Zoomed view of the USS *Arizona* Memor[...]

The back nine offers not only the finest views of Pearl Harbor, but also the finest string [...] holes on the course (#16-#18). The greens are grainy Bermuda, and you'll find yourself with lots [...] sidehill lies, no matter where you place your ball off the tee. However, that's about the most di[f-] cult thing about this course, other than dealing with the crowds, which can try anyone's patienc[e].

Be sure not to leave valuables in your car (or your cart unattended with valuables in it).

THE HOLES

#5

The par-5 5th is the first really compelling hole on the course. It doglegs sharply left and dow[n] which makes the green reachable in two for those with well-placed drives. The green sits down [...] a big gully, with several apartment buildings towering overhead, which brings a certain grand sc[ale] to the hole. Hitting a long drive to the corner as far left as you can see will give you sight distance [to] the green, or else you will be faced with a blind approach.

#7

The 7th is the signature hole here, a straightaway short par-4 with an elevated tee and prevaili[ng] trades at your back. Moderate to long hitters should be able to think about driving the green, b[ut]

PEARL HARBOR

AS WE ALL KNOW, ON THE QUIET SUNDAY MORNING OF DECEMBER 7, 1941, THE JAPANES[E] IMPERIAL NAVY LAUNCHED A PREEMPTIVE STRIKE ON THE UNITED STATES PACIFIC FLEE[T] BASED AT PEARL HARBOR. TODAY, THE SITE IS BEST MARKED BY THE USS ARIZONA MEMO[-] RIAL AND NEARBY USS MISSOURI, ON WHICH THE JAPANESE SURRENDERED TO THE UNITE[D] STATES IN 1945. PEARL HARBOR REMAINS THE MOST FREQUENTLY VISITED TOURIST ATTRAC[-] TION ON THE ISLAND, WITH OVER 4,500 VISITORS A DAY AND OVER 1.5 MILLION PEOPL[E] ANNUALLY.

PEARL COUNTRY CLUB OFFERS SOME WONDERFUL VIEWS OF PEARL HARBOR AND TH[E] MEMORIAL, WITH THE BEST VIEWS FROM THE CLUBHOUSE, THE 9TH BACK TEES, THE 11T[H] GREEN, AND THE COMMANDING VIEW FROM THE 15TH GREEN. NO OTHER COURSE ON TH[E] ISLAND OFFERS SUCH AN EXPERIENCE, WHICH GOES A LONG WAY TOWARD MAKING THI[S] COURSE WORTH THE TIME AND MONEY TO PLAY.

ARE: there's a pot bunker-sized pond that guards the green short
If you fly that you are probably not going to stick the green, which
s chasing a drive up the right side of the green your only chance of
ing the green in one. Of course, the sane player will play a moderate
and pitch up with a sand wedge to birdie distance.

the 8th green, don't forget to give the *shaka* (a.k.a. the "hang loose"
signal) to all the folks rumbling along the H1 freeway!

The 5th pin

PEARL COUNTRY CLUB

ADDRESS		CONTACT	
98-535 Kaonohi Street		808-487-3802	
Aiea, HI 96701		WWW.PEARLCC.COM	
COURSE DETAILS		**SCORECARD**	
Architect	Akira Sato	Par	72
Year Opened	1967	Slope	136
Renovated	No	Course Rating	72.7
Reservations	30 days out	**TEES/YARDAGES**	
Online Times	Yes	Blue	6787
Greens Fees	$$	White	6232
Discounts	Twilight	Red	5536
Club Rentals	Yes		
Premium	Yes		
Houses	Yes		
WATER		**DISTANCES**	
Types	Creeks/Ponds	Well-marked	Yes
Water Holes	4	Yardage Book	No
Oceanfront	No	Sprinklers	No
		GPS	Sky Caddie
PRACTICE		**BUNKERS**	
Driving Range	Mats	How Many?	34
Practice Balls	Extra	Consistency	Hardpan
Putting Green	Yes	**GRASS**	
Chip Green	Yes	Greens	Paspalum
Practice Bnkr.	Yes	Fairways	Paspalum

#16

The 16th is a sweet little par-3 with a small strip of water short of the green on the right side that one would think would be out of play, but probably has to be emptied of balls on a monthly basis. The large green sits below the tee, and downwind, so it isn't overly demanding, but simply one of the prettiest settings on the course.

#17

The par-5 17th gives you a chance to score. It's a short one that dogs left. The second of only two fairway bunkers on the course can be seen from the tee and defines the left side. Hit a downwind three-wood straight out, or blast a drive if you have the ability to draw it around the corner. The green is downhill from there and open in front.

19th Puka

Ambiance:	None
Fully stocked:	No
Draft beer:	No
Menu:	Yes
Cost:	Par
Best bet:	PCC Special Pupu Platter
The Lowdown:	This place gets pretty quiet during the week, but if you catch it after a tour bus has dropped off a load of golfers it really heats up.

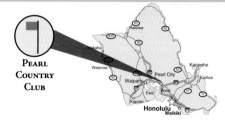

VIEW OF THE MEMORIAL FROM THE CLUBHOUSE | **1ST FAIRWAY (ABOVE) 3RD GREEN (BELOW)** | **THE FIFTEENTH**

Directions

From Waikiki, follow the H-1 West toward Pearl, proceed past the exit for H-3, and take exit #19b, following Hwy. 78 West to Hwy. 99 West (Kamehameha Hwy.). Follow Hwy. 99 past the Pearlridge Shopping Center and turn right onto Kaunohi St. Drive up the hill through one traffic light and enter the course on the right.

PEARL COUNTRY CLUB

The first green

Turtle Bay Resort—Palmer Course
~: Choke Hole: #18:~
Site of Turtle Bay Championship on the Champions Tour, SBS Open on the LPGA Tour

The Resort
Laid out on the damp and verdant northeastern tip of O'ahu, 800-acre Turtle Bay Resort is rare among O'ahu golf resorts. Along with Ko Olina, it's one of the very few major, full service golf resorts on the island. It's only an hour and a half from Honolulu, but feels like another world, surrounded by some of the least inhabited and most "country" areas on the most populated island in the archipelago. It's just a couple of bays away from legendary surf spot Sunset Beach, the first in a string that also includes Banzai Pipeline and Waimea Bay. The resort was originally established with the idea

FANATIC Ratings

Rating	
DESIGN INTRIGUE	★★★★
DIFFICULTY	★★★★
BEAUTY	★★★★
MAINTENANCE	★★★★
SERVICE	★★★★
SWANK FACTOR	★★★★

> " WHEN PLAYING IN KAMAKANI (WIND), REMEMBER TO BE CREATIVE. WINDY CONDITIONS CAN ALLOW YOU TO HIT SHOTS THAT YOU MAY NOT OTHERWISE TRY. FLOP SHOTS INTO THE WIND WILL STOP QUICKER. PLAYING WITH THE WIND CAN HELP YOU CURVE THE BALL AROUND A TREE INSTEAD OF PUNCHING OUT. TRY THE CHIP AND RUN WHEN HITTING AN APPROACH SHOT DOWN WIND. IT WILL ALLOW YOU TO CONTROL YOUR BALL BETTER. "
> —MATTHEW HALL, DIRECTOR OF GOLF

of introducing gambling to the island, but that didn't pan out, and what's left includes beaches, tennis courts, a slightly-outmoded hotel, a new spa and, the reason we're talking about it, 36 holes of golf.

The Course

The Champions Tour annually gathers at this Arnold Palmer and Ed Seay design for the Turtle Bay Championship, and the ladies follow soon thereafter for the SBS Open on the LPGA Tour. As such, the course has the cushy maintenance and demanding, thoughtful design that is necessary to accommodate that level of players. The course runs the gamut from a front nine that plays in a links style in a wide open plain, to the back nine that demands a much higher degree of accuracy as it horseshoes around a wildlife sanctuary. The Punaho'olapa Marsh is a 100-acre wetland area that is home to flocks of endangered Hawaiian birds. It's so soft, green, and lovely on the back half that you may be lulled into forgetting just how challenging it is. While you're lining up your putts, you'll hear everything from soft warbles and melodic tweets to avian choruses so wild and shrill they sound like the battle cries of ancient warriors. The wind is very much in play on the front, but on the back the thick trees protect you from the wind—until you play a high shot above the trees and your ball is suddenly blown abruptly in a new direction. Look to the tree tops to properly estimate the effect of the wind on your ball when you're playing a high shot.

I've played with some folks who were disgruntled that there are no oceanfront holes on this highly-praised course, but as long as you know that going in then you shouldn't be disappointed. So, consider yourself warned.

Turtle Bay doesn't offer on-board GPS systems, but they do provide caddies for a reasonable fee. A good caddy can save you strokes on a course you've never played, so give it some thought.

The approach on #

HOLES

u've played the Fazio course prior to the Palmer, you'll know immediately that you're in for
npletely different experience. The first hole cannot be considered a dogleg left, but a grove
es points you straight out to a cluster of fairway bunkers off the tee. This tee orientation
ands a left-to-right shot. Period. You have to be able to work the ball in that direction, or else
drive of reasonable length is bound for the sand. From that position, par is a near impossibility
o a large banyan tree between you and the green. At least Palmer lets you know what you're
gainst right out of the chute.

TURTLE BAY RESORT—PALMER COURSE

ADDRESS		CONTACT	
57-049 Kulima Drive Kahuku, HI 96731		808-293-8574 WWW.TURTLEBAYRESORT.COM	
COURSE DETAILS		**SCORECARD**	
Architect	Arnold Palmer/Ed Seay	Par	72
Year Opened	1992	Slope	141
Renovated	No	Course Rating	75.0
Reservations	1 month out	**TEES/YARDAGES**	
Online Times	Yes	Black	7199
Greens Fees	$$$$	Blue	6795
Discounts	Twilight/Resort	Gold	6225
Club Rentals	Yes	White	5574
Premium	Yes	Red	4851
Houses	No		
WATER		**DISTANCES**	
Types	Creeks/Lakes	Well-marked	OK
Water Holes	14	Yardage Book	Yes
Oceanfront	No	Sprinklers	No
		GPS	Sky Caddie
PRACTICE		**BUNKERS**	
Driving Range	Grass	How Many?	66
Practice Balls	Included	Consistency	Nice, fluffy
Putting Green	Yes	**GRASS**	
Chip Green	Yes	Greens	Paspalum
Practice Bnkr.	Yes	Fairways	Paspalum

#4

The lake left and long on the par-3 4th is like a ball magnet, particularly because the hole plays straight downwind. While the hole is named "Daring," there's no reason for you to be. Just hit a low skipper and take the wind out of the equation.

#11

It's hard to keep your ball dry on the par-4 11th. A creek holds tight to the right side of a fairway that dogs 90 degrees right—less than a full drive out. That leaves a long iron into a green on the far side of another arm of the creek. There are no bunkers on the hole, but with all that water you won't even notice.

#17

With nine shaped fairway bunkers to navigate around on the par-4 17th, you will have the opposite problem as you had on the 11th. A prevailing wind at your back gives you a reasonable chance of flying the two bunkers in the center of the fairway that guard the landing area. However, the hole jogs slightly right, so an overdriven ball is bound for the trees. From there it's just a short-mid-iron into a two-tiered green that sits adjacent to some shapely beach-side dunes.

19th Puka

Ambiance:	Casual fancy
Fully stocked:	Yes
Draft beer:	Yes
Menu:	Yes
Cost:	Pricey
Best bet:	Coconut Crunchy Shrimp with Plum Sauce
The Lowdown:	Lei Lei's is a casual breakfast and lunch spot on the course that fancies it up for dinner.

TURTLE BAY
PALMER COURSE
❦
(FROM RIGHT)
......
THE PAR-3 13TH
......
TEE MONUMENT
......
WILD GINGER IN
BLOOM
......
GOTTA GO?
......
THE 12TH PIN

The 11th green sits by the beach

URTLE BAY RESORT—FAZIO COURSE
~:Choke Hole: #2:~

THE COURSE

he only George Fazio design in the state of Hawaii occupies similar
al estate to the Palmer Course next door, but the course has a straight-
rward, archaic design that is light-years away from the modern and
triguing layout next door. Additionally, while playing the Fazio, you
ay start to feel like a second-class citizen. Despite very little difference
greens fees, the experiences between the two courses are stark and
ewildering. The Fazio carts are older (lacking in such amenities as ice
nests, though we were told we could beg a bag of ice from the bar), and
appears (judging from the condition of the fairways) that the Fazio

FANATIC Ratings

DESIGN INTRIGUE
★★★
DIFFICULTY
★★✦
BEAUTY
★★★
MAINTENANCE
★★★
SERVICE
★★✦
SWANK FACTOR
★★★

> *WITH BERMUDA GRASS COMES GRAIN. GRAIN AFFECTS BOTH DISTANCE
> AND DIRECTION IN REGARDS TO PUTTING. WHEN YOU PUTT YOUR
> GOLF BALL TOWARDS THE SUNSET, THE PUTT TENDS TO BE A BIT
> QUICKER THAN NORMAL AND VICE VERSA. THE GRAIN WILL ALSO
> MOVE TOWARDS THE BROWNED OR ROUGHENED EDGE OF THE CUP. IF
> ALL ELSE FAILS, HIT IT STRAIGHT AND FIRM AND IF YOU MISS THE
> PUTT, REMIND YOURSELF WHAT THE WEATHER IS LIKE BACK HOME.*
> —KEVIN CARLL, HEAD GOLF PRO

receives a slimmer share of the water than the Palmer does. Most of the holes play straight away with token doglegs, and lack much to stimulate the golfer's senses. There are a few fun holes, ar the frank and guileless nature of the course means scoring well is a good possibility. So, if you' just out for a day on the links, and aren't too discriminating, this course may serve you well. If o the other hand, you came to Hawaii to play challenging golf, you'll want to direct your attention t the neighboring Palmer design.

UPDATE: *A MAJOR UPGRADE AND RENOVATION IS BEING PLANNED FOR THE FAZIO COURSE, BUT A START DATE FOR THE WORK HAS YET TO BE ANNOUNCED. STAY TUNED.*

Turtle Bay Fazio

TURTLE BAY RESORT—FAZIO COURSE

ADDRESS		CONTACT	
57-049 Kulima Drive		808-293-8574	
Kahuku, HI 96731		WWW.TURTLEBAYRESORT.COM	
COURSE DETAILS		**SCORECARD**	
Architect	George Fazio	Par	72
Year Opened	1971	Slope	131
Renovated	No	Course Rating	71.2
Reservations	1 month out	**TEES/YARDAGES**	
Online Times	Yes	Blue	6535
Greens Fees	$$$	White	6083
Discounts	Twilight/Resort	Red	5355
Club Rentals	Yes		
Premium	Yes		
Houses	No		
WATER		**DISTANCES**	
Types	Lakes	Well-marked	OK
Water Holes	4	Yardage Book	No
Oceanfront	Yes	Sprinklers	No
		GPS	Sky Caddie
PRACTICE		**BUNKERS**	
Driving Range	Grass	How Many?	81
Practice Balls	Included	Consistency	OK, thin
Putting Green	Yes	**GRASS**	
Chip Green	Yes	Greens	Bermuda
Practice Bnkr.	Yes	Fairways	Paspalum

The Holes

5

When the trades are up, the green on the downwind par-4 at #5 is nearly drivable. The only problem is that Fazio has dropped two big bunkers into the center of the fairway 30 yards from the green that need to either be carried or hit safely short. It's fun to try to get in there for an eagle putt, but if you don't clear the sand, you're faced with one of the toughest shots in golf: the long bunker splash.

14

The short 14th is exactly the kind of par-4 I can't get enough of. The green is tantalizingly close, only a fairway wood away for reasonably long hitters, but there are bunkers directly in front and left of the green. Ample fairway space is available out to the right, which will leave only a little pitch into the green, but that's over two of those massive bunkers. The ideal shot is one that starts toward the bunkers that front the right side of the green, then comes left in the crosswind and finds the small gap in the bunkers on the left side of the green. If you can bounce it in there just right, it's eagle-putt city!

18

The 18th is a satisfying finisher that plays directly downwind. Tee it up high and let it rip to clear the marshes that demand a sizeable carry. The trades will help high balls reach the fairway, then it's a short iron into the green for an easy par, unless you drop one into another one of those cratered bunkers on the left and right sides!

TURTLE BAY RESORT—FAZIO COURSE

6TH GREEN | MARSHES ON #18 FROM THE TEE | BIG BUNKER ON #1

Directions

From Waikiki, it takes about 90 minutes to drive to Turtle Bay. Follow the H-1 West towards Waianae, and take the H-2 N at exit #8a for about 8 miles, then take exit #8 onto Hwy. 83 (Kamehameha Hwy.). Continue along the coastal highway northeast for about 21 miles and enter the resort on your left.

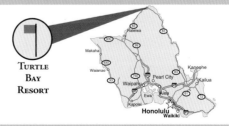

TURTLE BAY RESORT

The oceanfront links at Kaluakoi are left lonely after shutting down in mid-200

Moloka'i

he lightly populated "Friendly Isle" has a different pulse rate than the ther islands in the chain. Moloka'i remains proudly local, and possesses w of the tourist offerings of the other islands. What it lacks in modern ay conveniences, however, it makes up for in beauty, solitude, and the ociability of its people. The two courses on Moloka'i represent two diver-nt worlds: the resort-style Kaluakoi Golf Club (which has recently closed definitely), with its oceanside links, and the fun and quirky nine-holer at onwood Hills. Moloka'i is a special place, retaining the slower pace of "Old Iawai'i"—signs at the airport urge you "Slow Down, this is Moloka'i."

STOP PRESS

As *The Golf Fanatic's Guide to Hawaii* was being readied for press, word came out of Moloka'i that ll of the holdings of Moloka'i Ranch were being closed immediately. This, unfortunately for golf-rs, included the lovely Kaluakoi Golf Course, a Ted Robinson design with some of the finest ocean oles in the state, as well as the most modern accommodations on the island, The Lodge at Moloka'i Ranch. Hopefully a new investor can be found soon to reopen this gem of the Hawaiian links.

Moloka'i

Nickname: The Friendly Isle
Area: 260.0 square miles
Highest Point: Kamakou, 4,961 feet
Population: 7,404 (2000 census)
Flower: Kukui

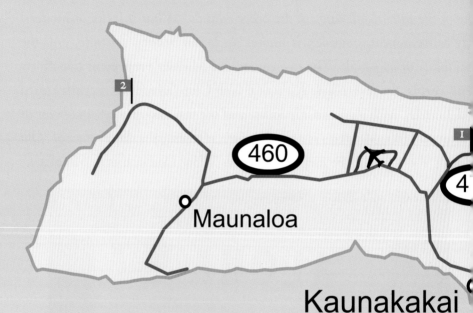

1 - Ironwood Hills Golf Club

2 - Kaluakoi Golf Course
   CURRENTLY CLOSED

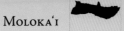

The top of #

Ironwood Hills Golf Club

Ironwood Hills, Moloka'i's little nine-holer, wasn't on my list of the top 50 public golf courses I wanted to include in this book, but I couldn't help golfing there on my day off (I am a Golf Fanatic, after all). It was an extremely fun, borderline goofy experience, so I'm mentioning it here as a little something extra, in case you find yourself on the Friendly Isle.

Half the fun of playing the course is scavenging for the back tees—they're never next to the gentlemen's tees but waaaay back in the woods. There's also a pervasive low-brow golf vibe that's a hoot. The carts are sputtery, and the sand dispensers, that are usually filled with sand or divot mix, are stuffed with cigarette butts (better there than flicked onto the course!). At Ironwood Hills, a pair of bright orange traffic pylons on either side of the fairway marks the 150-yard distance. This is a perfectly serviceable technique, but one that I'd never previously encountered.

Holes are either wide enough to land a 747 on, or so narrow that it's like driving a ball down a hallway. The layout takes advantage of the hilly landscape to create rarely seen challenges, like the

Ironwood Hills Golf Club	
Contact	
Kalae Hwy.	
Kaulapuu, HI 96751	
808-567-6000	
Course Details	
Greens Fees	$
Par	34
Slope	64
Course Rating	35.0
Tees/Yardages	
Blue	3088
White	2616
Red	2409

Ironwood Hills

ar-3 7th, a 272-yard barn burner that would seem absurdly out-of-reach for the average player if the green wasn't located far below and straight downwind of the lofty tee box.

Unlike most of Hawaii's courses, which are tended and staffed by an army of trained personel, the entire staff at Ironwood Hills Golf Course is a single man. Darrell Rego, who reportedly as come within a hair's breadth of qualifying for the Champions Tour, acts as Head Pro, Course uperintendent, Starter ... you name it. There's something charming about starting your round at Hawaiian-style trailer rusting happily away beneath some shady trees. If Darrell is out mowing r performing another of his myriad duties, just drop your token greens fee into the jar, grab a cart ey, and head to the first tee.

IRONWOOD HILLS

(FROM RIGHT)

2ND GREEN

FIND THE NEXT TEE!

WELCOME

THE CLUB TRAILER

DRIVING DOWN THE HALLWAY ON THE 6TH

Directions

From Kaunakakai, take Hwy. 460 (Maunaloa Hwy.) toward the airport. About 4 miles out of town, turn right on Hwy. 470 (Kalae Hwy.). Turn left into the driveway (which is so long and rutted that you almost need a 4WD vehicle) for the golf course in about 3.5 miles.

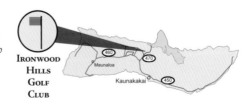

IRONWOOD HILLS GOLF CLUB

The Ocean nine at Princeville's Makai Course

Kaua'i

Kaua'i, the "Garden Isle," possesses some of the world's most compelling natural features, from the Na Pali coastline, to Waimea Canyon, to Mt. Waialeale, the wettest place on earth. The dense rainforest, gushing water-falls, and fabled beaches are the epitome of paradise. For the golfer, these same natural wonders help shape the kind of golf most people can only dream about. The Prince Course is a jungle golf experience like no other; the Kiele Course at Kauai Lagoons boasts the kind of over-the-water ocean shots that tend to induce drooling; Kukuiolono is the least expensive course in this book. It's all here, lushly encompassed by the green and varied island of Kaua'i.

THE ULTIMATE	THE FIND	THE MUNY
PRINCEVILLE PRINCE	**PUAKEA GOLF COURSE**	**WAILUA MUNICPAL**
Robert Trent Jones, Jr.'s "found" course on the verdent north shore of Kaua'i is the finest rainforest golf you'll play.	It may be tucked between a subdivision and a strip mall, but it still looks like Kaua'i and plays like a dream.	Come play with the locals and discover one of the best bargains in the state.
Page 159	Page 164	Page 168

Kaua'i

Nickname: The Garden Isle
Area: 552.3 square miles
Highest Point: Kawaikini, 5,243 feet
Population: 58,303 (2000 census)
Flower: Mokihana

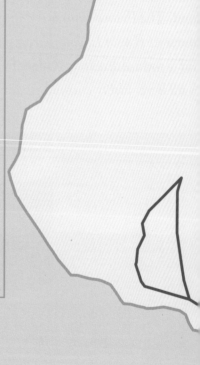

1 - KAUA'I LAGOONS GOLF CLUB

2 - KIAHUNA GOLF CLUB

3 - KUKUIOLONO GOLF COURSE

4 - POIPU BAY GOLF COURSE

5 - PRINCEVILLE—MAKAI COURSE

6 - PRINCEVILLE—PRINCE COURSE

7 - PUAKEA GOLF COURSE

8 - WAILUA MUNICIPAL GOLF COURSE

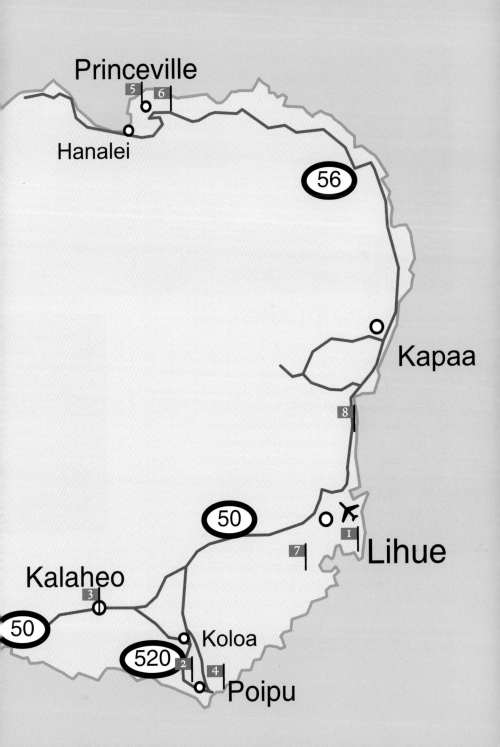

The 13th from the t

Kaua'i Lagoons Golf Club—Kiele Course
~:Choke Hole: #13:~

With a back nine that plays along some of the most awe-inspiring coastline in the state, the Kiele Course offers golfers the chance to inject some adrenaline into their swings. Located just minutes from Lihue and the Kaua'i airport, the resort at Kaua'i Lagoons was perhaps the most opulent of all of hotelier Chris Hemmeter's creations. Two Jack Nicklaus-designed golf courses were interwoven between prime ocean views and man-made lagoons with islands full of exotic animals, and custom-made Chris Craft boats ferried guests through the canals. There was a time when travel journalists couldn't help but compare this place to Disneyland.

FANATIC Ratings
DESIGN INTRIGUE
★★★★
DIFFICULTY
★★★★
BEAUTY
★★★★
MAINTENANCE
★★★★
SERVICE
★★★✦
SWANK FACTOR
★★★✦

Times have changed, however, and as the ostentatious '80s gave way to the tentative early '90 Hurricane Iniki dealt a savage direct hit to Kaua'i, stopping progress in its tracks. Hemmeter creations were nearly abandoned, until the Internet boom made it once again feasible for guests t afford such luxuries. Today the economic boom is in real estate, and the development of condo

> " On the Bermuda grass greens at Kaua'i Lagoons judge your distance first, about two feet past the hole, then choose your line. The greens are pretty slow, so playing the putt a bit longer will give you a better chance than trying to die it at the hole. "
> —Todd Stewart, Head Golf Professional

meshares, and luxury residences has begun in earnest. The kangaroos and monkeys are gone, d the islands that were their homes are now for sale as high-end personal estates.

Along with this new influx of investment came plans for changes to the two golf courses. Prosals have included halving the Mokihana Course while giving the championship Kiele Course major upgrade by routing additional holes along the ocean to make room for development along e 14th hole's inland fairway. Also, the "19th hole" is currently being reworked.

HE COURSE

s too easy to say that this course is all about the back nine. The holes that precede the 12th are fine, allenging Jack Nicklaus golf holes, but the final third of the course includes so much breathtak- g oceanfront acreage that the rest of the course sometimes gets overlooked. That seems unfair, hen Nicklaus has seamlessly interwoven the existing natural features with man-made attributes ke mounding, undulations, devilish bunker placement, and lagoons. The layout gets progressively ore intense as you play, culminating with the ocean holes on #12, #13, #15, and #16. The finish is rong: the demanding 18th plays into the wind to a green stranded on an island in a lagoon.

Each hole is marked at the tee with an extravagant marble statue. The only figure that isn't an nimal is the Buddha at the first tee. Be sure to rub his belly for good luck. With all the wind and ater you have ahead of you, you'll need the karma.

The 15th green

HE HOLES

3

Vhat was friendly and pretty at the 12th turns dramatic and threatening at the par-3 13th. Playing ith a quartering crosswind that wants to take your shot long and left into the breaking waves, ou'll be wise to club down one or two clubs and play it out toward the bunker on the right and atch it float back in. Balls that don't make it will eventually be crushed to sand by the ceaseless reaking waves in the inlet below.

#16

The 16th is one of those holes that you'll want to play again and again. It's short and plays downwind, which may make you think about trying to drive the green. However, you can't see the green off the tee, which should make you think twice. A hybrid or iron off the tee toward the right side is the logical move, and will yield a short wedge from the middle of the fairway. Be

The 16th gre

KAUA'I LAGOONS—KIELE COURSE (key-ay-lay)			
ADDRESS		**CONTACT**	
3351 Hoolaulea Way		800-634-6400	
Lihue, HI 96766		WWW.KAUAILAGOONSGOLF.COM	
COURSE DETAILS		**SCORECARD**	
Architect	Jack Nicklaus	Par	72
Year Opened	1987	Slope	134.7
Renovated	No	Course Rating	73.7
Reservations	30 days out	**TEES/YARDAGES**	
Online Times	No	Gold	7070
Greens Fees	$$$$	Blue	6674
Discounts	Resort/Twilight	White	6164
Club Rentals	Yes	Red	5417
Premium	Yes		
Houses	No		
WATER		**DISTANCES**	
Types	Lakes/Ocean	Well-marked	Yes
Water Holes	5	Yardage Book	Yes
Oceanfront	Yes	Sprinklers	Yes
		GPS	In-cart
PRACTICE		**BUNKERS**	
Driving Range	Grass	How Many?	89
Practice Balls	Included	Consistency	Good
Putting Green	Yes	**GRASS**	
Chip Green	Yes	Greens	Tifdwarf
Practice Bnkr.	Yes	Fairways	Bermuda 328

Kaua'i Lagoons Kiele Course

ntle with your approach, as the wind will carry the ball, and the green is below you. Shots that nd on the green and appear to bounce over into the ocean below will likely be caught by a dratic unseen bunker that's carved into the hillside above the ocean. Rather than risk that eventulity with a high wedge shot, consider a bump-and-run off of the sloping fairway neck and bounce ur ball into the green.

8

8 is one tough finisher, just as Jack would have it. The statue that marks this hole is, of course, bear, and that's exactly what this hole is. It's a long par-4, made longer by the trades, which you lay directly into. The lagoon will catch tee shots that leak to the right for those who muscle up in n attempt to give themselves a decent chance at a mid-iron approach shot. The well-bunkered reen is on a small island in the lagoon. While it's true that the longer you go off the tee, the better hance you have of coming in with a club that isn't your 3-wood, the truth is that for most of us this ole will be a three-shotter. Drive, lay it up, and try to stick your pitch close to have a shot at saving ar. I hope you rubbed the Buddha belly on #1. You're going to need a little help on this one.

| THE GOLDEN BEAR | #17 FROM THE TEE (ABOVE) 13TH GREEN (BELOW) | TEE MARKER |

Directions

From the Lihue Airport, turn left on Hwy. 51. Continue on Hwy. 51 by turning left at the stop sign on Rice St. The entrance to Kaua'i Lagoons Resort is about ½-mile down on the left.

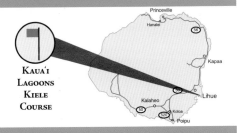

KAUA'I LAGOONS KIELE COURSE

The 8th gree

KIAHUNA GOLF CLUB
~:Choke Hole: #12:~

Constructed back in 1984 when Poipu was just a sleepy little beach community, Kiahuna is now at the heart of some of the area's most intense growth. Development is occurring along nearly every fairway at Kiahuna, and it will soon be another of those Hawaiian courses that is hemmed in by luxury homes and condos. However, that would be better than its current state, where heavy machinery pounds away incessantly. That said, the course owners cannot be blamed for being greedy, as they don't actually own any of the land that is being developed just off of their fairways. So, while it is certainly annoying, don't take it out on the guys in the pro shop.

FANATIC Ratings
DESIGN INTRIGUE
★★★
DIFFICULTY
★★★
BEAUTY
★★★
MAINTENANCE
★★★
SERVICE
★★★
SWANK FACTOR
★★✦

THE COURSE
This was once a really short course that played more like an executive than a normal 18-hole However, that's not the case anymore. Along with new owners in 2003 came a renovation that ha

> *KEEP YOUR TEMPO SMOOTH TO CUT DOWN SPIN WHEN PLAYING INTO THE WINDS THAT FREQUENT THIS PART OF THE ISLAND. THE COURSE CAN PLAY 200 YARDS LONGER IN THE WIND, AND TRYING TO HIT IT HARDER INTO THE TRADES WON'T HELP.*
> —MATTHEW TORRY, HEAD GOLF PROFESSIONAL

ded new sets of tees, and the course now plays fairly long from those back tees. The course
eatures unique junior tees that play 2,633 yards. These tees can also be used to play the course
ar-3, which could be good fun as a second round of the day, or if you opt for one of the terrific
ly membership plans. The club also offers reduced "bounce back" rates that are good for an
e week after you have paid full price.

The course has some unusual attributes, such as the various archaeological sites that are scat-
around the layout. Also, there's a lava tube located off the second hole with a community of
spiders that dwell within. Many of the golf shirts in the shop include an embroidered spider
e back of the collar, which makes them a bit more distinctive than some of the other standard
shirts available in the shops around the island. The archaeology and blind spiders are nice

KIAHUNA GOLF CLUB (KEY-uh-HOO-nuh)

ADDRESS		CONTACT	
2545 Kiahuna Plantation Drive Poipu, HI 96756		808-742-9595 WWW.KIAHUNAGOLF.COM	
COURSE DETAILS		**SCORECARD**	
Architect	Robert Trent Jones, Jr.	Par	70
Year Opened	1984	Slope	134
Renovated	2004	Course Rating	73.5
Reservations	30 days out	**TEES/YARDAGES**	
Online Times	Yes	Gold	6885
Greens Fees	$$$	Blue	6183
Discounts	Twilight/Replay	White	5560
Club Rentals	Yes	Red	4887
Premium	Yes	Green	2633
Houses	Yes		
WATER		**DISTANCES**	
Types	Lakes/Creeks	Well-marked	Yes
Water Holes	8	Yardage Book	Yes
Oceanfront	No	Sprinklers	Yes
		GPS	In-cart
PRACTICE		**BUNKERS**	
Driving Range	Grass	How Many?	59
Practice Balls	Included	Consistency	Good
Putting Green	Yes	**GRASS**	
Chip Green	Yes	Greens	Paspalum
Practice Bnkr.	Yes	Fairways	Paspalum

enhancements, but the golf is a bit lacking. Still, Kiahuna remains a relatively affordable place to hit the ball on the sunny part of the island.

THE HOLES

#7

The par-3 3rd has a double green that it shares with #7, so first, be aware that you are playing to the flag on the right and avoid the embarrassment and irritation that I endured when I incorrectly played to the wrong flag. After sticking a sweet 5-iron to birdie distance on t wrong green, I grumpily back-tracked and played to the correct flag, dropping my ball into t water when the right-to-left crosswind threw my Titleist into the lake along the left side.

19th Puka	
Ambiance:	Breezy hot spot
Fully stocked:	Yes
Draft beer:	Yes
Menu:	Yes
Cost:	Par
Best bet:	Local Joe's Special
The Lowdown:	At this mega-popular breakfast and lunch joint, try to get a sea at the koa wood bar.

#10

The tenth is a lovely par-4 of manageable distance with some attractive landscaping, lava ro walls, and a wide, narrow green. There's water off to the left, but it's only in play if you let the eyes the diners packed into the wildly popular Joe's on the Green unnerve you as you tee off.

#12

#12 is a tough, picturesque one-shotter with a creek that fronts a two-tiered green. When the pi placement is on the back right on the upper tier, this one can be brutal since the trades whip fro right to left. A safe shot that's left on the lower tier is at risk of a 3-jack.

CLOCK AT JOE'S ON THE GREEN	OUT OF A BUNKER ON #14	HOLE MONUMENT

Directions

From the Lihue Airport, follow Ahukini Rd. across Hwy. 51 for 1 mile. Turn left on Hwy. 56 (Kuhio Hwy.) and follow for 7 miles as it turns into Hwy. 50. Turn left at the "tree tunnel" onto Maluhia Rd. toward Poipu. Follow for about 5.5 miles as it becomes Poipu Rd. Turn left onto Kiahuna Plantation Dr. and turn left into the entrance less than a ½-mile down.

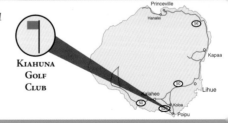

KIAHUNA
GOLF
CLUB

The 9th green

KUKUIOLONO GOLF COURSE

Are you in need of a warm-up round before plunking down big coin to play one of the resort tracks? Or do you merely enjoy simple, affordable golf? For less than a round of drinks at one of the resort bars, golfers can play all day up and down the nine holes of Kukuiolono Golf Course. This little find is situated high on an extinct cinder cone in South Kauaʻi and affords mountain and ocean views, vistas of Niʻihau (the Forbidden Isle), and sight lines all the way down to Poipu.

Once part of a large sugar plantation, it was the dream of owner Walter D. McBryde to leave his course to the people of Kauaʻi. He willed the land to the public upon his death in 1930, along with his life savings to pay for the maintenance. He is buried on site, next to the Japanese Garden.

Kukuiolono Golf Course	
CONTACT	
854 Puu Road Kalaheo, HI 96741 808-332-9151	
COURSE DETAILS	
Greens Fees	$
Par	36
Course Rating	35.0
TEES/YARDAGES	
Blue	3173
White	2981
Red	2708

The course is in the plantation style, with wide, tightly-mown (some may say burned out) fairways and few bunkers. The layout is studded with a varied collection of mature trees such as Cook pines, *kukui*, ironwoods, palms and eucalyptus, which are used to roughly delineate the fairways. Most of the holes play straightaway with little thrown in your way, so your fiercest opponents are yourself and the trade winds (not counting the aggressive chickens). The course is situated on pa[...] grounds, and you'll encounter lots of friendly people walking their dogs or simply out for a str[...] The park aspect is a great opportunity to turn the family loose while you squeeze in a quick ni[...] There's a Japanese garden, sacred Hawaiian stones, and foot paths to occupy their time while y[...] sharpen your game.

If you go, leave your resort fashions behind. You may even opt to go shirtless (*kane* only), [...] play in your *slippas* (flip flops) like some locals. A modest cart fee will get you a gas-powered ri[...] (you pay for the cart per nine), or you can walk the course all day for the one price. A friendly 19[...] hole is located in the plantation-style clubhouse, and serves up ice-cold beer and local dishes, su[...] as teriyaki beef and a *mahi mahi* plate.

KUKUIOLONO
GOLF COURSE

(FROM RIGHT)
·······
HIGH ABOVE
POIPU
·······
THE ENTRANCE
·······
THE 6TH
·······
STATUE IN
THE JAPANESE
GARDEN
·······
ROOSTER GONE
WILD

Directions

From the Lihue Airport, follow Ahukini Rd. across Hwy. 51 for 1 mile. Turn left on Hwy. 56 (Kuhio Hwy.) and follow for 12 miles as it turns into Hwy. 50. Kukuiolono is located in the funky locals' town of Kalaheo. Follow Papalina St. from the center of town for a ½ mile to the old school entrance into the park on your right.

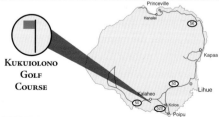

KUKUIOLONO
GOLF
COURSE

The 16th green

POIPU BAY GOLF COURSE
~: Choke Hole: #18 :~
Former Site of the PGA Grand Slam of Golf

There are three things that a golfer can be virtually assured of when playing Poipu Bay: rugged coastal beauty, blazing sun, and wind (with emphasis on the latter.) Located on the south shore of Kaua'i—the sunny side—this is where golfers head when they want to bring at least a little tan home from their vacation to Kaua'i, an island where sunshine is an uncertain commodity. This is probably why the housing around Poipu has burgeoned in recent years, with subdivisions and condo complexes springing up like a desert boomtown. Poipu also has some of the best beaches on the island, as well as great accommodations, dining, and even waves. It's the main tourist hub of the island, rivalling Princeville probably exclusively because of its sunnier clime.

FANATIC Ratings

Category	Rating
DESIGN INTRIGUE	★★★★
DIFFICULTY	★★★★
BEAUTY	★★★★
MAINTENANCE	★★★★
SERVICE	★★★★
SWANK FACTOR	★★★★

> *LIKE MOST COURSES ALONG THE OCEAN, EXPECT TO PLAY IN A LITTLE WIND. WHEN HITTING AN APPROACH SHOT AGAINST THE WIND, DON'T BE AFRAID TO TAKE AS MUCH AS TWO EXTRA CLUBS AND SWING EASIER. THIS WILL CREATE LESS SPIN ON THE GOLF BALL AND PRODUCE A MORE CONTROLLED AND MANAGEABLE BALL FLIGHT.*
> —CRAIG SASADA, DIRECTOR OF GOLF

THE COURSE

The first hole begins downwind, though you may not even notice that. Or perhaps, if you're like me, you may think, "Gee, I've got some extra whomp on the ball today." Cling to that notion, a you're not going to get much more of it. The course is oriented in such a way that nearly every hole plays directly into the trade winds or tacks relentlessly back and forth against them. The trades are such a factor here that they are actually indicated on the scorecard. You may ask, is this course really so much windier than the others on the island? Maybe not, but the layout makes it seem that way. However, this is just architect Robert Trent Jones, Jr.'s strategy to set up the final four holes. When you finally, blessedly reach the 15th tee, the clubhouse (and 19th hole) lie 1,800 yards straight downwind. This makes for a wonderful end to the round, assuming your muscles and score aren't too aggravated from the climb up to this point, and there's a blissful feeling of floating downstream while playing the final holes.

THE HOLES

#8

The par-4 8th isn't a long hole, but it plays directly into the teeth of the trades. The fairway is narrow with bunkers left and right off of the tee. Assuming you stay in bounds, the approach is really the more difficult shot. Take a full two clubs extra when the trades are pumping, and try to keep it low. Take it from someone who hits high iron shots — there's no room for that here. Such shots on this hole will be pushed short and to the sides, where, conveniently, there are five bunkers around the green awaiting blown balls from folks like me who haven't mastered the low punch shot.

#9

#9 is another short par-4, but it is also the #1 handicap hole on the course. Fairway bunkers left and right off of the tee pinch the fairway to a narrow 24 yards, so you'd better be straight, long, or short. A *heiau* (Hawaiian temple) is located along the right side of the fairway, and any ball hit into it can-

The 13th green.

be played. You must take a drop along with a
-stroke penalty. That may seem harsh, but it is
re tolerant than the traditional Hawaiian *kapu*
s where commoners who cast their shadow upon
ali'i (royalty) were killed in unpleasant ways.

nding on the 15th tee with the wind at your back
d the miserably long/uphill/upwind 14th also
ind you), smile and know that the final four holes

The Grand Slam of Golf is the world's most exclusive tournament, with only the winners of the four majors invited to play each year.

POIPU BAY GOLF COURSE (POY-poo)

ADDRESS		CONTACT	
2250 Ainako Street		800-858-6300	
Koloa, HI 96756		WWW.POIPUBAYGOLF.COM	
COURSE DETAILS		**SCORECARD**	
Architect	Robert Trent Jones, Jr.	Par	72
Year Opened	1994	Slope	129
Renovated	No	Course Rating	73.9
Reservations	30 days out	**TEES/YARDAGES**	
Online Times	Yes	Gold	7123
Greens Fees	$$$$	Blue	6612
Discounts	Resort/Afternoon/Twilight	White	6127
Club Rentals	Yes	Red	5372
Premium	Yes		
Houses	No		
WATER		**DISTANCES**	
Types	Lakes/Ocean	Well-marked	Yes
Water Holes	5	Yardage Book	Yes
Oceanfront	Yes	Sprinklers	Yes
		GPS	In-cart
PRACTICE		**BUNKERS**	
Driving Range	Grass	How Many?	85
Practice Balls	Included	Consistency	Dense/fluffy
Putting Green	Yes	**GRASS**	
Chip Green	Yes	Greens	Tifdwarf
Practice Bnkr.	Yes	Fairways	Bermuda

Poipu Bay Golf Course

are all downwind. With that knowledge, tee high and let the wind carry it far and long. Just don't tangle with the left side, where a stark lava cliff drops abruptly down to the crashing Pacific below.

#16

The signature 16th would be obscenely long if it weren't for the wind at your back and an elevated tee. As it is, the bunker directly behind the green has a lot of rake scratches, suggesting players are still flying this hole on approach.

19th Puka	
Ambiance:	Modern Asian
Fully stocked:	Yes
Draft beer:	Yes
Menu:	Pupus
Cost:	Pricey
Best bet:	Veggie tempura
The Lowdown:	A large bar and dining room with windows overlooking the 18th green. Turns into a Chinese place in the evening.

The sheer cliffs that run the entirety of the left side of the hole are both stunning and intimidati. Those who avoid the left side bring the lake on the right into play as well as a duo of fairway bunke The green is large enough that even if you find the putting surface in regulation, you are not assur an easy par.

#18

#18 is a great par-5 finisher. The prevailing trades give you plenty of distance off the tee, and will h a second shot come into the green with a possible eagle putt. But a lake lurks on the right, and de bunkers protect the left. It's risk/reward all the way, and no matter if you sink or swim, the 19th hole close at hand for a celebration or to ease your pain.

POIPU BAY GOLF COURSE

LOCAL *NENE* | #18 WITH THE CLUBHOUSE | WATCH YOUR STEP

Directions

From the Lihue Airport, follow Ahukini Rd. across Hwy. 51 for 1 mile. Turn left on Hwy. 56 (Kuhio Hwy.) and follow for 7 miles as it turns into Hwy. 50. Turn left at the "tree tunnel" onto Maluhia Rd. toward Poipu. After 3 miles, turn left onto Ala Kinoiki for 3 miles, and turn left at the end onto Poipu Rd. Proceed past the Poipu Hyatt to the entrance to the golf course on your right.

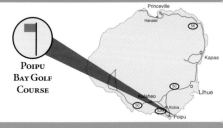

POIPU BAY GOLF COURSE

Ocean #3 from the tees

PRINCEVILLE AT HANALEI—MAKAI COURSE
~:Choke Hole: Ocean #7:~

FANATIC
Ratings

DESIGN INTRIGUE
★★★¹⁄₂
DIFFICULTY
★★★¹⁄₂
BEAUTY
★★★★
MAINTENANCE
★★★¹⁄₂
SERVICE
★★★
SWANK FACTOR
★★★

THE RESORT

Princeville is the stuff of legends. Located on the north shore of Kaua'i, adjacent to the fabled valley of Hanalei (where Puff the Magic Dragon lived by the sea), the Princeville Resort offers golf so scenic you may be inspired to write your own song about it. This is rainforest country, and the windward side of Kaua'i averages over 80 inches of "liquid sunshine" per year. Keep in mind, however, that all that moisture is precisely what makes this area so lovely. This is the kind of green that tropical island dreams are made of, and, yes, it has to rain in order to achieve this. On the other hand, sunlight is also required for such lush growth, and when the sun shines here, there isn't a more beautiful place on earth. The prodigious jade mass of Namolokama towers above the coast and is often adorned with gushing white necklaces of waterfalls after heavy rains, while Hihimanu (the mountain that looks to these SCUBA diver's eyes like a massive green manta ray) adds to the exotic backdrop.

> « *DRIVING THE BALL WELL MAY GIVE YOU A BETTER OPPORTUNITY TO SCORE. PLACEMENT, RATHER THAN DISTANCE, IS THE KEY TO GIVING YOURSELF A GOOD SECOND SHOT TO SET UP A BIRDIE OPPORTUNITY.* »
> —MIKE CASTILLO, DIRECTOR OF GOLF

THE COURSE

The Makai Course at Princeville was designed by Robert Trent Jones, Jr. as his first solo design endeavor way back in 1972. It has weathered the years admirably, despite the constant encroachment of development. The course is broken into three nines comprising 27 holes of solid resort golf. Each of the nines winds through various resort

The par-3 Ocean 3r[...]

complexes, so you won't find too much in the way of solitude here, but there are neverthe[...] less many beautiful holes and excellent golf to be played, including some of the finest coasta[...] holes in the state. You can't always choose which nines you play if you're only playing 18, bu[...] if you want to squeeze in a full 27 they'll usually work with you to try and make it happen.

The Ocean Nine is the most scenic of the three nines, as it plays down to the hotel which has fantastic vistas, then back up and out to another high panorama with a coupl[...] holes with cliff-side views. The Lakes Nine has water coming into play on three holes an[...] some real length to it, but the fairways are wide and forgiving. You can score well here if you[...] just keep your ball dry. The Woods Nine, as the name suggests, plays through some attrac[...] tive stands of trees, and while there is still plenty of resort housing along this segment, i[...] doesn't have the same claustrophobic feeling as the Lakes Nine sometimes has.

THE HOLES

OCEAN #3

The third hole of the Ocean Nine is a short par-3 that usually plays downwind of the trade[...] with a huge, 2-club drop to the green. For a lot of players, that means you're looking at some[...] sort of a wedge off of the tee, which is a bit awkward but also fun. A small lake short right[...] demands that you pay attention, which is a problem considering the view looks out over the[...] shoulder of the Princeville Hotel to Hanalei Bay. Also visible on the opposite side of the[...] bay, directly behind the hotel, is the distinctive rock structure known as Bali Hai, which[...] was featured in the classic film "South Pacific".

OCEAN #7

The Ocean's par-3 7th is cut on the side of a steep cliff above the Pacific, with a forced shot[...] over a deep gorge filled with tropical vegetation. The views are thrilling and with the trade[...] winds screaming from left to right, this hole is tough. Be sure to do what your onboard[...] GPS will remind you to do: walk to the back tees for a picture, even if you aren't playing from the tips.

LAKES #5

The short par-4 5th on the Lakes Nine plays over a gorge that will rattle your nerves, but the green
is drivable if you really catch it squarely. There's plenty of sand to waylay a slight mis-hit, but its
defenses are pretty thin, and this is definitely a birdie hole. The views of the ocean from the tee
aren't bad, either.

LAKES #9

The Lake's par-5 finisher is a beauty. The trade winds should be at your back, which is good since a
lake in front of the tee requires some airborne yardage to keep you dry. Just play it up into the wind

PRINCEVILLE AT HANALEI—MAKAI COURSE (muh-KAI)			
ADDRESS		**CONTACT**	
4080 Lei Opapa Road		808-826-3581	
Princeville, HI 96722		WWW.PRINCEVILLE.COM	
COURSE DETAILS		**SCORECARD**	
Architect	Robert Trent Jones, Jr.	Par	See
Year Opened	1972	Slope	Box
Renovated	No	Course Rating	
Reservations	30 days out	**TEES/YARDAGES**	
Online Times	No	Blue	
Greens Fees	$$$/18 holes	White	See
Discounts	Resort/Pre-twilight/Sunset	Silver	Box
Club Rentals	Yes	Red	
Premium	Yes		
Houses	Yes		
WATER		**DISTANCES**	
Types	Lakes/Ocean	Well-marked	Yes
Water Holes	7/27 holes	Yardage Book	Yes
Oceanfront	Yes	Sprinklers	Yes
		GPS	In-cart
PRACTICE		**BUNKERS**	
Driving Range	Grass	How Many?	121/27 holes
Practice Balls	Included	Consistency	Thin/Variable
Putting Green	Yes	**GRASS**	
Chip Green	Yes	Greens	Bermuda 328
Practice Bnkr.	Yes	Fairways	Bermuda 328

Princeville Makai Course

and when you catch up to it, you may just be looking at a mid-iron into the green in two, with the wind. The only problem with that is the lake is puddled between you and the green, which is backed by lovely Cook pines and the clubhouse.

WOODS #4

On the Woods Nine, the par-4 4th is a knee-buckler, as a 100-yard carry is required to clear the lake on approach, and the drop area still demands water clearance. The view from the fairway is memorable, with the lake reflecting an idyllic green backed by trees and jagged green mountains and waterfalls. Got a camera?

WOODS #8

The eighth hole on the Woods is a pretty par-3 that plays downwind. There's a ton of sand, but the presence of a triplet of Zen rocks in the largest bunker may finally induce the sound of one hand clapping in your golf swing.

Makai Course			
Ocean			
Blue		3497	
White		3157	
Red		2802	
Lakes			
Blue		3456	
White		3149	
Red		2714	
Woods			
Blue		3445	
White		3208	
Red		2829	
18 Hole Combos	**Par**	**Slope**	**Ratin**
Ocean/Lakes	72	132	73.2
Ocean/Woods	72	131	72.9
Lakes/Woods	72	129	72.5

Approach on the Lakes #9

Approach on the Woods #

Directions

From the Lihue Airport, turn right on Hwy. 51. Merge onto Hwy. 56 and follow it for 25 miles toward Princeville. Proceed less than a mile past the entrance to the Prince Course and turn right into the entrance to Princeville at Hanalei Resort. The entrance to the course is ½-mile down on the left.

PRINCEVILLE
MAKAI
COURSE

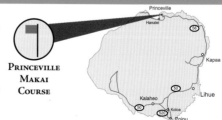

The epic carry over jungle on the 10th

RINCEVILLE AT HANALEI—PRINCE COURSE
~:Choke Hole: #7:~

ur first clue that you're in for something special at the Prince Course
't the spectacular clubhouse, which is constructed in the same opu-
t style as the Princeville Hotel. Nor is it the first glimpse you catch of
e practice facilities, which feature three teeing areas that allow you to
t your shots from different wind angles. It may be when you hear the
al guys joking on the range that they should maybe bag a few hand-
s of practice balls so they don't run out on the course. But you'll know
u've got it when the starter points at the deep green vegetation spread
ng the landscape beyond the range and says, "That is the course."
here, exactly, could a course fit into that? You are about to find out.

HE COURSE
bert Trent Jones, Jr. has created something unique at the Prince Course, and all of the awards (it's

FANATIC Ratings	
DESIGN INTRIGUE	★★★★☆
DIFFICULTY	★★★★☆
BEAUTY	★★★★☆
MAINTENANCE	★★★★
SERVICE	★★★★
SWANK FACTOR	★★★★

" ON THE 13TH, CLUB SELECTION IS KEY. THIS CHALLENGING PAR-4
REQUIRES A LAY-UP SHOT OF ABOUT 205 YARDS UP THE LEFT SIDE. YOU
CAN REACH THE ANINI STREAM IF YOUR SHOT GOES 210 YARDS. TAKE
ONE EXTRA CLUB ON YOUR APPROACH TO THE GREEN BECAUSE IT IS WELL
PROTECTED BY BUNKERS ON THE LEFT AND THE STREAM ON THE RIGHT.
—STEVE MURPHY, HEAD GOLF PROFESSIONAL

often called the best resort course in Hawaii),
lists, and press copy can't really do it justice.
You need to play it. Suffice to say, thick jungle
awaits your golf balls. Twists, doglegs, forced
carries, and elevation drops abound. Multi-
tiered greens, rolls and undulations, grass bunkers, and abrupt drop-offs into the heart of
darkness make even the most thoughtfully
considered shots highly unpredictable. There's

Trying to find the 13th fairw

even a dose of oceanfront golf thrown into the mix for those who don't consider it a Hawaii
golf experience unless they can hear the surf from the tee. It's all here, even some negatives in are
where the course lapses into generic development-sullied holes. But just when you think the exp
rience has been cheapened, you tee off on #12, leave it all behind, and don't look back.

The fairways are narrow, so you'd better bring your directional game. Distance contro
equally important, and sheer power isn't going to help you very much. As the starter told me
the tee, "People come here and want to beat this course. Well, you can't beat it. The course alw
wins." That may be true, but as long as you choose the right tee for your ability (out of the five t
are offered), you will at least have a reasonable chance of escaping with your ego mostly intact. Ju
heed this advice: watch out for the aggressive feral chickens and bring plenty of balls.

THE HOLES

#1

The par-4 1st is an apt introduction to what lies before you. That thick vegetated area that cu
right across the fairway is reachable on the downhill tee shot, so consider a fairway-wood and l
up. You'll have to come over the waste approach, but take care not to be short. The green is de
and beyond the putting surface is a gentle gathering area, but shots that come up even an in
short will plummet into the dense foliage and creek below the green.

The 6th gre

s a Golf Fanatic, don't miss the Robert rent Jones, Jr. Signature Tee on #7. The long ar-3 offers the experience of blasting off a iff (into a stiff headwind) to a distant green ver a gulch filled with thick jungle plants nat seem to thrive on a steady diet of golf alls. Take a shot at it with a shag ball, then nake your way to your chosen tee for your

The 7th green

Princeville Prince Course

PRINCEVILLE—PRINCE COURSE

ADDRESS		CONTACT	
5-3900 Kuhio Highway Princeville, HI 96722		808-826-5001 WWW.PRINCEVILLE.COM	

COURSE DETAILS		SCORECARD	
Architect	Robert Trent Jones, Jr.	Par	72
Year Opened	1987 front/1990 back	Slope	140
Renovated	No	Course Rating	75.2
Reservations	90 days out	TEES/YARDAGES	
Online Times	No	Black	7309
Greens Fees	$$$$	Blue	6960
Discounts	Resort/Afternoon/Twilight	White	6521
Club Rentals	Yes	Gold	6029
Premium	Yes	Red	5346
Houses	Yes		

WATER		DISTANCES	
Types	Lakes/Streams	Well-marked	Yes
Water Holes	4	Yardage Book	Yes
Oceanfront	Yes	Sprinklers	Yes
		GPS	In-cart

PRACTICE		BUNKERS	
Driving Range	Grass	How Many?	73
Practice Balls	Included	Consistency	Thin/Variable
Putting Green	Yes	GRASS	
Chip Green	Yes	Greens	Bermuda
Practice Bnkr.	Yes	Fairways	Bermuda

real shot. There's a safe landing area to the right, but anything left is gone. The view is spectacula
from the green, too, with Anini Beach below to the left and long waves breaking over the reef.

#10

#10 is a standout par-5 that opens one of the most intriguing back nines you will ever play. Big hi
ters will want to drive to the left, leaving open the possibility of getting home in two by taking
shortcut over the jungle growth. Notice that there's some room to the left to fudge a mistake, bu
anything right needs to be long enough. For those who lack the will or the way, drives center-rigl
are best. The second shot is a little hard to judge as the hole curves steadily around to the left, wit
lots of sand to catch your miscues. The views of mountains are awesome from this fairway. Thi
hole is a strategic—and scenic—jewel.

The plunging 12th from the te

#12

What the par-4 12th lacks in distance it makes up for in character. The tee is 100 feet above the
narrow fairway, where shoulders of vegetation pinch the fairway close to the green: selecting your
driver is a foolish move. A fairway wood, hybrid, or iron will be enough to ensure a short-iron or
wedge shot into the green, but accuracy is key, as Anini Stream snakes around the right side and
behind the green. A warning: beware the voracious chickens that will incessantly blitz your cart
like a scene from "Night of the Living Dead." Notice the sandwich bags and assorted shrapnel scattered along the length of the hole that is evidence of their insatiable appetites. Please people, safety
first.

3

3 is why you are playing this course. This r-4 lies in the deepest, darkest jungle of e track. Anini Stream cuts the hole in two, manding a lay-up off the tee that's as close to e end of the fairway as you are comfortable ith. You'll be left with a long-iron approach a green that is tucked into a tropical grotto. huge mango tree guards short right, and e stream winds behind the green while two g bunkers punish those who bail out left. wildly picturesque waterfall gushes just hind the putting surface. Check your map and compass, plot your route, and don't miss.

19th Puka

Ambiance:	Tropical Terrace
Fully stocked:	Yes
Draft beer:	Yes
Menu:	Yes
Cost:	Pricey
Best bet:	Fried sweetbread with powdered sugar
The Lowdown:	While "casual golf" is the breakfast and lunch vibe, they fancy it up a notch after sunset.

PRINCEVILLE PRINCE COURSE

(FROM RIGHT)

THE 7TH FROM THE SIGNATURE TEES

FERAL ROOSTER

PLUMERIA TEE MARKER

OCTOPUS TREE

THE 5TH GREEN

Directions

rom the Lihue Airport, turn right on Hwy. 51. Merge onto Hwy. 56 and follow it for 25 miles toward Princeville. The Prince Course is on the right just before entering the resort own of Princeville.

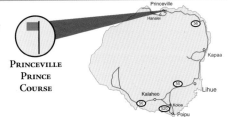

PRINCEVILLE PRINCE COURSE

The 6th gre

PUAKEA GOLF COURSE
~:Choke Hole: #6:~

FANATIC Ratings

DESIGN INTRIGUE	★★★★
DIFFICULTY	★★★⯨
BEAUTY	★★★⯨
MAINTENANCE	★★★⯨
SERVICE	★★★
SWANK FACTOR	★★⯨

Puakea Golf Course has a terrific layout that rolls and plunges amidst the type of suburban environment that has encumbered much of modern Hawaii. This master-planned community, pooled at the foot of the dramatic Ha'upu Mountains—which have been the backdrop for movies like "Jurassic Park" and "6 Days 7 Nights"—is stuffed with residences, and, most conspicuously, a handful of mainland box stores. While teeing off on the first hole, straight toward Costco, it may be difficult to avoid the idea that you didn't come all the way to Hawaii to gawk at the same developed views as you may have back home, but don't let that sense prevail. This is an excellent course that boasts some lovely views, is a fantastic challenge, and provides a high quality Hawaiian golf experience. Simply reali that Hawaii isn't any more immune to commercial development than your hometown.

> " BE SURE TO SPEND SOME TIME ON THE PUTTING GREEN BEFORE TEEING OFF. OUR BERMUDA GRASS GREENS ARE GRAINY AND WILL HAVE AN IMPACT ON YOUR PUTTS. THE EASIEST WAY TO IDENTIFY WHICH WAY THE GRAIN IS RUNNING IS TO LOOK AT THE COLOR OF THE GREENS. THE SURFACE WILL APPEAR SHINIER DOWN-GRAIN, AND DARKER UP-GRAIN. "
> —PAUL ITO, DIRECTOR OF GOLF

Mr. Hawaii himself, course architect Robin Nelson, began work on a beautiful chunk of real estate located on Grove Farm, a former sugar plantation. Ten holes had been completed by the time Hurricane Iniki devastated the island on September 11, 1992. Subsequently, development stopped at Grove Farm, and the golf course became overgrown and lay fallow until the economy on the island recovered and the original 10 holes were opened for play in 1997. The course became known as one of the best nine-holers in the country, but it wasn't until Steve Case of America Online bought the property in 2002 that Robin Nelson was brought back in to complete the final holes. The course reopened with its full eighteen holes in 2003, and the development around it soon began again in earnest.

The Course

Despite the development, Puakea remains a very strong track, a delight to play, and an excellent bargain. Many of the holes, including the original ten, play with lush mountain views, and the layout and strategy required to play well here outweigh the fact that, for instance, the ninth tee is

The 13th green

right across the street from the island's Borders Books and Music. The course features voluptuous mounding, slopes, elevation changes, well-placed bunkers (filled with fluffy white Australian sand), and strong trade winds, which add up to a compelling and fun round of golf. Advanced golfers will certainly find a challenge from the back tees here, but average golfers will appreciate that there are few truly punishing aspects to the course.

Puakea also prides itself on being the friendliest course on the island, and the staff goes out of its way to make you feel welcome. This attitude and Aloha Spirit go a long way toward making your day here a pleasant Hawaiian experience. By the end of your first round, you may already feel like it's the course where everybody knows your name.

THE STARTER'S SLOGAN:
"Kahi o makou e ho'okipa aloha ai."
—*Where we host and care with aloha.*

The Holes
#6

The fun on the front nine goes into high gear at the par-3 6th, where a wide, shallow green sits two to three clubs downhill across a pond. Greenside bunkers left and right punish way off-center shots, but guessing the right club on the tee is the key. For those who lose one into the lake, the drop area is down at the bottom of the hill, but it still requires a shot over the water. Look for the red-striped face and yellow-tipped beak of the endangered Hawaiian Common Moorhen stalking prey around the edges of the lake, and take a moment to admire the huge mango trees short and left of the green. (Think twice before plucking a ripe mango, as the juice from the leaves contains a toxin similar to poison ivy and gives a nasty rash.)

PUAKEA GOLF COURSE (poo-uh-KAY-uh)

ADDRESS		CONTACT	
4150 Nuhou Street		866-773-5554	
Lihue, HI 96766		WWW.PUAKEAGOLF.COM	
COURSE DETAILS		**SCORECARD**	
Architect	Robin Nelson	Par	72
Year Opened	1997 10 holes/2003 18	Slope	135
Renovated	No	Course Rating	73.3
Reservations	3 months out	**TEES/YARDAGES**	
Online Times	Yes	Green	6954
Greens Fees	$$$	Blue	6471
Discounts	Afternoon/Twilight	White	6061
Club Rentals	Yes	Red	5225
Premium	Yes		
Houses	Yes		
WATER		**DISTANCES**	
Types	Lakes, creeks	Well-marked	Yes
Water Holes	7	Yardage Book	Yes
Oceanfront	No	Sprinklers	Yes
		GPS	Sky Caddie
PRACTICE		**BUNKERS**	
Driving Range	Grass	How Many?	80
Practice Balls	Extra	Consistency	Good
Putting Green	Yes	**GRASS**	
Chip Green	Yes	Greens	Bermuda
Practice Bnkr.	Yes	Fairways	Bermuda

Puakea Golf Course

12

he twelfth is a mid-length par-4 with a two-
ered, divided fairway and a lake along the
ght side. The sensible shot is to the upper
ortion of the left fairway, but bunkers at the
d of the tier keep you from going too long.
g hitters may opt for the right fairway, but
e slope is toward the lake, and any right-
inning shot into the prevailing headwind
ill probably be fish food. For those who shy
vay from the lake on approach, there are
vo large bunkers left of the green to punish
ur cowardice.

19th Puka	
Ambiance:	Friendly Neighborhood Club-house
Fully stocked:	Yes
Draft beer:	No
Menu:	Yes
Cost:	Par
Best bet:	Ahi Poke (POH-kay)
The Lowdown:	A no-frills spot to melt away those pre-round butterflies (you're on vacation, no?)

13

he 13th is a long par-3 that plays with the trades at your back, so it may be a couple shots shorter
an the yardage reads. The green is long and narrow, and the fairway runs all the way up to the
utting surface, so a bit of miscalculation on the length won't ruin your day. The shot plays over a
ke and between a narrow opening in some large trees, which makes for a dramatic view — and
emands a straight shot.

PUAKEA GOLF COURSE

12TH GREEN   THE 3RD   11TH GREEN

Directions

From the Lihue Airport, turn left on Hwy. 51. Continue
on Hwy. 51 by turning left at the stop sign on Rice St. and
follow about 1 ½ miles as it turns into Hwy. 58. Turn left at
Pikake St. Turn left at Borders Books onto Pikake St., then
take your next left on Nuhou St. to the entrance on the left.

PUAKEA
GOLF
COURSE

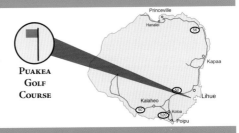

17th green from the te

WAILUA MUNICIPAL GOLF COURSE
~:Choke Hole: #17:~

FANATIC Ratings

DESIGN INTRIGUE	★★★
DIFFICULTY	★★★✦
BEAUTY	★★★
MAINTENANCE	★★★
SERVICE	★✦
SWANK FACTOR	★✦

As the oldest course on the island, and one of the oldest in Hawaii, Wailua is a classic. The course is located just a couple miles north of the main town of Lihue, right on the eastern shore of Kaua'i, where it receives the strong trade winds that blow from the northeast. This is a real municipal, with loads of locals shelling out $45 a month for unlimited rounds. This offers a great chance to get to know some nice local folks, who'll do a better job of cluing you in on the subtleties of the course than I can. The course can play tough, especially when the winds are blowing, but you can't escape the fact that it's a great deal. Golf has been played here for nearly 100 years; there's a palpable history to go along with the abundance of mature trees and plants.

THE COURSE

The trade winds are a big factor on the course and will work into every shot you make on a typical day. The bunkers here look like they were blown out with dynamite; just massive crater filled with beach sand. The front nine is the newer of the two, added in 1966, and plays mor

> *KEEP THE BALL IN THE FAIRWAY, AND PLAN TO USE EVERY CLUB IN YOUR BAG. ALSO, STAY OUT OF THE BUNKERS, THEY'RE BIG AND DEEP.*
> —ED OKAMOTO, GOLF COURSE ADMINISTRATOR

raightaway. The original nine is now the ack nine, and here you'll need more varied nots, particularly a right-to-left ball flight f the tee, since five out of seven driving oles dog to the left.

The beach fronting the course

HE HOLES

3

he par-3 third plays straightaway from the each, giving you an excellent opportunity o enjoy the sights and sounds of a day on the sand while you wait for your turn to play. (While I aited for a group ahead to putt out, I watched as an octogenarian, using an old golf club as a cane, odded past a pickup truck loaded with beat up surfboards.) The shot to the green is a simple, vel poke, with two large bunkers covering both front sides of the green, but the wind is usually reaming at your back, giving you some grief in club selection.

9

tanding on the tee of the par-5 9th, take a look at the fairway and try to judge which way the wind blowing. Yeah, the leaning trees make it pretty obvious. Fortunately, the hole jogs left along with le crosswind, so a straight, high tee shot ought to bounce down the middle of the fairway. The nly obstacles to getting home in two here are the limitations of the golfer and the two clamshell unkers in front of the green.

3

he 13th is a long 3-shotter that doglegs left, just like most of the holes on the back. If you want to raw your drive around the corner, you'll have to do it against the trade winds. There's a ditch a

The 15th green

long drive out that will keep you from making too much ground off the tee. Shots that are too far to the right will have a tough time with a second-shot approach, as a cluster of ironwood trees blocks the right side of the green.

#17

The par-3 17th is the finest hole on the course. The tee sits above the green tight against the trees, which mask the crosswinds that won't hit your ball until it

Banyan tr

WAILUA MUNICIPAL GOLF COURSE (why-loo-uh)			
ADDRESS		**CONTACT**	
3-5350 Kuhio Highway		808-241-6666	
Lihue, HI 96766		WWW.KAUAI.GOV/GOLF	
COURSE DETAILS		**SCORECARD**	
Architect	Toya Shirai/Others	Par	72
Year Opened	1928 front/1961 back	Slope	129
Renovated	No	Course Rating	73.3
Reservations	7 days out for two plus	**TEES/YARDAGES**	
Online Times	No	Blue	6981
Greens Fees	$	White	6585
Discounts	Twilight	Red	5974
Club Rentals	Yes		
Premium	No		
Houses	No		
WATER		**DISTANCES**	
Types	Lakes	Well-marked	Yes
Water Holes	6	Yardage Book	No
Oceanfront	Yes	Sprinklers	No
		GPS	Sky Caddie
PRACTICE		**BUNKERS**	
Driving Range	Mats	How Many?	37
Practice Balls	Extra	Consistency	Good
Putting Green	Yes	**GRASS**	
Chip Green	Yes	Greens	Bermuda 328
Practice Bnkr.	Yes	Fairways	Bermuda 328

Wailua Municipal Golf Course

ses above the treetops. Then, only a ball that hung way out to the left will find its way the middle of the green. Three massive unkers guard the front and right side, beckning the hapless hacker who fires straight the pin and watches helplessly as his ball ushes into the sand: trapped. Expect a wait n this hole, and be ready for the foursome ehind you to scramble up onto the tee to atch you have a go. Word to the wise: if you rop it into the hole off the tee, as I almost id, you may have to "Buy whiskeys for all!"

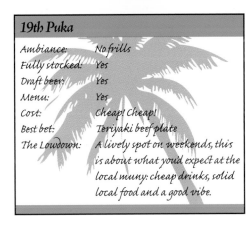

19th Puka

Ambiance:	No frills
Fully stocked:	Yes
Draft beer:	Yes
Menu:	Yes
Cost:	Cheap! Cheap!
Best bet:	Teriyaki beef plate
The Lowdown:	A lively spot on weekends, this is about what you'd expect at the local muny: cheap drinks, solid local food and a good vibe.

WAILUA
MUNICIPAL
✿
(FROM RIGHT)
······
THE 17TH GREEN
······
LOCAL TURTLE
······
COMMON
MOORHEN
······
FAT TOAD
······
THE 5TH WITH
LILIES

Directions

From the Lihue Airport, turn right on Hwy. 51. Merge onto Hwy. 56 and proceed just over a mile to the entrance on the right side.

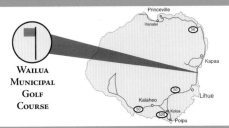

WAILUA
MUNICIPAL
GOLF
COURSE

Princeville
Hanalei
56
Kapaa
50
Lihue
Kalaheo
50
Koloa
520
Poipu

The luxurious Four Seasons Resort Hualalai along the Big Island's Kohala Coast

Big Island

The island of Hawai'i, aptly nicknamed the "Big Island," is nearly twice the combined size of all the other Hawaiian Islands. Millions of people come to the Big Island every year to view Kilauea, the world's most active volcano. While they're here, they also find legendary Hawaiian waterfalls, idyllic valleys, perfect beaches, Kona Coffee Country . . . and golf. From the upscale resort courses along the sunny Kohala Coast, to the cool upcountry courses such as Big Island Country Club, to fairways near one of the world's most active volcanic vents at Volcano Country Club, golf on the Big Island is as diverse as the massive island itself.

THE CLASSIC	TO DYE FOR	PURE LUXURY
MAUNA KEA	**BIG ISLAND C.C.**	**HUALALAI**
Robert Trent Jones, Sr. defined the black lava/green fairway look of Kohala Coast golf way back in the '60s.	Pete and Perry Dye's verdant mountain course is great fun, but the island green at the par-3 17th will make or break your round.	This Nicklaus course at the swankiest resort on the island will keep you coming back—if you can afford it.

Page 200 ☞   Page 176 ☞   Page 184 ☞

Big Island

Actual Name: Hawai'i
Area: 4028.0 square miles
Highest Point: Mauna Kea, 13,796 feet
Population: 148,677 (2000 census)
Flower: Lehua

1 - Big Island Country Club

2 - Hapuna Golf Course

3 - Hualalai Golf Course

4 - Kona C.C.—Ocean Course

5 - Kona C.C.—Mountain Course

6 - Makalei Golf Club

7 - Mauna Kea Golf Course

8 - Mauna Lani—South Course

9 - Mauna Lani—North Course

10 - Waikoloa Kings' Course

11 - Waikoloa Beach Course

12 - Waikoloa Village Golf Club

13 - Waimea Country Club

14 - Volcano Golf & Country Club

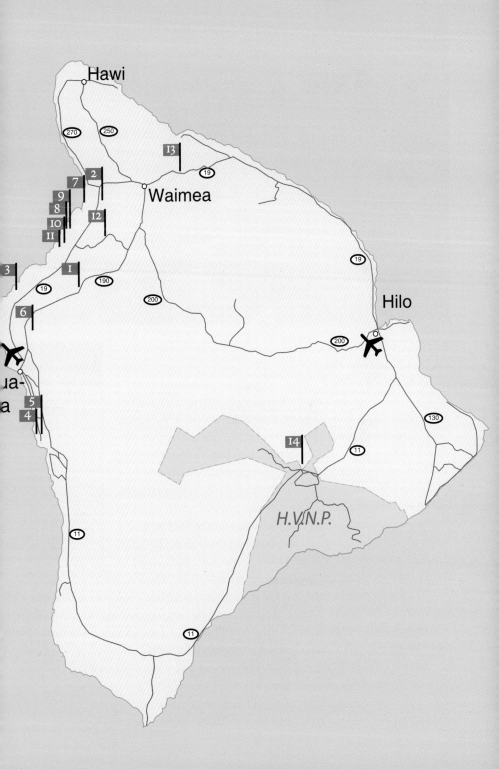

Hawi

270

250

13

19

7 2

Waimea

9

8

12

10

11

19

3

1

19

190

6

200

Hilo

19

200

ua-
a

5

4

130

14

11

H.V.N.P.

11

11

The par-3 island 17

BIG ISLAND COUNTRY CLUB
~:Choke Hole: #17:~

FANATIC
Ratings

DESIGN INTRIGUE
★★★★✦
DIFFICULTY
★★★★
BEAUTY
★★★★
MAINTENANCE
★★★★
SERVICE
★★✦
SWANK FACTOR
★★

At 2,500 feet above sea level, the Big Island Country Club can be a welcome departure from the harsh, lava-ridden courses of the Kohala Coast. Just a short drive up the slopes from the major resorts, the course sits in a lush ecosystem. The area is plush with large flowering trees and wild birds, such as turkeys and *nene* (the state bird), which freely roam the fairways. The air generally turns to rain and mist in the afternoons, and cooler temperatures are virtually assured. Folks turn up just to stroll the area, usually armed with binoculars for the fine bird watching, or to catch a break from the sun-drenched coast below. Golfers are drawn here for the same reasons, and, of course, for a world-class Dye design that is rewarding and satisfying.

The master plan for the course was put into motion in the mid-nineties, and called for a private layout for the owners of the 100 lots that surround the property. However, the developer ran out of funds, and never made any progress on the houses, or the pool or lavish clubhouse. Instead they brought in some trailers and erected a "temporary club tent."

> ONLY READ THE SLOPE OF THE GREENS, THERE IS NO GRAIN
> UP HERE. AND DUE TO THE ELEVATION, USE A HALF CLUB
> LESS SINCE YOUR BALL WILL FLY A LITTLE FARTHER.
> —NOA GALDEIRA, DIRECTOR OF GOLF

THE COURSE

At the Big Island Country Club, Perry Dye has created a course in the same fine tradition that has made his father, Pete, one of the most distinguished architects in golf. This track features many of the familiar Dye characteristics that make their courses so special. The par-3 island green 17th the most instantly recognizable Dye feature, but the emblematic Dye railroad ties are also conspicuous around the central lake and in several bunkers. Other Dye characteristics: friendly, bowl-shaped contours on several holes that funnel errant shots back into the fairway, blind tee shots, and risk/reward propositions.

WHAT IS THAT?

IT'S YOUR BIG MOMENT: YOUR BUDDIES HAVE EACH DEPOSITED A PRO V1 INTO THE POND ON #17, AND YOU HAVE A CHANCE TO BE THE LONE SURVIVOR. YOU MAKE A SWEET SWING, BUT THE WIND COMES OUT OF NOWHERE AND HANGS YOUR SHOT UP. IT PLUMMETS FROM THE SKY LIKE A NENE DROPPING AND LANDS SHORT AND WET. THEN, JUST WHEN IT COULDN'T GET ANY WORSE, A FIENDISH LAUGH ERUPTS FROM THE BRUSH, MOCKING YOUR FAILURE. YOU LOOK AROUND, BUT DON'T SEE THE FOURTH-GRADE BULLY HIDING IN THE BOUGAINVILLEA, SO WHAT IS IT? THAT'S THE HARMLESS CALL OF THE ERCKEL'S FRANCOLIN, A PARTRIDGE THAT CALLS THESE DAMP VOLCANIC SLOPES HOME. BUT TAKE HEART, THERE'S AN OPEN SEASON ON THE AFRICAN GAME BIRDS FROM NOVEMBER THROUGH JANUARY.

Fairway on the par-5 2nd

THE HOLES

7

On the par-4 7th, a lake runs along the right side and a creek crosses the fairway about 200 yards out. This situation demands either a sensible lay up, or an incredibly accurate drive that clears the creek, avoids the lake, and sticks to a narrow neck of fairway that tilts toward the water.

#15

The 15th is a short par-4 of a drivable distance, but the green juts above the fairway, leaving room for error. Can you stick a green with your driver? The putting surface is large and there's expanse of fairway around the green, which makes the moon shot more alluring. If you miss, course, you're in real trouble. Rational-minded folks will stroke a mid-iron down the middle to full wedge position.

#17

The par-3 17th, with its island green, is a major draw to the course and does not disappoint. Wh

Big Island Country Club				
Address			**Contact**	
71-1420 Mamalahoa Highway Kailua-Kona, HI 96745			808-325-5044	
Course Details			**Scorecard**	
Architect	Perry Dye		Par	72
Year Opened	1997		Slope	140
Renovated	No		Course Rating	76.3
Reservations	1 week out		**Tees/Yardages**	
Online Times	No		Black	7075
Greens Fees	$$$		Blue	6578
Discounts	Twilight/Replay		White	6041
Club Rentals	Yes		Green	5287
Premium	Yes		Red	4837
Houses	No			
Water			**Distances**	
Types	Creeks/Lakes		Well-marked	Yes
Water Holes	9		Yardage Book	Yes
Oceanfront	No		Sprinklers	Yes
			GPS	Sky Caddie
Practice			**Bunkers**	
Driving Range	Grass/Mats		How Many?	50
Practice Balls	Extra		Consistency	Variable
Putting Green	Yes		**Grass**	
Chip Green	Yes		Greens	Bent/Poa
Practice Bnkr.	Yes		Fairways	Bent

Big Island Country Club

green is moderately sized, the drama of the moment combines with the unpredictable winds to create a disproportionately difficult shot. There is only one bunker on the and, short right, and the golfer who finds the sand here will have to summon a lot of courage to blast out, especially when the pin cut short: blading the ball into the water after staying dry off the tee shot is a bitter ze. I've watched foursome after foursome me through here and dunk all of their tee shots, take second whacks and miss those,

19th Puka

Ambiance:	Tent
Fully stocked:	No
Draft beer:	No
Menu:	No
Cost:	Cheap! Cheap!
Best bet:	$3 can of beer & a bag of Doritos
The Lowdown:	Grab a brew out of the icebox and head back out the driveway to sit above the 17th and watch the pond fill up with balls.

, then go to the chipping area and sink those into the pond. However, they seem to enjoy the le anyway, posing for pictures and soaking in the view, which is highlighted by multi-colored ugainvillea and purple-blooming jacaranda trees.

NENE LOVE   #17 THROUGH JACARANDA TREES APPROACH ON #16 (BELOW)   THE COURSE ENTRANCE

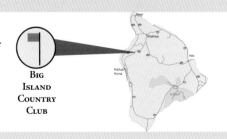

Directions

om Kailua-Kona, head up the hill at the intersection of lenry St. and Hwy. 19 by Borders Books. Turn right at the tersection with Palani Rd. and continue for about 18 miles it becomes Hwy. 190. From the Kohala Coast resorts, llow Hwy. 19 to the intersection with Waikoloa Rd. and rn up the hill for 12 miles. Turn right at the intersection ith Hwy. 190 and proceed for about 9 miles.

BIG ISLAND COUNTRY CLUB

The 1st gr

HAPUNA GOLF COURSE
~:Choke Hole: #3:~

The little sister to neighboring Mauna Kea is a unique, xeriscaped offering from Arnold Palmer and Ed Seay that winds its way through the dry, *kiawe* desert of the Kohala Coast. More and more construction is springing up along the fairways of the course, but traditionally this course has been striking for the contrast between the lush green fairways and the desiccated landscape that it occupies. The views are lovely at the apex of the course, with all viewable peaks of the Big Island visible, as well as the summit of Haleakala on Maui hovering in the haze across the channel.

Both the Hapuna and Mauna Kea resorts are owned and operated by Prince, but they are effectively two adjacent resorts. It's easy enough to travel between the tv for a day at the beach or a fine meal, but the resorts have distinctly different feels. While Maui Kea is the elder statesman, the Hapuna Resort (and its golf course) is more modern and a lit more family friendly.

FANATIC Ratings		
DESIGN INTRIGUE		
★★★★		
DIFFICULTY		
★★★★		
BEAUTY		
★★★★		
MAINTENANCE		
★★★★✓		
SERVICE		
★★★		
SWANK FACTOR		
★★★★		

> *DRIVER, USUALLY, IS NOT YOUR BEST OPTION HERE. YOUR BEST BET IS TO PLAY FOR POSITION OFF THE TEE, WHICH WILL USUALLY REQUIRE A FAIRWAY WOOD OR EVEN AN IRON. THEN, YOU CAN SCORE ON APPROACH.*
> —BRAD BAPTIST, HEAD GOLF PRO

ᴇ Course

ᴇ course isn't long, even from the back
s, and a player with big distance can dom-
ᴀte, especially since many holes feature
wnhill landing areas that will bounce long
ives even farther. The rub, of course, is
ᴀt the landing areas are narrow and loads
waste areas and high grass punish any-
ʼing that isn't right on the money. There's
mewhat of a links feel to the design, but,

The 6th green

with so many of the links-style courses in Hawaii, the ubiquitous heat melts any feeling of Scot-
ᴛh golf right off the course map. Nevertheless, lots of mounds, dips, and contours constitute the
ᴋs impression.

ᴇ Holes

ᴇ short par-4 1st sets the tone for the day. You'll likely be tempted to drive it close, but it's an
hill shot that gets narrower the closer you try to land it to the green. The final uphill neck is
out as heavily bunkered an area as you'll see on this course, and you may take away from this
ᴛe the lesson that ample length could seriously help you or completely destroy your round at
ᴀpuna.

ᴇ 3rd is risk-reward all the way. A narrow chute is your landing area off the tee, and if you split
ᴇ middle, your ball may take the downhill bounce and bump a *looong* way. From there, get-
ᴦg on in two should be a no-brainer, but the hole curves tightly around a lake on the left, and
approach that balloons up into the wind too much might be carried over the water and sunk.
ᴏrtals should be able to plunk their way through this one with a solid chance at par.

The pin at #4 with Maui in the haze

#14

The par-5 14th is another of the great par-5s on this course. The tee shot is uphill, but a nice drive leaves you with a deceptively short shot uphill over a ravine to the green. Be sure to take at least two extra clubs to get the ball all the way up to the putting surface, as the final swooping rise to the green is more ample than it looks. Coming up short will cause your ball

The approach on #

Hapuna Golf Course (huh-poo-nuh)			
Address		**Contact**	
62-100 Kauna'oa Drive		808-880-3000	
Kamuela, HI 96743		WWW.PRINCERESORTSHAWAII.COM	
Course Details		**Scorecard**	
Architect	Arnold Palmer/ Ed Seay	Par	72
Year Opened	1992	Slope	136
Renovated	No	Course Rating	73.3
Reservations	1 year out	**Tees/Yardages**	
Online Times	Yes	Black	6875
Greens Fees	$$$	Blue	6534
Discounts	Twilight/Resort	Orange	6029
Club Rentals	Yes	White	5067
Premium	Yes		
Houses	Yes		
Water		**Distances**	
Types	Lakes	Well-marked	Yes
Water Holes	4	Yardage Book	Yes
Oceanfront	No	Sprinklers	Yes
		GPS	Sky Caddie
Practice		**Bunkers**	
Driving Range	Grass	How Many?	37
Practice Balls	Included	Consistency	Soft, fluffy
Putting Green	Yes	**Grass**	
Chip Green	Yes	Greens	Tifdwarf
Practice Bnkr.	Yes	Fairways	Bermuda 328

Hapuna Golf Course

roll back down the hill or deflect into the
arge bunker on the left side of the neck.

8

he par-4 finisher slips left and down off the
ee, offering another opportunity to bounce
ne a long way off the tee. There's plenty of
rouble to find for those of us who always try
o end strong. For those who do bang out a
ice one, a downhill approach to a green that
ronts the clubhouse is an attractive close to a
atisfying round.

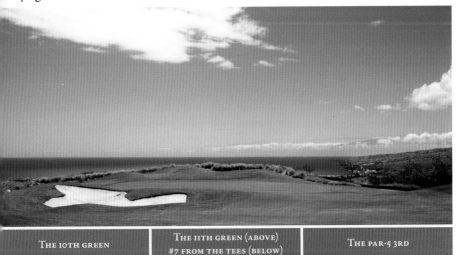

THE 10TH GREEN

THE 11TH GREEN (ABOVE)
#7 FROM THE TEES (BELOW)

THE PAR-5 3RD

Directions

From the Kona Airport, turn left on Hwy. 19 (Queen
Kaahumanu Hwy.) and drive about 25 miles, entering the
Hapuna Prince Resort on your right. The clubhouse is on
your right just before the hotel.

HAPUNA
GOLF
COURSE

The lovely par-3 17

HUALALAI GOLF COURSE
~:Choke Hole: #17:~
Site of Champions Tour MasterCard Championship

THE RESORT

With a spectacular level of service, facilities, and golf, this sumptuous Four Seasons Resort is the top destination in this book. There is simply nothing to dislike here. Need a few more minutes to warm up? Your starter will accommodate you, while filling your bag with logoed ball markers, repair tools, tees, yardage books, and pointing out the cooler filled with complimentary waters and sodas.

To make the most of your Hualalai experience, don't forget to relax in the locker room. If you're staying for a few days, get a locker and bring a change of clothes. Have your shoes shined. Drink some chilled citrus water and vegetate on the couch while watching the Golf Channel on the widescreen TV. Do you have any other idiosyncratic desires (related to golf, ahem) that could be fulfilled? Merely ask, and you will be indulged.

Of course, this leads to the major problem with playing here: you must be a resort guest in order to get a tee time. While shelling out for one of these lavish rooms adds greatly to the already steep greens fees, it ensures the course is seldom crowded.

FANATIC
Ratings

DESIGN INTRIGUE	★★★✦
DIFFICULTY	★★★★
BEAUTY	★★★★✦
MAINTENANCE	★★★★✦
SERVICE	★★★★★
SWANK FACTOR	★★★★★

> *THE GREENS DON'T BREAK AS MUCH AS THEY MAY AT FIRST APPEAR TO BREAK, ESPECIALLY UNDER 10-15 FEET. DON'T OVER-READ THE GREENS.*
> —BRENDAN MOYNAHAN, HEAD GOLF PROFESSIONAL

THE COURSE

st as the service is personal, friendly, and ever-present, the maintenance of the course is nearly wless. You won't find many crusty spots or disparate lengths of rough from hole to hole, Nick-us's design is thoughtful and fits well with the physical features that he encountered here. The urse plays naturally up and down the lava flows, rather than cutting awkwardly across them, d lava features are used playfully and attractively.

And then there are the greens. Many players find grainy Hawaiian greens difficult to read, it these greens are large and flat, with little break and minimal grain implication. They're reason-ly quick, roll true, and are a relief after playing places where you'll swear the grain carries your ll uphill through the break! The most beguiling aspect of the greens is the tendency to over read em, expecting a break that isn't there.

There are many intricately shaped bunkers, but few places where you will find yourself ueezed on two sides and forced to land your shot in a tight spot, as one side is nearly always open. you should happen to find the beach, which is likely with nearly 100 bunkers, you'll discover the xury of soft, playable sand. Finally you'll know why the PGA players make getting out of the inkers look so easy.

#12 with the "Bear Trap" bunker in the green

HUALALAI VOLCANO

HE FOUR SEASONS RESORT HUALALAI IS NAMED FOR THE SLOPES OF THE VOLCANO ON WHICH T SITS. HUALALAI IS THE THIRD TALLEST VOLCANO ON THE ISLAND, PEAKING AT 8,271 FEET. TS LAST ERUPTION OCCURRED IN 1801, AND FLOWED WIDELY THROUGH THE AREA AROUND HE KONA AIRPORT, SPARING MOST OF THE PRESENT-DAY RESORT AREA. BUT DON'T RELAX TOO IUCH: EXPERTS BELIEVE THAT SLUMBERING HUALALAI IS OVERDUE FOR A MAJOR ERUPTION OMETHING TO THINK ABOUT WHILE YOU'RE SIZING UP A DELICATE DOWNHILL PUTT).

THE HOLES

#5

One of the few water holes, the fifth is a one-shotter with a lake that runs tight along the right sid
The single bunker on the left side of the green only comes into play if you hit away from the wate
It's not surprising that there are always a lot of raked areas in that trap. The volcano Hualalai tov
ers to the left off the tee, while palm trees and multi-million dollar homes back the wide green.

#12

The 12th is a short par-3 with a whimsical twist: a bunker lodged in the middle of the green. Th

HUALALAI GOLF COURSE (hoo-AH-luh-lye)			
ADDRESS		**CONTACT**	
100 Ka'upulehu Drive		808-325-8480	
Ka'upulehu-Kona, HI 96740		WWW.FOURSEASONS.COM/HUALALA	
COURSE DETAILS		**SCORECARD**	
Architect	Jack Nicklaus	Par	72
Year Opened	1996	Slope	139
Renovated	No	Course Rating	73.7
Reservations	3 months out	**TEES/YARDAGES**	
Online Times	No	Mahope	7117
Greens Fees	$$$$	Championship	6632
Discounts	None	Regular	6032
Club Rentals	Yes	Mua	5374
Premium	Yes		
Houses	Yes		
WATER		**DISTANCES**	
Types	Lakes/Fish pond/Ocean	Well-marked	Yes
Water Holes	3	Yardage Book	Yes
Oceanfront	Yes	Sprinklers	Yes
		GPS	In-cart
PRACTICE		**BUNKERS**	
Driving Range	Grass	How Many?	93
Practice Balls	Included	Consistency	Soft, nice
Putting Green	Yes	**GRASS**	
Chip Green	Yes	Greens	Tifdwarf
Practice Bnkr.	Yes	Fairways	Bermuda

Hualalai Golf Course

ear Trap" adds an interesting wrinkle to
a otherwise straightforward hole and may
st your skills with a lob wedge from the
ghtest lie there could be: from on the green.

7

he 17th is one of the most beautiful holes
the state. Carved out of rugged shoreline
va, this par-3 plays from an elevated tee to
huge green backed by crashing surf. There
n't too much to the shot, but the drama of
e setting always makes it more difficult
an it should be.

HUALALAI GOLF COURSE
♣
(FROM RIGHT)
......
APPROACH ON #13
......
THE 18TH GREEN
......
THE PAR-3 8TH
......
THE 10TH GREEN
......
THE 3RD FROM THE TEES

Directions

From the Kona Airport, turn left on Hwy. 19 (Queen Kaa-
humanu Hwy.) and drive just over 6 miles, turning left onto
Kaupulehu Dr. into the Hualalai Resort and follow into the
Four Seasons Hualalai Resort at the end of the road.

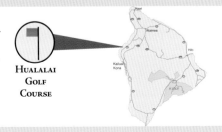

HUALALAI
GOLF
COURSE

The par-3 3rd from the te

KONA COUNTRY CLUB—OCEAN COURSE
~:Choke Hole: #17:~

THE RESORT

Kona Country Club is located just a few short miles south of Kailua-Kona, the largest town on the sunny side of the Big Island. The resort-style 36-hole layout is smack dab in the middle of the laid-back tourist enclave of Keauhou. The weather tends to be pretty humid down here, more so than along the Kohala Coast, but when the trade winds are battering golfers there, there's usually little more than a light breeze in Keauhou. You won't find the same level of service here as you will in the posh resorts along the Kohala Coast, but the courses have fun layouts that are worth a look.

THE COURSE

The Ocean Course boasts four ocean-front holes, which is more than the sum total on the islan of O'ahu. The Pacific isn't really in play on these holes in the same way as, say, #3 at Mauna Kea

> " ALWAYS PLAY TO BELOW THE HOLE WHEN YOU'RE ON
> APPROACH. IF YOU FIND YOURSELF ABOVE THE HOLE ON
> THESE GREENS, YOUR PUTTS MAY NEVER STOP.
> —DUANE OTTE, HEAD GOLF PROFESSIONAL

it's still really nice to play along the water, and this tends to e visitors a satisfying feeling of playing a "Hawaiian" course. e fairways are wide and the rough is closely mown. Bunker- is sparse, basically-shaped and not placed anywhere you uldn't expect.

The golf here is about as forgiving as you'll find in the state, ept for one thing: the grain on the greens. Both Kona courses greened with Bermuda 328, which was the most popular orid in the '60s when William Bell designed them—and is e of the grainiest Bermuda hybrids. On the upside, it is easy identify which way the grain is running by observing which e of the cup is rough: the grain runs that way, which is pretty ich toward the setting sun. On downhill, down-grain putts, u may roll yourself right off the green.

14th tee

The yardages on the course are poorly marked, and the carts lack an on-board GPS system, bring your range finder or Sky Caddie.

IE HOLES

he 3rd is a long par-3 that plays along rough lava shoreline. It would take a wicked slice to actu- y put one into the surf off the tee, so the proximity of the ocean is really just a lovely reminder of iere you are. Coconut palms shake and shimmy at the edge of the fairway and around the green, ntle breezes do little to affect your ball flight, and the wide blue sea extends far out of sight. It's a reet hole that's simple to play, which equals idyllic Hawaiian resort golf.

2

he par-3 12th also plays tight against the sea with no real risk of pulling your ball into it. It's mid- ngth and plays from an elevated tee to a large green that tilts back to front to hold balls. Its meager

The 12th green

defenses are a few clamshell bunkers on the left and right. Enjoy the view and play to the center of the green.

#13

The 13th is one of the most distinctive holes in the state. While it's really just a straight-away par-4, there's an actual blowhole in play off the tee. If the surf is up (usually during the summer on this side of the island), waves create a geyser effect that sends a wet, salty sneeze high into the air. From the middle and forward tees, this is only a distraction, but from the back

18th

Kona Country Club—Ocean Course (KOH-nuh)				
ADDRESS		**CONTACT**		
78-7000 Ali'i Drive		808-322-2595		
Kailua-Kona, HI 96740		WWW.KONAGOLF.COM		
COURSE DETAILS		**SCORECARD**		
Architect	William Bell	Par		72
Year Opened	1966	Slope		129
Renovated	No	Course Rating		72.8
Reservations	2 weeks out	**TEES/YARDAGES**		
Online Times	Yes	Blue		6748
Greens Fees	$$$	White		6281
Discounts	Twilight	Red		5436
Club Rentals	Yes			
Premium	Yes			
Houses	Yes			
WATER		**DISTANCES**		
Types	Ocean	Well-marked		No
Water Holes	4	Yardage Book		Yes
Oceanfront	Yes	Sprinklers		No
		GPS		Sky Caddie
PRACTICE		**BUNKERS**		
Driving Range	Grass	How Many?		64
Practice Balls	Extra	Consistency		Good, playable
Putting Green	Yes	**GRASS**		
Chip Green	Yes	Greens		Bermuda 328
Practice Bnkr.	Yes	Fairways		Bermuda 328

Kona C.C. Ocean Course

es you must actually play through that air-
ace, so time your tee shot accordingly.

7

he 17th is just a short-iron uphill pop to a
rge green. However, the gaping black lava
rge you are forced to hit over attracts loads
balls. Coconut palms, flowering trees, and
e landscaping make this a plush hole that
es far fewer birdies than it should.

8

he finisher is a short par-5 that plays longer than its yardage due to an uphill approach shot. The
y on this one is to leave yourself below the hole, which will be to the right side of the flagstick.
ot heeding this advice will turn many eagle opportunities into bogies. That's not the way to end
ine round.

19th Puka

Ambiance:	Open-air lounge
Fully stocked:	Yes
Draft beer:	Yes
Menu:	Yes
Cost:	Par
Best bet:	Fish and Chips
The Lowdown:	Situated in the elevated club-house, the sunset views are awesome and attract a sizable early-dinner crowd.

16TH GREEN

PAR-5 2ND GREEN (ABOVE)
CARTS (BELOW)

THE PAR-3 17TH

The 7th gre

KONA COUNTRY CLUB—MOUNTAIN COURSE
~:Choke Hole: #13:~

THE COURSE

Tumbling up and down these fairways it becomes clear why this course is a locals' favorite. It is not only more challenging and generally less trafficked than its sister course, but also possesses phenomenal vistas and a sense of precariousness that can only come from playing on the side of a mountain. The front and back nines were designed by different architects and built six years apart, and this comes across vividly. The front nine is surrounded by condos and large private residences, while the back winds away from the developments and has much more of the "mountainous" feel for which the course is named. The holes on the front play primarily back and forth across the face of the mountain, so all balls want to run towar the ocean. It is wise to consider this both off the tee and on approach. Lava is used more on th Mountain Course, and it's well blended into the layout, adding an attractive contrast to the ja fairways and greens. This is one of the most scenic courses on the island.

FANATIC Ratings		
DESIGN INTRIGUE		
★★★↲		
DIFFICULTY		
★★★★		
BEAUTY		
★★★★		
MAINTENANCE		
★★★		
SERVICE		
★★		
SWANK FACTOR		
★★↲		

> **THE MOUNTAIN IS A COURSE YOU JUST DON'T HAVE TO HIT DRIVER ON. PLACEMENT IS KEY OFF THE TEE, AND A WILD DRIVE CAN GET YOU IN TROUBLE QUICK.**
> —DUANE OTTE, HEAD GOLF PROFESSIONAL

KONA COFFEE COUNTRY

THE MOUNTAIN COURSE AT KONA COUNTRY CLUB CLIMBS UP INTO THE VERDANT HILLS ABOVE THE SOUTHERN KONA COAST. JUST A BIT FARTHER SOUTH IS THE ECOSYSTEM THAT PRODUCES ONE OF THE WORLD'S FINEST COFFEES. WARM MORNING SUN, COOL AFTERNOONS, EVENING RAINS, AND FECUND VOLCANIC SOIL ADD UP TO NEAR-PERFECT GROWING CONDITIONS. TOURING COFFEE PLANTATIONS IS A GREAT WAY TO SPEND THE AFTERNOON AFTER A MORNING ROUND AT THE KONA COUNTRY CLUB, AND YOU'LL BE ALLOWED TO TASTE BEFORE YOU BUY. LOOK FOR THE 100% KONA COFFEE LABEL AND AVOID THE 10% BLENDS THAT ARE FILLED IN WITH CHEAPER BEANS. TO REALLY APPRECIATE THE SUBTLETIES OF THE COFFEE, YOU'LL NEED TO TASTE THE FINEST GRADES, WHICH ARE "EXTRA FANCY" AND "FANCY." ALSO TRY THE POPULAR AND DELICIOUS PEABERRY.

THE HOLES

1

The 1st lets you know how it's going to be. It's a straight-away par-4, but the fairway slopes steeply right to left. Judging from the amount of divots in the left-hand rough, most players clearly find it difficult to keep their tee shot in the fairway. Tee up on the left side of the tee box and aim right of center.

5

The par-5 5th is short, fun, and always difficult. The tee shot is an uphill right twister to a fairway that slopes right to left. Aim just inside the trees on the upper-right side of the fairway. A good tee shot could hit the upper slope and roll down and across the fairway for extra yards. It will be tempting to go for the green in two, but it's a tough shot with trees protecting the left-short side of an elevated green that falls away to the left. You'll be looking for a birdie, but be happy with par.

13

The par-3 13th features an elevated tee with a shot over a lake to an oblong green with a couple deep

#13 from the back tees

bunkers sandwiching the neck. This hole is pretty much a cupcake when the pin position is in the front, but when they move it to the back this is a challenging hole. The view is excellent from the tee, with the Pacific far below and a view toward south Kona almost to Kealakekua Bay, where Captain James Cook, who commanded the first European ship to visit Hawaii, met his death at the hands of the Hawaiians in 1779.

13th p

#18

The par-4 18th is one of my favorite holes in the state. It plays straight

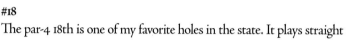

Kona C.C. Mountain Course

KONA COUNTRY CLUB—MOUNTAIN COURSE (KOH-nuh)				
ADDRESS		**CONTACT**		
78-7000 Ali'i Drive		808-322-2595		
Kailua-Kona, HI 96740		WWW.KONAGOLF.COM		
COURSE DETAILS		**SCORECARD**		
Architect	William Bell–front nine	Par	72	
Year Opened	1985	Slope	135	
Renovated	1991 R.Nelson/R. Wright	Course Rating	72.9	
Reservations	2 weeks out	**TEES/YARDAGES**		
Online Times	Yes	Blue	6634	
Greens Fees	$$$	White	5976	
Discounts	Twilight	Red	5038	
Club Rentals	Yes			
Premium	Yes			
Houses	Yes			
WATER		**DISTANCES**		
Types	Lakes	Well-marked	OK	
Water Holes	4	Yardage Book	Yes	
Oceanfront	No	Sprinklers	No	
		GPS	Sky Caddie	
PRACTICE		**BUNKERS**		
Driving Range	Grass	How Many?	46	
Practice Balls	Extra	Consistency	Variable	
Putting Green	Yes	**GRASS**		
Chip Green	Yes	Greens	Bermuda 328	
Practice Bnkr.	Yes	Fairways	Bermuda 328	

ownhill, and all it takes to score well is straight shot off the tee. But trees mark oth sides of the narrow fairway, punish-g any squirts off the tee. Somehow, just nowing that a long straight drive will run rever adds a lot of pressure, but pull-g it off is rewarding. The hole plunges en more steeply down to the green on pproach, so take at least a club less on pproach.

View of the Kona Coast from the 5th green

KONA COUNTRY CLUB MOUNTAIN COURSE

(FROM RIGHT)
•••••••
OUT OF THE BUNKER ON #2
•••••••
IN THE FAIRWAY ON #7
•••••••
GOATS OVER KONA
•••••••
10TH GREEN
•••••••
THE ELEVATED APPROACH ON #18

Directions

From the Kona Airport, turn right on Hwy. 19 (Queen Kaahumanu Hwy.) and drive for 12 miles as the road be-omes Hwy. 11. Take a right at the light onto Kamehameha II. Follow it to the bottom of the hill and take a right at the ight onto Alii Dr. The course is a mile down on the right.

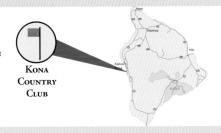

KONA COUNTRY CLUB

The par-3 15th from the te

MAKALEI GOLF CLUB
~:Choke Hole: #15:~

Laid out at nearly 3,000 feet above the sunny Kona Coast, Makalei Golf Club rolls and tumbles through forests teeming with peacocks and wild game. This course is kind of like Wild Kingdom meets a petting zoo, while offering unique golf and respite from the incessant heat on the coast.

Like several other excellent courses in the state, Makalei was originally intended as a private Japanese country club. When the Asian markets collapsed, the club instead opened to the public. Makalei has been through a number of transformations since its original opening in 1992, including some poor management and ill maintenance, but it is now stronger than ever and about as playable as it gets. The clubhouse (a collection of temporar structures, since the planned "grand" clubhouse was never built) sits at about 2,500 feet while th

FANATIC Ratings

DESIGN INTRIGUE	★★★★✰
DIFFICULTY	★★★★✰
BEAUTY	★★★★✰
MAINTENANCE	★★★✰
SERVICE	★★
SWANK FACTOR	★★

> " MAKALEI IS A WELL-DESIGNED COURSE IN THE SENSE THAT THE AVERAGE PLAYER AND GOOD PLAYER CAN PLAY TO A SIMILAR LEVEL BY UTILIZING THE TERRAIN. THIS IS ONE OF THE FEW COURSES YOU'LL FIND WHERE WEAKER PLAYERS CAN HIT 300-YARD DRIVES BY HITTING THE BALL IN THE RIGHT SPOT AND LETTING IT RIDE. "
> —KEVIN GINOZA, DIRECTOR OF GOLF

inth crests above the 2,900-foot level, translating into cool, damp golf – get here early before the afternoon clouds roll in. However, Makalei is sheltered from the trade winds, so this is an ideal place to come when winds are battering the coast.

Take note of the trees, as you won't see many of these types on other golf courses in the state, and will have little opportunity to view them without grabbing a compass and doing some hiking. Silver oak, with its yellowish bottlebrushes dominate, but jacaranda, classic *koa*—the ultimate Hawaiian hardwood with its sickle-shaped leaves—as well as *kukui* and *ohia* are also amply represented. Also, note the lava features, such as a full-blown lava tube on the right side of the 8th green.

THE COURSE

Makalei comes from the same mind that carved the tortuous Koʻolau on Oʻahu: architect Dick Nugent. The course ranks as the third most difficult course in the state, which means that the shot values are high, and even very well-struck shots, if not precisely orchestrated, may be lost forever.

The first is a strange opener, playing short and straight uphill, but the course finds its pace after that. The front plays a bit longer than the back, since it winds up several hundred feet, but the back is no pushover, as there are still a couple holes that play relentlessly uphill. There are picturesque lava walls running along and through some holes, and lots of sidehill lies; Nugent seems to have created something in the Doaks/Crenshaw style of having "found" the course and revealed it rather than taking a bulldozer and sculpting something more artificial.

THE HOLES

#2

From the tee at the second, a gap in the trees behind the green allows a glimpse of the Kona Coast and the Pacific Ocean far below. The green is a steep plunge below the lofty tees and is narrow, deep and well-guarded left and right. The carded yardage is long, but the hole really plays two to three clubs shorter than that.

The 14th green

#11

The par-4 11th is a sweet hole, primarily because of the expansive views of the coast below. Yo ought to be able to squeeze out some extra distance from the elevated tee and have a mid- to low iron into the two-tiered green. Aim down the left side off the tee, as the fairway slopes left to rig and will feed your ball toward the fairway bunker.

#12

I've taken shot after shot on the par-3 12th without being able to hit this narrow green. It's not to difficult when the pin is in the front, but when it's cut in the back upper tier of the green you ca

MAKALEI GOLF CLUB (MAH-kuh-lay)				
ADDRESS		**CONTACT**		
72-3890 Hawaii Belt Road Kailua-Kona, HI 96740		808-325-6625 WWW.MAKALEI.COM		
COURSE DETAILS		**SCORECARD**		
Architect	Dick Nugent	Par		72
Year Opened	1992	Slope		144
Renovated	No	Course Rating		74.3
Reservations	6 months out	**TEES/YARDAGES**		
Online Times	Yes	Black		7091
Greens Fees	$$	Blue		6698
Discounts	Twilight	White		6161
Club Rentals	Yes	Red		5242
Premium	Yes			
Houses	No			
WATER		**DISTANCES**		
Types	Lakes	Well-marked		Yes
Water Holes	2	Yardage Book		No
Oceanfront	No	Sprinklers		Yes
		GPS		Sky Caddie
PRACTICE		**BUNKERS**		
Driving Range	Grass	How Many?		39
Practice Balls	Extra	Consistency		Good, playable
Putting Green	Yes	**GRASS**		
Chip Green	Yes	Greens		Bent
Practice Bnkr.	No	Fairways		Bermuda 328

Makalei Golf Club

se your ball left, right, or long. The green is queezed between two exposed lava features ad guarded by a bunker on the left. Your est shot may be to drop your ball onto the ont and make the tough uphill putt to the pper tier (when the pin is in the back).

5

he lovely 15th is yet another par-3 from an evated tee to a green below, but this time he putting surface is both wide and deep. Iowever, a lake on the left and gaping bunkers on the right still demand accuracy from your tee shot. The views from the tee on clear days unnot be beat, with sight lines all the way down to the Kona Coast.

19th Puka

Ambiance:	Break room
Fully stocked:	No
Draft beer:	No
Menu:	Yes
Cost:	Cheap! Cheap!
Best bet:	Teriyaki Burger
The Lowdown:	The 19th here isn't much to look at, but homemade-style Hawaiian grinds make it worth your while for breakfast or lunch.

MAKALEI GOLF CLUB
❀
(FROM RIGHT)
••••••
2ND GREEN WITH KONA COAST BELOW
••••••
PEACOCKS ABOUND
••••••
18TH FROM BEHIND THE GREEN
••••••
LAVA TUBE ON #8
••••••
4TH GREEN

Directions

From the Kona Airport, turn right on Hwy. 19 (Queen Kaahumanu Hwy.) and drive for just over 3 miles. Turn right at the light onto Hinalani Rd. and continue 3.5 miles to the top of the hill. Turn left at the intersection with Hwy. 190 (Hawaii Belt Rd.) and drive 4 miles to the entrance on the right.

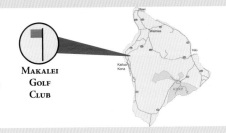

MAKALEI
GOLF
CLUB

The legendary par-3 3rd, with Maui in the distan

MAUNA KEA GOLF COURSE
~:Choke Hole: #3:~

THE RESORT

Mauna Kea, the *grande dame* of Hawaiian golf courses, was constructed in 1964 by Robert Trent Jones, Sr., one of only three full-length golf courses he ever designed in the state (Royal Ka'anapali on Maui and the defunct Discovery Harbor on the Big Island are the others). Laurance S. Rockefeller hired Jones to build an epic golf course to embellish his vision of the Mauna Kea Resort on the Kohala Coast of the Big Island, where, at the time, there was no other resort. Centered around Kauna'oa Beach, a stunning crescent of white sand on an island not known for its beaches, the resort set a high standard for the resorts that followed. With a fiercely faithful clientele, the hotel has continued to provide an exquisite experience, though its smallis

FANATIC Ratings	
DESIGN INTRIGUE	★★★★
DIFFICULTY	★★★★
BEAUTY	★★★★
MAINTENANCE	★★★★
SERVICE	★★★★
SWANK FACTOR	★★★★

> " BRING A SENSE OF HUMOR. JUST KIDDING. THIS COURSE ISN'T ONE WHERE YOU'RE GOING TO LOSE A LOT OF BALLS OFF THE TEE. THE FAIRWAYS ARE WIDE AND THE COURSE IS LONG, SO YOU'LL WANT TO HIT DRIVER OFF THE TEE. IT'S THE APPROACH SHOTS WHERE YOU HAVE TO BE CAREFUL. WITH THE WINDS, ELEVATION CHANGES, AND FALSE FRONTS, HITTING POOR APPROACHES IS A SURE WAY TO RUN UP YOUR SCORE.
> —BRAD BAPTIST, HEAD GOLF PROFESSIONAL

ooms and cracker-sized pool have lagged behind modern resort trends. A major earthquake off
he coast of the Big Island on October 15, 2006 put a large crack through the middle of the hotel.
econstruction is underway: the resort is scheduled to reopen in early 2009.

THE COURSE

With huge elevation changes, narrow fairways, severe bunkering, and the knee-buckling ocean- carry
quired on #3, playing Mauna Kea is an uncompromising test. It is also wildly beautiful, a majestic course
f emerald fairways and blinding white sand cut through a harsh lava and *kiawe*-treed landscape. On clear
ays, perfect views of the summit of Mauna Kea, with its observatories dotting the peak, can be glimpsed
om several holes. It always appears closer than it is, and seems impossible that it's nearly 14,000 ft. high. You
nay even see a crown of snow during winter.

Control, rather than distance, is the key to scoring well here. Elevation changes, roller-coastering
airways, penal bunkers, doglegs, curls, and few straightaway holes mark the course. Brutal grains used to
efine the greens, but kinder, gentler greens are reportedly on the way.

Since the hotel is closed for repairs, Mauna Kea Golf Course is also being renovated and is scheduled
o reopen in the spring of 2009. There will be a new clubhouse, with locker rooms and a restaurant, but
hat about the course changes? Rees Jones, son of original architect Robert Trent Jones, Sr., (and brother
f the prolific architect Robert Trent Jones, Jr. who helmed a softening of the course in the mid-70s) is
verseeing the renovation, which is considered to be more of a "face lift" than a redesign of this classic layout.
he back tees are being moved farther back; fairway bunkers that have been rendered obsolete by modern
quipment are being put back into play. Additionally, green complexes will be softened to accommodate
he new TifEagle putting surfaces that will have less grain than the previous, brutal Bermuda greens (I hear
hat the member owners clamored loudly for this). Beyond that? Well, look for the greens fees to increase.

THE HOLES

3

he legendary third hole at Mauna Kea is the holy grail of Hawaiian ocean holes. From any of the
e positions, it's all about carry. Rough black lava in the water makes the ocean more agitated and
olent—the last thing you want to notice when concentrating on not dropping your ball into it.

The par-3 11th from the back tees

The green sits at the top of a steep lava wall that will happily knock your ball back into the surf if you carry the water, but don't quite get enough of it to chase it all the way up the face. The putting surface is massive and multi-tiered, and your goal should be to just land somewhere on it. Or in one of the seven bunkers that surround the green. Or in the hole, of course.

#11

The par-3 11th is another classic. From an elevated tee, your shot is down

11th pin with bea[...]

MAUNA KEA GOLF COURSE (MAH-nuh KAY-uh)			
ADDRESS		**CONTACT**	
Kohala Coast Highway		808-882-5400	
Kamuela, HI 96743		WWW.MAUNAKEARESORT.COM	
COURSE DETAILS		**SCORECARD**	
Architect	Robert Trent Jones, Sr.	Par	72
Year Opened	1964	Slope	TBA
Renovated	'75 RTJ II, '07-'08 R. Jones	Course Rating	TBA
Reservations	1 year out	**TEES/YARDAGES**	
Online Times	Yes	Black	7124
Greens Fees	$$$$$	Blue	6737
Discounts	Twilight/Resort	Orange	6365
Club Rentals	Yes	White	5277
Premium	Yes		
Houses	Yes		
WATER		**DISTANCES**	
Types	Ocean	Well-marked	OK
Water Holes	1	Yardage Book	No
Oceanfront	Yes	Sprinklers	No
		GPS	Sky Caddie
PRACTICE		**BUNKERS**	
Driving Range	Grass	How Many?	130
Practice Balls	Included	Consistency	TBD
Putting Green	Yes	**GRASS**	
Chip Green	Yes	Greens	TifEagle
Practice Bnkr.	Yes	Fairways	Bermuda 419

Mauna Kea Golf Course

a green that appears to be right on the edge of the ocean. The green falls away from the center, d four deep bunkers can trap you right, left, or long. The view of the beach and hotel from the een is gorgeous. This is why you're in Hawaii playing golf.

8

ove the finisher here. It's tough but kind of a rush, as your tee shot is downhill and twists away to e right. Play a fade, but don't bite off too much or you may find the waste on the right. The hole liberally bunkered on both sides, so, you know, try to find the middle of the fairway. Consider a irway-wood off the tee, as any well-struck ball should bounce a considerable distance down the irway.

| CART LOGO | OBSERVATORIES ON MAUNA KEA APPROACH ON #1 (BELOW) | PACIFIC GOLDEN PLOVER |

Directions

From the Kona Airport, turn left on Hwy. 19 (Queen Kaahumanu Hwy.) and drive about 25 miles. The entrance to the Mauna Kea Resort is on your right just after the entrance to the Hapuna Prince Resort on your right. Follow he resort road to the clubhouse at the end of the road.

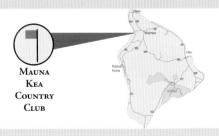

MAUNA
KEA
COUNTRY
CLUB

The signature par-3 15

MAUNA LANI RESORT
FRANCIS H. I'I BROWN—SOUTH COURSE
~:Choke Hole: #15:~
Former site of the Senior Skins Game

FANATIC
Ratings

DESIGN INTRIGUE
★★★★
DIFFICULTY
★★★✦
BEAUTY
★★★★✦
MAINTENANCE
★★★★✦
SERVICE
★★★★
SWANK FACTOR
★★★★

THE RESORT

The Mauna Lani Resort is well-loved by folks looking for understated luxury. It's a spectacular coastal area that boasts a rich history. Hawaiian fish ponds, lava rock shelter caves, petroglyphs, and a traditional fishing village are some of the anthropological goodies that make this region a cultural treasure. The resort carries on this tradition by being one of the "greenest" resorts in Hawaii. They have piled up awards and accolades for their stewardship, including their complex of solar energy cells that generates much of the resort's electricity, and their endearing *honu* program that breeds, raises, and, ultimately, sets free the local endangered green sea turtles.

Of more interest to golfers, the Mauna Lani courses were brought to the national consciousness when the Senior Skins Game arrived in 1990. The tournament was initially played on th

> *THE SOUTH COURSE IS SO BEAUTIFUL, JUST RELAX AND ENJOY THE JOURNEY. BUT USE CAUTION WHEN THE WIND BLOWS, AS THIS BEAUTIFUL OCEANSIDE VENUE CAN TURN INTO A MONSTER. DO NOT BE AFRAID TO VARY YOUR CLUB SELECTIONS BY UP TO THREE OR MORE CLUBS WHEN THE WIND KICKS UP.*
> —TOM SURSELY, HEAD GOLF PRO

iginal 18 holes, but in 1992, when the course was split
to two 18s, it moved to the South Course. The winners
t reads like a "who's who" of golf's legends, including Jack
icklaus, Arnold Palmer, and a five-year run of victories
Raymond Floyd. Be sure to peek behind the Senior
kins monuments (on select holes) to see which year these
gends won big dollars. Jim Colbert won $180,000 on the
th hole of the South Course in 1996. That's not bad for
tirement golf!

The 7th green

THE COURSE

Vith harsh, barren lava fields contrasted by bright, emerald-green fairways, the South Course
nbodies the essence of Kohala Coast golf. And with such eye-candy holes as the par-3 7th and
th, you'll also encounter some of the finest oceanfront golf in the state. The course is a forgiving
sort track, but when the trade winds come up it can be tough to keep your ball out of the lava.
ine maintenance is a trademark here and means that all views are picture-perfect; the fairways
e always fair, and the rough is rarely particularly spiteful. Seashore paspalum greens are a big
us, as the grass possesses little noticeable grain, unlike the various strains of Bermuda grass that
ersist on most courses on the Coast.

The ocean holes here are spectacular — just what the majority of golfers are looking for when
ey book a ticket, pack their clubs, and fly off to Hawaii with visions of crashing waves, blinding-
hite bunkers, and comely greens dancing in their heads. Coconut palms are everywhere, throw-
g a little shade over a course that otherwise bakes in the sun. Wear sunscreen.

THE HOLES

7

he par-3 7th gives you your first look at the stunningly beautiful coast at the Mauna Lani. The
acific Ocean plays along the hole from an elevated tee to a large, multi-tiered green. The winds

The 13th green with #15 behind

can do some funky things to the ball on its way to the narrow putting surface. If you jerk it left, you may be saved by a long strip bunker left of the green; if not, your ball is fish food. (As someone who has snorkeled in the ocean here, I can assure you that your ball would join thousands of others.)

1st tee mark

#13

The 13th is one of the prettiest par-4s you're likely to see. From the tee, the fairway looks as wide as the Great Plains. Tall coconut palms are

MAUNA LANI RESORT—SOUTH COURSE (MAH-nuh LAH-nee)

Mauna Lani South Course

ADDRESS			CONTACT	
68-1310 Mauna Lani Drive			808-885-6655	
Kohala Coast, HI 96743			WWW.MAUNALANI.COM	
COURSE DETAILS			**SCORECARD**	
Architect	H. Flint/R. Cain		Par	72
Year Opened	1981		Slope	133
Renovated	1991 R.Nelson/R. Wright		Course Rating	72.8
Reservations	3 weeks out		**TEES/YARDAGES**	
Online Times	No		Black	6938
Greens Fees	$$$$		Blue	6436
Discounts	Twilight/Resort		White	5940
Club Rentals	Yes		Yellow	5128
Premium	Yes			
Houses	Yes			
WATER			**DISTANCES**	
Types	Ocean/Lakes		Well-marked	Yes
Water Holes	6		Yardage Book	Yes
Oceanfront	Oh, yeah		Sprinklers	Yes
			GPS	Sky Caddie
PRACTICE			**BUNKERS**	
Driving Range	Grass		How Many?	80
Practice Balls	Included		Consistency	Nice, playable
Putting Green	Yes		**GRASS**	
Chip Green	Yes		Greens	Paspalum
Practice Bnkr.	Yes		Fairways	Paspalum

rched on the cliffs that mark the end of
e fairway and the endless blue Pacific fills
ur vision beyond. A tee shot that starts
the fairway bunkers on the left and fades
ck into the fairway is ideal. It leaves a short
pproach into a green with the often seem-
gly disembodied peak of Maui's Haleaka-
floating above it. The green seems easy
ough to hit from there, but I've managed
jerk it straight off the cliff from the middle
the fairway. Enjoy the view of the upcom-
g 15th from the 13th green.

5

et your cameras ready. The par-3 15th offers the kind of gorgeous postcard image that can get
any a Golf Fanatic through long North American winters. A shot over the crashing waves is
quired from all except the forward tees, but no matter which tees you're playing, proceed all the
ay back to the tips to absorb the full impact of this classic golf hole. You'll need length, accuracy,
d friendly winds to score well on this one.

MAUNA LANI
SOUTH COURSE
❀
(FROM RIGHT)

······

THE PAR-3 12TH
FROM THE TEES

······

CART ART

······

THE 11TH GREEN

······

THE UNDER-STATED
CLUBHOUSE

······

THE 5TH PIN WITH
THE 13, 796' PEAK OF
MAUNA KEA

The par-3 signature 17

Mauna Lani Resort
Francis H. I'i Brown—North Course
~:Choke Hole: #17:~

The Course

The North Course at Mauna Lani doesn't quite get the recognition or the amount of play as its more attractive sister to the south, but it poses a more interesting test of golf. The course plays through an ancient lava flow as well, but thick *kiawe* (mesquite) trees give the links a more solitary feeling. It also is more punishing, with more forced carries, tighter fairways, and more situations that call for shaped shots. Prior knowledge of the course pays off here, and first-timers may have their *'okoles* handed to them. The green complexes run the gamut from reasonably flat and gently sloped to multi-tiered and steeply graded. The fine maintenance of both courses exemplified by the attention paid to the bunkers, which is the most labor-intensive aspect of keeping golf courses in shape. The lips are well designed, carefully cut, and kept clear and clean of creep

FANATIC Ratings

DESIGN INTRIGUE	★★★★⌐
DIFFICULTY	★★★★
BEAUTY	★★★★
MAINTENANCE	★★★★⌐
SERVICE	★★★★
SWANK FACTOR	★★★★

> *Mauna Lani North is a position shotmaker's layout. I really advise some preshot planning before attacking any hole. The course has many subtle hazards that must be navigated to score well, so take your time and think your way around.*
> —Tom Sursely, Head Golf Professional

g grass. The sand is consistent, which is no simple feat considering the fierce trade winds that
[t]en whip through the area.

FRANCIS H. I'I BROWN

THE BUSINESSMAN AND STATESMAN WHO WAS KNOWN AS THE "LAST ALI'I" PURCHASED THE
[L]AND THAT THE MAUNA LANI NOW OCCUPIES IN THE 1930S. BROWN WAS A LARGER-THAN-
[L]IFE PERSONALITY WHOSE FRIENDSHIPS RANGED FROM ISLAND LOCALS TO EUROPEAN ROY-
[A]LTY. HE WAS ALSO A GOLFER, AND AT ONE TIME HELD CONCURRENT AMATEUR CHAMPION
[S]TATUS IN HAWAII, CALIFORNIA, AND JAPAN. KALAHUIPUA'A, AS THE MAUNA LANI WAS
[K]NOWN BACK THEN, WAS BROWN'S PERSONAL RETREAT, WHERE HE ENTERTAINED FRIENDS
[A]ND FAMILY ALONG WITH VISITING DIGNITARIES. IN THE MID-SIXTIES HE HAD THE IDEA TO
[D]EVELOP A WORLD-CLASS RESORT ON THE SITE, A PLACE WHERE PEOPLE FROM AROUND THE
[W]ORLD COULD COME AND RESTORE THEIR SPIRIT "HAWAIIAN-STYLE." THE RESULT WAS THE
MAUNA LANI RESORT. THE TWO GOLF COURSES AT THE RESORT ARE NAMED FOR FRANCIS I'I
[B]ROWN.

The 14th green

THE HOLES

[Fr]om the back tees, the par-4 4th demands a scorching tee shot over a lava gully of archaeological
[si]gnificance to a shallow fairway that twists left. Tee off right toward the nearly 14,000-foot peak of
[M]auna Kea and draw it around the trees and into the fairway. The green is elevated, heavily bun-
[ke]red up front, and plays directly into the trade winds, so don't be shy on approach.

#14

The 14th is a dainty one-shotter to a small green horseshoed on the right side by a lovely blue lava lake, and bunkers left and long that are nearly as large as the green. It shouldn't take much more than a wedge from the elevated tees, especially when the trades are pushing at your back. No problem, right? Sure, unless I'm not the only one who grows uneasy picking a sand wedge off a tee.

Teeing off on the par-4 12

Mauna Lani North Course

MAUNA LANI RESORT—NORTH COURSE (MAH-nuh LAH-nee)			
ADDRESS		**CONTACT**	
68-1310 Mauna Lani Drive Kohala Coast, HI 96743		808-885-6655 WWW.MAUNALANI.COM	
COURSE DETAILS		**SCORECARD**	
Architect	H. Flint/R. Cain	Par	72
Year Opened	1981	Slope	135
Renovated	1991 R.Nelson/R. Wright	Course Rating	74.0
Reservations	3 weeks out	**TEES/YARDAGES**	
Online Times	No	Black	6913
Greens Fees	$$$$	Blue	6579
Discounts	Twilight/Resort	White	6057
Club Rentals	Yes	Yellow	5307
Premium	Yes		
Houses	Yes		
WATER		**DISTANCES**	
Types	Lakes	Well-marked	Yes
Water Holes	7	Yardage Book	Yes
Oceanfront	No	Sprinklers	Yes
		GPS	Sky Caddie
PRACTICE		**BUNKERS**	
Driving Range	Grass	How Many?	68
Practice Balls	Included	Consistency	Nice, playable
Putting Green	Yes	**GRASS**	
Chip Green	Yes	Greens	Paspalum
Practice Bnkr.	Yes	Fairways	Paspalum

7

he signature 17th is wee but
ighty. A massive green sits in a
tural lava amphitheater, and the
ort shot from the elevated tee is
nple enough. But if you blow it,
d land your shot behind the lava
mb in the middle of the bunker
ort left, this birdie hole becomes a
gistical nightmare.

The 9th green

#15 FROM BEHIND THE GREEN	THE PAR-3 14TH (ABOVE) CART LOGO (BELOW)	#10 FROM THE TIPS

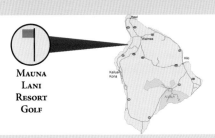

MAUNA LANI
RESORT

Directions

rom the Kona Airport, turn left on Hwy. 19 (Queen
aahumanu Hwy.) and drive about 20 miles, entering the
Mauna Lani Resort on your left. At the roundabout, take
our third right. The entrance to the clubhouse is about a
alf-mile down on your right.

MAUNA
LANI
RESORT
GOLF

DARRIN GEE'S SPIRIT OF GOLF ACADEMY

866-GOLF-433
808-887-6800
Big Island, HI
www.spiritofgolfhawaii.com

As golfers, we all come to a point when our physical approach to the game can no longer bring better scores. We've taken the lessons and the clinics, bought the books and DVDs, put thousands of conflicting swing thoughts in our heads. Now what?

As the pros know, there comes a time when the inner game must be addressed to achieve o next scoring goals. At Darrin Gee's Spirit of Golf Academy, this is what it's all about. Throug a two-hour lesson, Darrin will show you how to "get grounded," "find your natural swing," a other key elements that will help you master your mental game. You'll start your lesson on t putting green as Darrin starts introducing you to his "Seven Principles of Golf," before movi onto the driving range where you'll apply the principles to your full swing.

Anticipate plenty of "A-ha!" moments, from sinking six-foot putts with your eyes closed discovering the wonders and joys associated with not gripping your golf club like you're choki that guy who always talks in your backswing. Darrin is an enthusiastic and positive instruct who continuously churns out interesting nuggets of golf wisdom that ring true. Some of what y hear will certainly sound familiar ("grip the club like you're holding a baby bird"), but the progra is very effective at reminding Golf Fanatics that the more relaxed and focused you are, the bet you play.

The academy claims that students have achieved such radical results as a twenty-stroke swi reduction in the course of a single lesson, which very well may be true. I didn't have results th were quite so dramatic, but I can testify that I took things away from the experience that ha absolutely stripped strokes from my game, and also helped me to enjoy my rounds more fu while playing them.

And, if after all that, you still want a book and a DVD, well, Darrin's got those, too.

Directions

Darrin Gee's Spirit of Golf Academy operates from two locales: The Big Island Country Club and the Hapuna Golf Course.

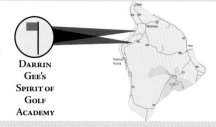

17th at Big Island Country Club: one of the locations
of the Spirit of Golf Academy

18th green and the clubhou

WAIKOLOA KINGS' COURSE
~:Choke Hole: #4:~

FANATIC
Ratings

DESIGN INTRIGUE	
★★★★	
DIFFICULTY	
★★★★	
BEAUTY	
★★★	
MAINTENANCE	
★★★	
SERVICE	
★★★	
SWANK FACTOR	
★★★↲	

THE RESORT
Bustling Waikoloa Resort is South Kohala's tourist hub. Packed with high-end residences, acres of timeshares, two large hotels (including the massive Hilton Waikoloa Village), and two shopping malls, odds are good that you'll find yourself here at some point during your vacation. Anaeho'omalu Beach (generally referred to as "A-Bay") is an attractive slice of sand that fronts the southern end of the resort, and makes for a nice respite from the crowds and an ideal sunset spot. At Waikoloa, you'll not only have access to all of the trappings of a solid Hawaiian resort experience, you'll also discover 36 holes of excellent Hawaiian golf.

THE COURSE
Tom Weiskopf and Jay Morrish conspired to design this links-style layout, which is carve out of the harsh lava desert. It's a fun and challenging track that consists of an interesting m

> *THE KINGS' COURSE IS A SECOND-SHOT GOLF COURSE. RIP YOUR TEE SHOT AND GET CREATIVE ON YOUR APPROACH TO SCORE WELL.*
> —SCOTT HEAD, DIRECTOR OF CLUB OPERATIONS

holes. There are few parallel fairways and
ome rarely seen elements that make this an
ngaging course to play. Look for a compel-
ng use of lava features, big pot bunkers, and
isk-reward opportunities. All in all, there's
lenty of trouble to get into. The wind often
amps up here in the afternoon, so morning
an be a better time to play. There's also less
eat and direct sunlight in the a.m.

The 4th tees

THE HOLES

#2

The par-5 2nd plays into the prevailing trade winds, which can leave you struggling to generate
enough distance to challenge the green in two shots. A lake down the left side is in play off the tee
on your second shot (and even on approach if you start it left and the wind worsens your pain).

#5

With little doubt, the most intriguing hole on the course is the short par-4 5th. The carded distance off the tee suggests this hole is drivable, but the winds will usually demand a reality check.
The largest bunker on the course lurks down the left side of the fairway, and seems to suck balls its
way with magnetic attraction. Perhaps it's the two lumpy mounds of lava within the bunker that
pull balls that way. For those who play short or right, there are less perverse bunkers to catch anything offline there, too. This always seems like it should be a birdie hole, so it rarely is.

#10

The fairway that opens the back nine always seems particularly difficult to hit. It blindly dogs a bit

Brutal bunkering on #5

left, while the trades want to blow the ball right. A high drive over the fairway bunker straight down the left side seems to be the best play. Then again, I rarely find the short grass here, so perhaps you'll want to try your own shot on this one.

The 3rd gree

#13

Ah, the 13th. This one I see in my dreams. It's another short par-4, and when the trades are howling they're at your back with a free escalator of air for your ball. This is the kind of hole you'd see Tiger Woods

WAIKOLOA KINGS' COURSE (WHY-koh-LOH-uh)			
ADDRESS		**CONTACT**	
600 Waikoloa Beach Drive		877-WAIKOLOA (924-5656)	
Waikoloa, HI 96738		WWW.WAIKOLOABEACHRESORT.COM	
COURSE DETAILS		**SCORECARD**	
Architect	Tom Weiskopf/J. Moorish	Par	72
Year Opened	1990	Slope	135
Renovated	Ongoing	Course Rating	73.4
Reservations	1 year out	**TEES/YARDAGES**	
Online Times	Yes	Black	7074
Greens Fees	$$$$	Gray	6594
Discounts	Twilight/Resort	White	6010
Club Rentals	Yes	Orange	5459
Premium	Yes		
Houses	Yes		
WATER		**DISTANCES**	
Types	Lakes	Well-marked	OK
Water Holes	6	Yardage Book	Yes
Oceanfront	No	Sprinklers	Yes
		GPS	Sky Caddie
PRACTICE		**BUNKERS**	
Driving Range	Grass	How Many?	71
Practice Balls	Included	Consistency	OK
Putting Green	Yes	**GRASS**	
Chip Green	Yes	Greens	Tifdwarf
Practice Bnkr.	Yes	Fairways	Bermuda

Waikoloa Kings' Course

ll a 6-iron and stick it under 8 feet. Just rip high and hard and it should carry all the ay to the green. Of course if it doesn't, it will op into the lake. You can always bail out to e right as there's a wide expanse of fairway ere. But what fun is that?

8

he picturesque par-5 18th gives you a last ance to get under par. If the trade winds en't howling, getting home in two is a possibility. However, deep bunkers guard the ont of the putting surface, so don't be short into this triple-tiered green.

THE 7TH GREEN	THE 10TH GREEN (ABOVE) THE RANGE WITH MAUNA KEA	THE TANTALIZING 13TH

Directions

From the Kona Airport, turn left on Hwy. 19 (Queen Kaa-umanu Hwy.) and drive 17 miles, entering the Waikoloa Resort on your left. Take your first right and follow the maintenance road until it intersects with Waikoloa Beach Dr. Turn right and enter the course on your right.

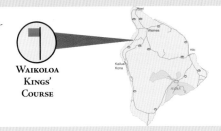

WAIKOLOA KINGS' COURSE

The green at the par-3 4

WAIKOLOA BEACH COURSE
~:Choke Hole: #12:~

THE COURSE

The Waikoloa Beach Course is a friendly resort layout that twists
and turns through the most visited resort area on the Big Island. The
fairways are wide and the greens undulate gently. The rough is usually tightly mown, and nice views are abundant. The yardage from the
tips looks manageable enough, but Waikoloa Beach is one of the few
par-70 layouts in the state, so most holes play longer than you may
expect at 6,500 yards. In another oddity, following a front nine with
six par-4s, the back has only four of them (along with three par-3s and
two par-5s). This mix of holes seems a bit unbalanced on paper, but it
actually keeps things interesting as you play. In 2007, both Waikoloa courses underwent exte

FANATIC Ratings

DESIGN INTRIGUE	★★★
DIFFICULTY	★★★★
BEAUTY	★★★★
MAINTENANCE	★★★★
SERVICE	★★★★
SWANK FACTOR	★★★★

> " PLAYING WELL ON THE BEACH COURSE REQUIRES STRATEGIC
> PLACEMENT OF TEE SHOTS. THE BUNKERS THAT FRAME THE
> FAIRWAYS OFTENTIMES CREATE NARROW CORRIDORS TO FIT THE BALL
> INTO. KNOWING THE DISTANCE TO THESE BUNKERS IS CRITICAL.
> IT'S BETTER TO LEAN TOWARD THE CONSERVATIVE SIDE OFF THE
> TEE AND BE MORE AGGRESSIVE WITH THE APPROACH SHOT. "
> —SCOTT HEAD, DIRECTOR OF CLUB OPERATIONS

ve sand replacement, trading out a difficult-
-play crushed coral mix with standard sand,
welcome improvement. With one of the most
mous holes along the water in the state, the
Vaikoloa Beach Course is a consistently popu-
r track and a lot of fun to play.

The dogleg-left 12th from the tees

HE HOLES

2

he par-4 2nd provides a wake-up call after an unexceptional opening hole. The longer the tee
not, the better chance you have of carrying the lake that fronts the green on approach. The pre-
iling trades are in the golfer's face the whole way, and a well-placed fairway bunker sits at the
rner of the slight elbow left to punish those trying to gain an edge by cutting the corner. Mauna
ea appears to float above the green.

4

he 4th is a short- to mid-length par-3 over a small lake to a green ringed by a picturesque lava
nphitheater. The hole is more challenging and scenic from the back tee, which sits on a stone
dge above the lake. I once played this hole with my brother-in-law, who pulled his ball straight
to the lava where it rocketed high into the air, back into play, landed on the green, and rolled to
ithin 18 inches of the hole. I came up next and played the exact same shot, jerking my tee shot into
ne lava. Then Pele (the goddess of fire and lava), to show it's a woman's prerogative to change her
nind, bounced my ball high, out of the lava, and into the lake in front of the green. D'oh!

7

he 7th is another tough par-3 that plays into the prevailing trades with a forced carry over a lake
r the entire distance. Deep green ironwood trees back the green and cut down the wind a bit, but

The 12th at the green

you'll still need all of your distance on this long one-shotter.

#12

Waikoloa relentlessly markets the par-5 12th hole here as one of the finest holes in Hawaii, and they certainly have a point. It's not only lovely, but also offers some interesting options for scoring. The hole plays as an abrupt dogleg left, with the tee at a right angle away from the ocean. Moderately long hitters can drive a straight one through the fairway (though there is a fairway bunker straight out to save your *poi*), but

The 2nd p

WAIKOLOA BEACH COURSE (why-koh-LOH-uh)

ADDRESS			CONTACT	
1020 Keana Place			877-WAIKOLOA (924-5656)	
Waikoloa, HI 96738			WWW.WAIKOLOABEACHRESORT.COM	
COURSE DETAILS			**SCORECARD**	
Architect	Robert Trent Jones, Jr.		Par	70
Year Opened	1980		Slope	134
Renovated	Ongoing		Course Rating	71.6
Reservations	1 year out		**TEES/YARDAGES**	
Online Times	Yes		Blue	6566
Greens Fees	$$$$		White	5958
Discounts	Twilight/Resort		Orange	5122
Club Rentals	Yes			
Premium	Yes			
Houses	Yes			
WATER			**DISTANCES**	
Types	Lakes/Ocean		Well-marked	OK
Water Holes	5		Yardage Book	Yes
Oceanfront	Yes		Sprinklers	Yes
			GPS	Sky Caddie
PRACTICE			**BUNKERS**	
Driving Range	Grass		How Many?	78
Practice Balls	Included		Consistency	OK
Putting Green	Yes		**GRASS**	
Chip Green	Yes		Greens	Tifdwarf
Practice Bnkr.	Yes		Fairways	Bermuda

Waikoloa Beach Course

he ideal shot is a draw over the fairway bun-er on the inside corner. Prevailing trades low from behind and right-to-left, which ill help your ball around the corner, and ill then be straight at your back for your pproach, meaning a good tee shot can often e rewarded with the chance to take the reen in two. The green is backed by a hand-ul of statuesque coconut palms swaying in he breeze at the edge of the Pacific. Pause ere for photos.

19th Puka

Ambiance:	Dining room
Fully stocked:	Yes
Draft beer:	Yes
Menu:	Yes
Cost:	Stratospheric
Best bet:	Original "Trader Vic's" Mai Tai
The Lowdown:	The Waikoloa Beach Grill serves high-end Pacific Rim and fusion cuisine and offers a comparable wine list.

WAIKOLOA BEACH COURSE
❀
(FROM RIGHT)
••••••
THE 16TH PIN
••••••
FORCED LAVA CARRY ON #18
••••••
THE GOLF VAN
••••••
MAUNA KEA LOOM-ING OVER #1
••••••
LAVA MOUND GUARDING 10TH GREEN

Directions

From the Kona Airport, turn left on Hwy. 19 (Queen Kaa-humanu Hwy.) and drive 17 miles, entering the Waikoloa Resort on your left. Follow the resort road for just over a mile and take a right at Keana Place.

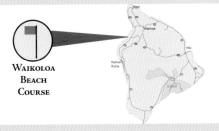

WAIKOLOA BEACH COURSE

The par-3 6

Waikoloa Village Golf Club
~:Choke Hole: #18:~

This Robert Trent Jones, Jr. design is tucked at the foot of towering Mauna Kea, and perched a thousand feet above the sun-baked lava desert of the Kohala Coast. This vantage point provides staggering views of the highest peak in the Hawaiian Islands, while at the same time allowing a few wide vistas of the coast below, the Hawaiian-blue ocean, and the island of Maui.

While the golf course has been choked by over-enthusiastic condo developers, it is nevertheless a solid track. You are still likely to encounter a wide array of wildlife, from the nene (the world's rarest goose and the state bird) and turkeys to bands of goats and the occasional "Kona Nightingale" (local wild donkey). During a recent round, one of my playing partners told me he'

FANATIC Ratings
DESIGN INTRIGUE
★★★
DIFFICULTY
★★★
BEAUTY
★★★
MAINTENANCE
★★★
SERVICE
★★↗
SWANK FACTOR
★★↗

> *Kikuya grass makes for some difficult rough. To give yourself the best chance to escape, take one more club than you would generally need from that distance and open up your clubface at address. When you swing through, the kikuya will pull the clubface closed, squaring it up, and the extra club will account for the deceleration of the club through the rough.*
> —Fran Cipro, Director of Golf

ace seen a donkey rolling around in a bunker scratching his back on the hard, coarse sand.

Lots of locals live up in the somewhat isolated area of Waikoloa Village, and the course offers me of the least expensive golf on the island. This can lead to some slow rounds, especially in the asy winter months. Fran Cipro, the director of golf at the course, believes in the importance of fordable golf (and will spend hours defending it), and his course provides great value and plenty bang for your buck.

THE COURSE

typical Jones, Jr. fashion, fairways are wide and forgiving, but a riskier shot is often required to ave a chance to birdie. Still, unlike many courses in the state, you're not likely to lose too many alls here. There simply aren't many places for your ball to hide. The bunkering is attractive and noughtful, but the high winds that are common here necessitate coarse, almost gravelly sand that hard, crusted, and sometimes so difficult to play out of that it borders on the ridiculous.

Warning: when the winds are up, this mild test of links skill becomes more akin to a test of urvival, sometimes literally. Not too long ago, I came up here for a round during a particularly asty blow, and the guys in the pro shop pleaded with me not to go out. Local knowledge is often he key when playing golf, so it was a no-brainer to heed their advice and head back to town for a old beer.

THE HOLES

6

The par-3 6th demands a shot over a *kiawe*-stuffed gully to a gargantuan green protected by two arge bunkers left and right. What makes this hole special are the views of the ocean with Maui off o your right. Winds can make this kind of tricky, but the green is so large that if you can't find a piece of it then maybe you shouldn't be out here.

The watery 18th

#7

Despite the fact that this course was one of Trent Jones, Jr.'s first, the short par-4 7th is still instant
recognizable as one of his. A shaped bunker sits plump in the middle of the fairway, forcing you
choose sides or attempt to beat one over the top. That shouldn't be too difficult on calmer days, b
when the trades are howling, you'll need to strike it cleanly to beat the beach. A semi-blind uph
approach to a well-bunkered green completes the hole.

#18

The par-5 finisher is the finest hole on the course. A large fairway bunker keeps most mortal h

Waikoloa Village Golf Club (WHY-koh-LOH-uh)

ADDRESS		CONTACT	
68-1792 Melia Street Waikoloa, HI 96738		808-883-9621	
COURSE DETAILS		**SCORECARD**	
Architect	Robert Trent Jones, Jr.	Par	72
Year Opened	1972	Slope	130
Renovated	No	Course Rating	73.9
Reservations	1 year out	**TEES/YARDAGES**	
Online Times	No	Blue	6814
Greens Fees	$$	White	6230
Discounts	Twilight	Red	5501
Club Rentals	Yes		
Premium	Yes		
Houses	Yes		
WATER		**DISTANCES**	
Types	Lakes	Well-marked	Yes
Water Holes	3	Yardage Book	No
Oceanfront	No	Sprinklers	No
		GPS	Sky Caddie
PRACTICE		**BUNKERS**	
Driving Range	Grass	How Many?	76
Practice Balls	Extra	Consistency	Kitty litter
Putting Green	Yes	**GRASS**	
Chip Green	Yes	Greens	Bermuda 328
Practice Bnkr.	Yes	Fairways	Kikuya

Waikoloa Village Golf Club

s from trying to cut the corner of the
rp dogleg left, but for those who are
ing especially macho, it is possible to hit
ng, high drive over the trees on the left,
ich would leave only a mid- to long-iron
r the lake that fronts the wide, shallow
en. Even for those who don't have the
rt or skill for such dramatics, a drive
l lay-up will leave you with wet palms
your final approach of the round.

Cart x-ing

A FUZZY DUCKLING

MAUI OVER THE 5TH GREEN
#7 FROM THE TEES (BELOW)

LOCAL GOAT

Directions

om the Kona Airport, turn left on Hwy. 19 (Queen
aahumanu Hwy.) and drive 18 miles. Turn right at
e light onto Waikoloa Rd. After 5.5 miles, turn left onto
niolo Ave. and take your next left onto Lua Kula St. The
bhouse is about a half-mile down on your left.

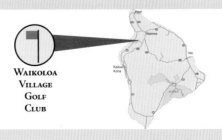

WAIKOLOA
VILLAGE
GOLF
CLUB

The 7th gr

WAIMEA COUNTRY CLUB
~:Choke Hole: #7:~

Waimea Country Club sits amid rolling green pastureland on the wet and breezy side of the town of Waimea. Home of the *paniolos* (Hawaiian cowboys), Waimea appropriately rides the saddle between the rainy windward side of the Big Island and the parched Kohala Coast on the lee. This is some of the loveliest cattle country in the world, and while it's a bit of a surprise to find quality golf hiding in such a non-touristed part of the island, it somehow seems to fit right in. After all, the sport of golf had its genesis amidst pastures not dissimilar to these.

Built by Japanese investors in the early '90s, Waimea Country Club now belongs to Andy Anderson, one of Hawaii's most stalwart businessmen-cum-politicians, who has stamped his mark on the course with the recent addition of so brutal bunkering. The clubhouse is a quaint old plantation house that offers little more than a sm snack window—nothing fancy, but the price is right. Remember to bring some extra layers and re gear, as precipitation is as common here as palm trees and lava are on the rest of the island.

FANATIC Ratings	
DESIGN INTRIGUE	★★★✦
DIFFICULTY	★★★✦
BEAUTY	★★★
MAINTENANCE	★★★
SERVICE	★✦
SWANK FACTOR	★★

> " *TRY AND CARRY YOUR BALL TO THE GREEN ON MOST HOLES BECAUSE YOU CAN'T REALLY RUN YOUR BALL ONTO THE GREENS HERE. IF YOU HIT SHORT OF THE GREEN YOUR BALL USUALLY STOPS BEFORE IT GETS TO THE GREEN.*
> —DAN O'CONNOR, CLUBHOUSE MANAGER

The Course

John Sanford has laid out a track complete with several elements that smack of real Scottish links golf: wind, rain, and high grass. The front nine is more wide open than the woodsier back nine, but don't think that adds up to forgiveness. Balls hit even a few feet offline are consumed by the kind of thick, knee-high grass that always seems to yield a few balls when searched (none of which are actually the ball you put into play).

The par-3 2nd

Elevations roll up and down, mounds deflect balls both favorably and unfavorably, and winds both help and hinder your efforts. I've seen flags blown out of the cups here.

The current owner has, apparently, deemed the course too easy, and has recently added or augmented some bunkers that are more in the Scottish links tradition (read, "you're screwed"). They aren't indicated on the course map, but pay special attention on #2, #6, and #8, and you could emerge unscathed. The odd thing is that these bunkers are in direct contrast to most of the other bunkers, which lie nearly level to the turf and have virtually no lips at all. Yes, the course is a bit quirky, but it's unique, and a fine test of skill.

The Holes

6

The par-4 6th is typical of the front nine, until you reach the green. It plays straightforward enough, but the freshly augmented bunker front left is to be avoided at all costs. Escape may be impossible if you plug one into the forward compartment of this cavity. At the very least you'll need to pop it out backwards, or else take a stroke penalty and drop it back where it's playable.

The 13th green

#7

The 7th is a beauty. This downwind par-5 may tempt you to try and get home in two, especially if your drive gets a nice ride on the trade winds. Any second shot will have to clear a reedy lake on approach, however. For those who choose to lay up, be sure to come up short of the ugly bunkers at the corner that see plenty of action from those who wuss out.

Resident turk

WAIMEA COUNTRY CLUB (wai-MAY-uh)			
ADDRESS		**CONTACT**	
47-5220 Mamalahoa Hwy. Kamuela, HI 96743		808-885-8777 WWW.WAIMEAGOLF.COM	
COURSE DETAILS		**SCORECARD**	
Architect	John Sanford	Par	72
Year Opened	1994	Slope	130
Renovated	Ongoing	Course Rating	71.7
Reservations	3 months out	**TEES/YARDAGES**	
Online Times	No	Blue	6661
Greens Fees	$$	White	6210
Discounts	Twilight/Replay	Red	5673
Club Rentals	Yes		
Premium	No		
Houses	No		
WATER		**DISTANCES**	
Types	Ponds/Lakes	Well-marked	OK
Water Holes	6	Yardage Book	No
Oceanfront	No	Sprinklers	No
		GPS	Sky Caddie
PRACTICE		**BUNKERS**	
Driving Range	Mats	How Many?	35
Practice Balls	Extra	Consistency	Playable
Putting Green	Yes	**GRASS**	
Chip Green	Yes	Greens	Bermuda 328
Practice Bnkr.	Yes	Fairways	Bermuda 328

Waimea Country Club

.8

he par-4 finisher is disarmingly short, but
quires a tricky tee shot to stick it onto the
ll that swoops down from the tee and back
p to the green. Even if the trade winds help
ur drive turn the corner, you won't get
uch run on this one. In fact, depending on
ow much it's been raining, your drive may
st plug right into the fairway. The approach
a steep uphill shot to a multi-tiered green
ith bunkers left and trees right.

19th Puka

Ambiance:	Ranch House Snack Window
Fully stocked:	Limited Cocktails
Draft beer:	No
Menu:	Yes
Cost:	Cheap! Cheap!
Best bet:	Spam Musubi (oh, yeah!)
The Lowdown:	Don't expect too much here, but it is a place to wet your whistle after a round, and it's cozy on a cool, rainy day on the "wet" side.

WAIMEA
COUNTRY CLUB
❀
(FROM RIGHT)
•••••••
THE 11TH
GREEN
•••••••
THE
CLUBHOUSE
•••••••
BIRD OF
PARADISE
•••••••
THE ENTRANCE
•••••••
THE 9TH GREEN

Directions

From the Kona Airport, turn left on Hwy. 19 (Queen
Kaahumanu Hwy.) and drive for 26 miles. Take a right
onto Kawaihae Rd. and drive about 10 miles into the
own of Waimea. Take a left at the first light onto Hwy. 19
(Mamalahoa Hwy.) and proceed for about 5½ miles. The
driveway to the course is on the left.

WAIMEA
COUNTRY
CLUB

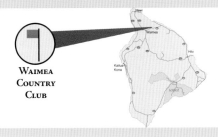

Mauna Loa over the 18th gree

VOLCANO GOLF AND COUNTRY CLUB
~:Choke Hole: #17:~

FANATIC
Ratings

DESIGN INTRIGUE
★★⯪
DIFFICULTY
★★★
BEAUTY
★★★★
MAINTENANCE
★★⯪
SERVICE
★
SWANK FACTOR
★★

It's not every day that you get the chance to tee off on the top of an active volcano. But indeed, when you are standing on the first tee of Volcano Country Club, Kilauea is beneath your feet and you're only about a full pitching wedge away from the boundary to Hawai'i Volcanoes National Park (and probably only a good Tiger Woods drive from the steaming maw of Halema'uma'u Crater). The experience, however, is very different than playing through the lava wastelands of the Kona and Kohala Coasts. Those courses seem much more volcanic. At Volcano C.C., the lava flows are *old*, and beautiful ancient trees grow tall and strong in the rich soil. It's cool, breezy, and damp. Aren't volcanoes supposed to be hot? But don't be fooled; massive amounts of molten lava are constantly churnir beneath the fairways here.

Views of towering Mauna Loa, the largest volcano in the world from base to summit (and live volcano that most recently erupted in 1984), makes it hard to forget where you are. The mour tains attract plenty of rain, and the elevation keeps it cool, especially in the morning when it ca

> *" AT 4,000 FEET, THE ELEVATION CAN COME INTO PLAY. GENERALLY,*
> *MOST PLAYERS WILL HIT THE BALL ABOUT A HALF-CLUB FARTHER.*
> *—KEN YOSHITOMI, PRO SHOP MANAGER*

below freezing. Temperatures usually rise to a pleasantly warm level in the afternoons, but it's a
ood idea to bring an extra layer or two just in case.

THE COURSE

he front plays pretty tightly through a forest of *ohia* trees, and that's where you'll sometimes
ncounter an array of wildlife. It can be an adventure finding some of the tees, like on #7, where
ushwhacking back to the blue tees is more akin to being on an ATV adventure than enjoying
relaxed round of golf. The action really gets going on the latter half of the back nine, however,
here the course is most scenic and the finest holes are showcased. Staggering views of Mauna
oa are everywhere on the back, and a few spectacular glimpses of Mauna Kea (snow-capped in
he winter) can be seen on clear days over the shoulder of the nearer volcano. Maintenance is utili-
arian, with a pickup truck dragging the mower, a technique that's practical, cheaper, and faster
han a tractor.

KILAUEA

ONE OF FIVE SHIELD VOLCANOES ON THE BIG ISLAND, KILAUEA IS THE MOST ACTIVE VOLCANO
ON THE PLANET. THE VOLCANO RISES TO ONLY A LITTLE OVER 4,000 FEET, AND IS DWARFED
BY NEARBY MAUNA LOA AND MAUNA KEA. HOWEVER, KILAUEA IS STILL VERY MUCH IN
ITS GROWING CYCLE, AND WILL EVENTUALLY BE A MASSIVE STRUCTURE LIKE ITS NEIGHBORS.
THE VOLCANO IS PRESENTLY THE MAIN OUTPUT OF THE VOLCANIC HOTSPOT THAT CREATED
ALL OF THE HAWAIIAN ISLANDS, WHICH IS SLOWLY MOVING NORTHWEST, IN THE DIRECTION
OF THE REST OF THE HAWAIIAN VOLCANOES THAT WERE ONCE OVER THIS SAME SPOT.

THE HOLES

#14

The trees just off the tee of the par-4 14th demand a left-to-right drive, or you may very well end
p in the strangest trap on the island: a volcanic crater down the right side that will catch tee shots
hat don't bend back into the fairway. It's pretty shallow, but it's steep getting to the bottom to

#17 from the tees

access your wayward shot (look for narrow switchbacks cut into the ledge). Grass at the bottom of the crater makes playing out not too tough, but you'll need to come over a bunker on the front right of the green on approach.

#15

#15 is another par-4 with the same crater in play, but you'll want to aim your shot down the left center anyway. A tall swamp mahogany marks an abrupt dogleg left, and both going over the tree and bending it around the corner are unlikely propositions. Just smack it past the tree and come in from there. Mauna Kea can often be seen beyond Mauna Loa, which frames the green.

Volcano Golf and Country Club

Address		Contact	
99-1621 Pi'i Mauna Drive		808-967-7331	
Volcano, HI 96718		WWW.VOLCANOGOLFSHOP.COM	

Course Details		Scorecard	
Architect	Arthur Jack Snyder (renov.)	Par	72
Year Opened	1921	Slope	128
Renovated	1967	Course Rating	70.8
Reservations	6 months out	Tees/Yardages	
Online Times	No	Blue	6547
Greens Fees	$$	White	6190
Discounts	Twilight	Red	5567
Club Rentals	Yes		
Premium	No		
Houses	No		

Water		Distances	
Types	Lake	Well-marked	No
Water Holes	1	Yardage Book	No
Oceanfront	No	Sprinklers	No
		GPS	No

Practice		Bunkers	
Driving Range	Mats	How Many?	31
Practice Balls	Extra	Consistency	Coarse
Putting Green	Yes	Grass	
Chip Green	Yes	Greens	Bermuda 328
Practice Bnkr.	Yes	Fairways	Kikuya

Volcano Golf and Country Club

17

The par-5 17th is simply beautiful. It's like walking beside some of the old-growth forests that are preserved nearby. The hole is a long uphill climb that features a tall *ohia* tree in the middle of the fairway on approach, making for an intriguing obstacle for those trying to get home in two. A grove of rare *koa* trees, which Hawaiians traditionally used to carve their seafaring canoes, stands to the right of the green.

19th Puka

Ambiance:	Warm country inn
Fully stocked:	Yes
Draft beer:	No
Menu:	Yes
Cost:	Par
Best bet:	Breakfast burger
The Lowdown:	As one of the few places to dine in tiny Volcano Village, this cozy place serves more than just golfers.

| NATIVE FERN BY 2ND GREEN | OUT OF THE CRATER ON #14
LOCAL TRACTOR (BELOW) | NENE BELOW MAUNA LOA ON #8 |

Directions

From the Kona Airport, it will take about 2 ½ hours to get to Volcano Golf and Country Club. Turn south from the airport onto Hwy. 19 (Queen K. Hwy.) and drive through Kailua-Kona (as it becomes Hwy. 11) for a total of 99 miles. Turn left onto Pii Mauna Dr. about ¼-mile past the Mauna Loa Rd. turnoff, and just before the entrance to Hawai'i Volcanoes Nat'l. Park. The course is on the right.

**VOLCANO
GOLF &
COUNTRY
CLUB**

The legendary 12th at the Challenge at Manel

Lana'i

ormerly owned entirely by the Dole family, the "Pineapple Isle" was once the world's *rgest pineapple plantation. That industry is now just another piece of history, and *day the economy is geared toward high-end tourists. The Four Seasons operates *o world-class resorts on Lana'i. Manele Bay is the picture of tropical luxury, *ith pools, beaches and dolphins in the bay, while the Lodge at Koele sits at nearly ,000 feet amidst Cook pines and retains the rustic vibe of an English hunting lodge. *he golf courses at each hotel are equally divergent, from Nicklaus's masterpiece at *Manele, which features holes with shots from cliff to cliff over surging ocean breaks, * Koele's upland layout, one of the most unusual and lovely courses in the state.

THE MOON SHOT	THE GUT WRENCHER	THE CHILL

KOELE - SEVENTEEN
Put your driver in your hand and see how close you can blast it on this narrow par-4 that drops nearly three stories.

MANELE - TWELVE
This do-or-die par-3 is what is what golf in Hawaii is all about for some folks, and even for those just here for the drinks.

MANELE - NINETEEN
This is about the sweetest spot you'll find to tip a few back while reliving your best shots of the day.

Page 245 ☞   Page 240 ☞   Page 241 ☞

Lana'i

Nickname: The Pineapple Isle
Area: 140.5 square miles
Highest Point: Lana'ihale, 3,366 feet
Population: 3,193 (2000 census)
Flower: Kauna'oa

1 - The Challenge at Manele

2 - The Experience at Koele

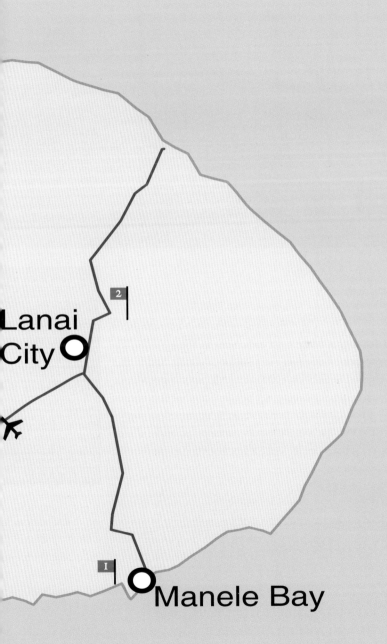

Lanai
City

2

Manele Bay

1

The signature par-3 12

THE CHALLENGE AT MANELE
~:Choke Hole: #12:~

Perched above the spectacular cliffs of one of Hawaii's least inhabited islands, The Challenge at Manele is a golf course for the ages. This signature design by Jack Nicklaus is a stunner both visually and from a golfing perspective. The clubhouse sits in an idyllic spot above Manele Bay and is a suitably swanky structure. They don't do too many rounds here on a daily basis, so take your time warming up, relax and enjoy a mellow day. By the way, the complimentary danishes and coffee offered to those teeing off in the morning make it worth getting to the course a little earlier in the a.m.

FANATIC
Ratings

DESIGN INTRIGUE
★★★★★
DIFFICULTY
★★★★
BEAUTY
★★★★⭒
MAINTENANCE
★★★★⭒
SERVICE
★★★★⭒
SWANK FACTOR
★★★★⭒

THE COURSE

Rarely is a golf course architect offered a canvas as fetching as this one, and thank heavens Ja Nicklaus was chosen for the job. Of course, Jack's designs are notorious for their demandi nature, and his brainstorm at Lana'i is certainly no different. From all tees except the forwa

> **AT THE CHALLENGE, THE FAIRWAYS ARE GENEROUS AND THE GREENS ARE FAIRLY EASY TO READ. THERE ISN'T TOO MUCH TROUBLE TO GET INTO UNLESS YOU STRAY FROM THE FAIRWAY.**
> —BRIAN BUECHLE, ASSISTANT GOLF PROFESSIONAL

nes, there is a forced carry on every single hole—most of them from off the tee—and some have
ore than one. The views are fantastic on both nines, with the front having the highest point on
e course, and therefore the finest panoramic views, and the back having the teeing-off-on-the-
de-of-the-world thing going on.

The wind is a factor here, and Jack's design definitely took that into consideration. Look at
ur cart GPS and understand what each hole demands before teeing off. As with most Nicklaus
urses, there are choices to be made off the tee that can give you an advantage if you recognize
em, thereby allowing you to get the most out of an already excellent setting and course.

HE HOLES

5

he 5th climbs to the highest point on the course, so even if you blow the hole it still can be enjoy-
le. Of course, not all people feel that way, so they have their work cut out for them on the #1
andicap hole. But really, what's so hard about a 462-yard, par-4 drive that plays into prevailing
eadwinds? Just drive it straight (but not too long) up a fairway that ends abruptly at a high ledge,
d leaves a mid- to short-iron to a green six stories below. Too easy. By the way, if you see what
oks like little rain drops far below you in the bay, those are the resident spinner dolphins putting
n a show!

DA KINE DIVING

IF YOU ALSO HAPPEN TO BE A SCUBA FANATIC, DON'T MISS DIVING ONE OF THE PREMIER DIVE
SITES IN THE STATE. AT THE LEGENDARY CATHEDRALS, LIGHT FILTERS THROUGH HOLES IN
THE CEILING OF A SUBMERGED LAVA TUBE TO GIVE THE APPEARANCE OF STAINED GLASS. A
LARGE, FLAT ROCK AT THE BACK OF THE CAVE RESEMBLES AN ALTAR, AND PEOPLE ACTUALLY
GET MARRIED DOWN THERE. EVEN IF YOU'RE NOT LOOKING FOR AN OFF-THE-WALL WAY TO
GURGLE YOUR VOWS, DESCENDING INTO THIS DIVE SPOT IS A RELIGIOUS EXPERIENCE.

Cliffside from the 17th tee

#7 & #8

The 7th and 8th holes are rare back-to-back par-3s that play over the same deep gully. #7 is 40 yards short er than #8, but you might just use the same club for both since #7 plays into the wind and #8 plays with th wind at your back. Interesting duet.

#12

The 12th is why you're here. The back tee is nestled at the edge of the cliffs, staring down at crashing wave 150 feet below, and toward a wide narrow green 200 yards downwind. This is the place where Bill an Melinda Gates tied the knot (renting out the entire Four Seasons to ensure their privacy), and it's easy t

THE CHALLENGE AT MANELE (muh-NELL-ee)			
ADDRESS		**CONTACT**	
P.O. Box 630310 Lana'i, HI 96763		808-565-2222 WWW.GOLFONLANAI.COM	
COURSE DETAILS		**SCORECARD**	
Architect	Jack Nicklaus	Par	72
Year Opened	1993	Slope	135
Renovated	No	Course Rating	73.7
Reservations	30 days out	**TEES/YARDAGES**	
Online Times	No	Nicklaus	7039
Greens Fees	$$$$	Gold	6684
Discounts	Resort	Blue	6310
Club Rentals	Yes	White	5847
Premium	Yes	Red	5024
Houses	Yes		
WATER		**DISTANCES**	
Types	Ocean	Well-marked	No
Water Holes	3	Yardage Book	Yes
Oceanfront	Yes	Sprinklers	No
		GPS	In-cart
PRACTICE		**BUNKERS**	
Driving Range	Grass	How Many?	87
Practice Balls	Included	Consistency	Nice, playable
Putting Green	Yes	**GRASS**	
Chip Green	Yes	Greens	Paspalum
Practice Bnkr.	Yes	Fairways	Paspalum

The Challenge at Manele

...e why they chose it. You'll never forget it: simply spectacular.

17

The par-4 17th plays straight away from the 12th and has a similar shot over the surging sea, into the wind, to a distant fairway. At least take a shot from the back tee for posterity (you might as well take a shot with your camera, too). Approach shots are murder here; with the green tucked tightly against the cliff, anything long or right has a chance of hitting one of the dive boats offshore.

19th Puka

Ambiance:	Fishbowl with a view
Fully stocked:	Yes
Draft beer:	No
Menu:	Yes
Cost:	Pricey
Best bet:	Hulupe Prawn, Bacon, Lettuce & Tomato
The Lowdown:	Watch the dolphins do flips while sipping a frozen cocktail at this swanky clubhouse spot.

THE CHALLENGE AT MANELE
♣
(FROM RIGHT)
· · · · · · ·
WIND SOCK FLAG STICK AT #2
· · · · · · ·
THE 13TH GREEN
· · · · · · ·
THE MANELE CLUBHOUSE
· · · · · · ·
INDIAN CORAL TREES ALONG #10
· · · · · · ·
APPROACH ON #7

Directions

For those who are staying at one of the Four Seasons resorts, a porter is usually at the dock on Maui to assist you with your bags on and off of the Expeditions ferry. The ferry makes several trips a day between Lahaina (Maui) and Lana'i, where your boat is met by a resort shuttle. Expeditions also offers day-trip golf packages. For tickets and schedules, visit www.go-lanai.com.

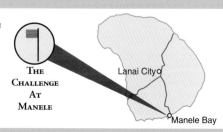

THE CHALLENGE AT MANELE

Lanai City

Manele Bay

The signature par-4 17

THE EXPERIENCE AT KOELE
~:Choke Hole: #17:~

Though both of Lana'i's golf courses offer unparalleled experiences, they are polar opposites. While The Challenge at Manele provides quintessential oceanfront golf, The Experience at Koele has an enchanted forest vibe. Perched at an elevation of over 2,000 feet, Koele has cooler temperatures and occasional fog that mists the tops of the tall pine trees. Architect Ted Robinson has added many of his signature waterscapes to the course, providing flourishes that make Koele a rare find.

While golf courses with names like "The Experience at Koele" sound pretentious, it must be said that playing Koele is, in fact, an experience (and a superlative one, at that). With stands of rare *koa*, Norfolk pines and ironwood trees, and views of Maui and Moloka'i—it's among the very best.

FANATIC Ratings	
DESIGN INTRIGUE	★★★★⯪
DIFFICULTY	★★★★
BEAUTY	★★★★⯪
MAINTENANCE	★★★★⯪
SERVICE	★★★★
SWANK FACTOR	★★★★⯪

THE COURSE
Why a golf course needs a designer (Greg Norman) and an architect (Ted Robinson) is difficult to say without getting cynical about the marketing value of name recognition, but the wide variety of

> *ONE THING MAKES KOELE DIFFERENT FROM ALL OF THE OTHERS: BENT GRASS GREENS. SO WHAT YOU SEE IS WHAT YOU GET. EXPECT TRUE ROLLS WITH CONSISTENT SLOPE AND SPEED.*
> —DOUG DAGUAUI, ASSISTANT GOLF PROFESSIONAL

atures used on this course seems to suggest that indeed two personalities had a hand in how the
urse came together. While some holes have intricately-shaped bunkers with fingers that claw
to the fairway to entrap balls you thought were safe, other holes use nothing but simple round
t-bunkers to accomplish the same thing.

Another duet of holes may feature a sharp dogleg left with a fairway bunker on the inside
rn, while the next dogs abruptly right with a collection of sand to capture shots that go long. This
not to suggest that there are wildly different faces on the course, merely that the course is varied,
d uses myriad strategies to provide a variety of experiences on each hole. With doglegs, multi-
ered greens, elevation changes, waterfalls, lakes, forced carries, blind tee shots, and beautifully
afted lava rock masonry, the Experience at Koele manages to be soft and sumptuous, demand-
g and thoughtful, all at the same time.

HE HOLES

here is a lot going on at the par-5 3rd. A lake is in play to the right off the tee, but a safe shot out to
e left will roll along the contour of the left side of the fairway and be longer, so there's no reason

Waterscape at #9

THE GOLDEN BEAR

N 1991, JACK NICKLAUS PLAYED AN INAUGURAL ROUND WITH GREG NORMAN. IT WAS A
FOGGY DAY, AND AS THE PLAYERS LOOKED OUT OVER THE 17TH HOLE, IT WAS DIFFICULT TO
EE WHERE THE FAIRWAY WAS. UNSURE OF WHICH DIRECTION TO PLAY, NICKLAUS HIT SEVEN
STRAIGHT BALLS INTO THE POND ON THE RIGHT SIDE OF THE FAIRWAY. HE EVENTUALLY HAD
TO BORROW A BALL FROM GREG NORMAN TO FINISH THE HOLE. NICKLAUS ENDED UP CARD-
NG A 17 ON THE HOLE!

to mess with the water. Longer drivers may feel they have a shot at the green in two, but the landscaped network of pools and waterfalls on the right of the green may encourage caution. For those who try to play a safe approach left, the only greenside bunker is there, and if you don't quite get enough of it, you may find a knotty old *koa* tree between you and the pin.

#8
The 8th is a short par-4, but the green is a sharp dogleg away to the right. It sits alluringly on a wooded island with pretty pot bunkers on both sides

Distance mark

THE EXPERIENCE AT KOELE (koh-EL-ee)			
ADDRESS		**CONTACT**	
PO Box 310 Lana'i City, HI 96763		808-565-4653 WWW.GOLFONLANAI.COM	
COURSE DETAILS		**SCORECARD**	
Architect	T. Robinson/Greg Norman	Par	72
Year Opened	1991	Slope	141
Renovated	No	Course Rating	75.3
Reservations	30 days out	**TEES/YARDAGES**	
Online Times	No	Black	7000
Greens Fees	$$$$	Blue	6617
Discounts	Resort/Replay	White	6128
Club Rentals	Yes	Red	5414
Premium	Yes		
Houses	Yes		
WATER		**DISTANCES**	
Types	Lakes/Creeks	Well-marked	No
Water Holes	9	Yardage Book	Yes
Oceanfront	No	Sprinklers	No
		GPS	In-cart
PRACTICE		**BUNKERS**	
Driving Range	Grass	How Many?	72
Practice Balls	Included	Consistency	Perfect
Putting Green	Yes	**GRASS**	
Chip Green	Yes	Greens	Bent
Practice Bnkr.	Yes	Fairways	Bermuda

The Experience at Koele

hat catch the big hitters who choose to try
nd ride the wind into the green off the tee.
'or the mortals among us, a long-iron will do
ne, leaving a short wedge to the green. Just
ow close you're willing to come to the water
ff the tee may indicate how much you're
villing to risk for a birdie.

17

The signature 17th is truly a jaw-dropping
ole, as the tee is perched 250 feet above the
arrow fairway, which sits in Lana'i's deepest

avine. A lake on the right side is in play for those who don't hit a driver, but why would you come
his far and pay this much money just to hit an iron down the middle?

| NIGHT HERON | MOLOKA'I OVER #11 (ABOVE) ISLAND GREEN ON #8 (BELOW) | FIRST TEE |

Directions

You're not likely to have a rental car on Lana'i, and you'll
most likely be coming from Maui. If you are staying at one
of the Four Seasons Resorts, they will probably have a porter
there to handle your bags as you board the ferry on Maui,
then they will direct you to a shuttle that will take you to your
hotel. The Experience is on the main road, past Lana'i City
and past the Lodge at Koele. You can also fly to Lana'i.

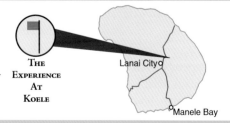

THE
EXPERIENCE
AT
KOELE

Lanai City

Manele Bay

Maui Hotels

Hyatt Regency Maui
Resort and Spa

200 Nohea Drive
Lahaina, Maui, HI 96761
808-661-1234
maui.hyatt.com

Essentials
-40 "tropically-landscaped," oceanfront
acres
-806 guest rooms, including 31 suites
-Four restaurants, three bars and lounges
-Spa Moana with in-room and oceanside massage, specialty treatments, salon services, boutique
and fitness center
-Camp Hyatt, for kids 5-12, with indoor, outdoor, and cultural activities
-Wildlife, including penguins, parrots, flamingos, African cranes, and a swan lagoon
-Nightly luau, banquet rooms, business center, Asian art collection, shopping, beach, pool com
plex with 150-foot lava tube water slide, and hot tub

The Scoop
As soon as you enter the lobby, you are inside a huge atrium filled with flowers, tropical plant
and the calls of birds. A jaunt around the courtyard reveals priceless antique Asian art (part of th
collection of legendary hotelier Chris Hemmeter), *koi* ponds, parrots, penguins, and a gawky, bril
liantly colored African crane. If that's not enough to get you or the kids into vacation mode, jus
take a stroll down to the pools.

With a series of waterfalls, a pool grotto with a swim-up bar, kids' water playground, and
150-foot lava tube water slide, the Hyatt's pool complex is exactly what a lot of people envision a
the quintessential Hawaiian resort experience. My wife and I made a pledge one morning that w
were going to go down the slide twenty-five times. That may not sound like much, but betweer
the Mai Tais, the sun, and the beach-side hammocks, we took our 25th slide right at five o'clock
when the slide closed.

The Hyatt is located on Ka'anapali Beach, which, at three miles long, is the largest beach o
Maui. The numerous restaurants and lounges are all good. I've been going to Spats Trattoria sinc
the mid-nineties, and visitors cannot miss the decadent breakfast at Swan Court, an open-air ea
ery on a lagoon filled with the majestic birds. The biggest problem I've ever had here is getting ou
of the perfect beds in the morning. As any visitor can attest, their comfort has a gravitational pul
And while it's worth it to bunk in while on vacation, there's plenty here to get you up.

Oh, and the hotel is located right on the 16th hole of the Ka'anapali Kai course. You can't ge
much closer to world-class golf.

MAUI HOTELS

GRAND WAILEA RESORT HOTEL AND SPA

3850 Wailea Alanui
Wailea, HI 96753
808-875-1234
www.grandwailea.com

ESSENTIALS

40 ocean-front acres
780 guest rooms, including 52 suites
Six restaurants, three bars
Spa Grande with 40 treatment rooms, hydrotherapy *terme* with
Roman Tub, waterfalls, Japanese Furon, saunas and five specialty baths, and fitness center
Camp Grande, a 20,000-square-foot "Children's Resort"
Seaside Chapel, banquet rooms, business center, art collection, shopping, beach, extensive pool
complex with water slides, and hot tub

THE SCOOP

Forget the splashy waterfall in the driveway. Ignore the massive, airy show of the lobby, with its fountains and sculptures and general grandiosity. Simply allow your eyes to pass over the frenzy of lively sights in the lobby and realize that, yes, this whole massive complex is centered around the bar. And what a bar! This perfect, booze-dispensing circle sits elegantly under a sort of modern, art deco pagoda, with Hawaiian murals and a fat old sun painted in the Italian-style atrium.

Of course, there's a lot more to the Grand Wailea than just its lobby bar. After getting your hand round a fresh Mai Tai at said bar, begin by taking a stroll around the lobby. Nine striking bronze sculptures by Fernando Botero are scattered around, in what might be called an "Ode to Large Women." Several steps down from the lobby lies the grand dining room and its stunning view over the upper grounds, including beautiful fountains, white gazebos, and quite a large church (they do a thriving wedding business here).

There are, of course, more bars down by the pool complex, which deserves its own paragraph. Two large water slides provide twisting, slippery descents into the bottom of the pools, where a "pool elevator" brings lounging swimmers back to the top pool, from where they can start their slow float back down to the bottom through a series of small slides and light rapids. There are plenty of waterfalls along the way, and a hot "Volcano Whirlpool" stuck in a lava tube for those who need to get their body temperature back up after too much time in the pool.

There are 740 rooms in this massive complex, as well as six restaurants and the famous Spa Grande, a 50,000-square-foot spa that offers pretty much anything you could want. What better way to ease your sore back and soothe your sunburned skin after a few rounds at the Wailea courses?

Maui Hotels

Kapalua Gold Villas
500 Office Road
Lahaina, Maui, HI 96761
800-545-0018
www.kapalua.com

Essentials
-One-, two-, and three-bedroom condo-
miniums available in oceanfront, ocean
view, and fairway view
-1,200 to 2,400-square-foot layouts featuring complete kitchens with high-end appliances, priva
lanais, washer/dryer, TVs with DVD or VCR, robes
-Discounted golf, preferred tee times, 24-hour reception center, free resort-wide shuttle service, fu
service concierge and activity desk, complimentary tennis, three pools with barbecue areas, acce
to three beaches

The Scoop
The Kapalua Gold Villas are a collection of fine condos scattered around three locations of th
Kapalua Resort. The accommodations all come with a full kitchen and include daily maid service, a
well as nightly turndown service. Each villa is privately owned, so the decor varies from unit to uni
and each feels like a home away from home. The Gold Villa designation is reserved for those villa
with the finest amenities, including flat panel TVs, DVD player, slippers and robes, and evenin
turndown service. Top-end appliances, furnishings and high-speed Internet service are also include

As most traveling golfers have discovered, sometimes it's nice to have a little more room to sprea
out than what a standard hotel room can provide. Each villa offers ample space for golf bags and gea
without having to piece everything in the room together like a puzzle in order to get around. With li
ing and dining rooms, large bedrooms, and spacious lanais, the Kapalua Gold Villas provide the kin
of space and comfort you crave while you're on a golf vacation.

The villas are located near shopping, restaurants, three white sand beaches, and three swimmin
pools and BBQ areas that are within the complex.

Kapalua Resort also offers private home rentals through their Kapalua Luxury Home progran
Several high-end three- and four-bedroom estate homes are available, and include such amenities a
private pool and whirlpools, and gourmet kitchens.

Additionally, all guests of the Kapalua Gold Villas and Kapalua Luxury Homes have access t
free tennis, discounted golf, resort-wide charging privileges, and private concierge service.

While the oceanfront villas possess an obvious charm, many of the golf course villas are within
short distance to my favorite restaurant in the state. Vino, located in the Village Clubhouse, is an Ita
ian tapas and wine bar, serving diminutive plates of fine food that are easily paired with vintage wine
available by the glass. *Bellissimo!*

O'AHU HOTELS

MAKAHA RESORT & GOLF CLUB

84-626 Makaha Valley Road
Waianae, HI 96792
808-695-9544
866-576-6447
www.makaharesort.net

ESSENTIALS

26-acre valley resort
173 guest rooms including 20 suites, plus vacation cottages
Two restaurants and lounges
Pool, banquet facilities, tennis courts
Spa services, laundry
Wireless Internet in lobby and poolside
Immediate proximity to Makaha Resort Golf Club

THE SCOOP

In the most remote corner of O'ahu, far from the hectic push and shove of Waikiki, sits one of the best golf resort values in Hawaii. Makaha Resort and Golf Club lies in the heart of the gorgeous Makaha Valley, hemmed in on three sides by steep green cliffs, with the other side open to the coast below. The resort is one of the original Hawaiian resorts, dating back to the late '60s, built at the behest of visionary Hawaiian businessman Chinn Ho. The resort was developed along with two excellent golf courses, which are now operated as separate businesses. However, resort guests receive fifty percent off green fees at the resort course and discounts at the adjacent Makaha Valley Country Club, offering prices that simply cannot be beat at any other resort in the state.

The rooms are spread over five main buildings and twelve two-story cottages. The resort features a nice pool and other amenities, including a restaurant and lounge, both with unpretentious food and drinks. The rooms are somewhat vintage, but they are spacious and include air conditioning, mini refrigerators, private lanais, coffee makers, hair dryers, and bathing amenities. Room prices are extremely reasonable by Hawaiian standards, and food and cocktails are as within-the-stratosphere as you can get at Hawaiian resorts. The service is generally very friendly and laid back. Time seems to move a bit slower this far from Honolulu, and both guests and employees move about at their own pace. This is an unhurried side of Hawaii.

The hotel is at least a 45-minute drive from the airport, but it can take significantly longer depending on traffic. Those looking to be right in the action will not find what they are looking for here, but for those who want to get away from it all and still find affordable lodging and plenty of golf action need look no further.

Hyatt Regency Waikiki Resort & Spa
2424 Kalakaua Avenue
Honolulu, HI 96815
808-923-1234, 800-55-HYATT
waikiki.hyatt.com

Essentials
-Twin forty-story towers and three-story open-air atrium
-1,230 guest rooms and suites
-Four restaurants and a bar and lounge on the sundeck
-Na Ho'ola Spa with 19 treatment rooms, spa and salon ser-
vices ranging from Gentlemen's Facials to Macadamia Nut
Bodyscrub to Lomi Lomi massages, fitness center, saunas, and
locker rooms
-Camp Hyatt, for kids 5-12, with activities that include ukulele
lessons to sand-castle making and catamaran rides
-Sundeck, pool, two whirlpools, business center, shopping, extensive banquet rooms and service
live music, prime location

The Scoop
For those who crave high-end luxury in the heart of Waikiki, it's hard to beat the Hyatt Regenc
Waikiki. Two skyscraping towers offer what may be the best view of the beach in the city. Room
above the beach afford dizzying vistas down to the sand and waves, and from your room's lanai, th
noise and electricity of Waikiki is hushed and awesome.

Despite its amazing proximity to everything that's going on in Waikiki, it's possible to find ever
thing you need within the hotel. The restaurants at the resort are delicious, top-end offerings. Th
lobby is situated in a breezy, three-story atrium that doubles as a mall, meaning even fancy Waiki
shopping is at your fingertips. And the spa facilities might just put you into the kind of near coma th
keeps you from venturing out.

The sundeck is a relaxed, urban fixture, with two hot tubs and a small, chilly pool, but with gre
views a couple stories above the street. The bar will keep you hydrated (so to speak), while live ente
tainment keeps you feeling festive while the sun sets.

Kuhio Beach Park, the surfing heart of Waikiki Beach, is steps away from the hotel. The wave
here are long and mellow, perfect for beginners and intermediates. Waikiki's famous surfboard loc
ers are located on this beach, as are some of the finest surfing instructors in the islands. Plus, Waiki
surfers tend to lack the sometimes aggressive attitude of surfers at places like the North Shore.

The Hyatt Regency Waikiki is centrally located for good access to the golf courses on the Ew
Plain, as well as the windward courses, which are just on the other side of the verdant Ko'olau Mou
tains to the northeast.

KAUA'I HOTELS

GRAND HYATT KAUA'I RESORT & SPA

1571 Poipu Road
Koloa, HI 96756
808-742-1234, 800-55-HYATT
kauai.hyatt.com

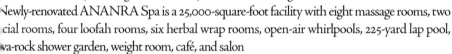

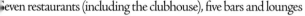

ESSENTIALS

o oceanfront acres

o2 guest rooms, 37 suites

Seven restaurants (including the clubhouse), five bars and lounges

Newly-renovated ANANRA Spa is a 25,000-square-foot facility with eight massage rooms, two cial rooms, four loofah rooms, six herbal wrap rooms, open-air whirlpools, 225-yard lap pool, va-rock shower garden, weight room, café, and salon

Camp Hyatt, for kids 3-12, with themed activities, group sports, and outdoor Theatre Nights

Two pools with waterfalls, meandering waterways, 150-foot water slide, whirlpools, five-acre salt-ater swimming lagoon, 500-yard beach, tennis courts, shopping, and luau

ndoor and outdoor banquet and meeting facilities including two ballrooms, breakouts, a board-om, and a business center

THE SCOOP

The Grand Hyatt Kaua'i has just about everything that most of us can think of when envision-g our ideal tropical resort. Stunning location? Check. Gauzy luxury? Check. Meandering pools, ach, waterfalls? Check. This is that kind of place.

From the moment you step into the massive, elegant lobby, it's clear that you have made the ght choice. Arriving in your room, that feeling is confirmed. And when you finally step out into e sunshine and settle into a lounge chair, you know that you're officially on vacation.

Every area of the resort is enjoyable. There are almost too many restaurants to get to in a ngle visit. The newly expanded spa is at the cutting-edge of spa decadence. The pool complex d landscaped grounds are so intricate you can almost get lost. Camp Hyatt will keep the kids ccupied while you spend the day golfing, and you can easily make it up to them by taking them to e of the best luaus in the state. The golf course, by the way, is right next door in case you want to queeze in an extra nine holes or spend a half-hour on the range. Too easy.

Guest rooms are, naturally, well appointed. The Hyatt beds are almost too comfortable (you on't want to sleep away your vacation here, trust me), while the bathrooms possess a formal, tiled xury that hits just the right note.

For those who crave more than a pillow after dark, don't miss the party at Stevenson's ibrary, the ultimate resort lounge. With wood panels, billiards, live music, grub and grog, you n't go wrong.

KAUA'I MARRIOTT RESORT AND BEACH CLUB

> 3610 Rice Street
> Lihue, Hawaii 96766
> 808-245-5050
> www.marriott.com/lihhi

ESSENTIALS

-85 oceanfront acres

-356 guest rooms, including 11 suites, plus 232 Beach Club suites

-Four restaurants and lounges, and many more within close proximity

-Day spa and salon

-26,000-square-foot swimming pool with five whirlpools, tennis, art collection, fitness cente shopping, water sports, baby sitting, Kalapaki Kids Program, biking and jogging trails, free ai port shuttle

-Cultural program featuring a variety of Hawaiian cultural activities such as hula lessons, ukule lessons, lei making, torch lighting ceremonies, koi feeding, and ancient Hawaiian games

-Three wedding ceremony sites and a full-service wedding staff

-Nearly 20,000 square feet of meeting and banquet space including a massive ballroom, 60,00 square feet of outdoor meeting space, Wi-Fi Internet, business center

THE SCOOP

The Kaua'i Marriott is another of legendary Hawaiian hotelier Chris Hemmeter's brillia constructs. This mammoth structure opened as a Westin amid the opulence of the 1980s befo Kaua'i was devastated by Hurricane Iniki in 1993. As is typical of Hemmeter projects, the hot features a lovely Asian art collection and features a modern Asian design scheme.

While the hotel is very nice, it's all about the water here (besides the golf, you understanc The beach is a nice soft sandy crescent with little surf, just right for families and lazy lounge alike. And then there's the pool. The largest and most ostentatious pool in the state, this eno mous puddle is the watery heart of the resort. It features five ornate columns that skyrock from the interior ring of the pool, under each of which is a bubbling whirlpool. Hours slip l easily here, as you make your way from hot tub to hot tub, enjoying listless floats in the po between times, and signaling for another frosty beverage whenever you happen to bottom o on your previous one. Nice.

Several fine restaurants are on site or just outside the resort, while more dining venues an shopping are just a few steps farther down the beach.

The Kaua'i Resort is located right next door to Kaua'i Lagoons and its 36 holes of golf. Di counts are available for guests of the resort.

G ISLAND HOTELS

OUR SEASONS RESORT HUALALAI
**72-100 Kaupulehu Drive
Kailua-Kona, HI 96740
808-325-8000; 888-340-5662
www.fourseasonsresort.com/
hualalai**

SENTIALS
prawling, ocean-side layout

43 guest rooms in 36 low-rise bungalows

ive restaurants and cafes, plus two bars and lounges

Hualalai Sports Club and Spa, with 25-meter lap pool, climbing wall, cold plunge pool, open-air assage *hales* with waterfalls

ive pools, including an "adults only" pool and whirlpool, sand-bottomed children's pool, and a ltwater snorkeling "aquarium"

Cultural center, lighted tennis courts, business center, banquet facilities, teen activity center, basrtball court, beach volleyball

Access to the "guests only" Hualalai Golf Course

HE SCOOP
or laid-back luxury in one of the world's most beautiful settings, there are few options that can val the Four Seasons Resort Hualalai. Accommodations are the definition of "low-rise," with zens of two-story bungalows spread across the resort, rather than a single concrete mass. The sort is only minutes from the airport and the bustle of Kailua-Kona, but the feeling is more of Robinson Crusoe-style modern beach resort that feels worlds away from everyday life.

Guest rooms are large and plush, with indoor and outdoor showers, as well as a bath. All oms are fitted with wide-screen flat-panel TVs and high speed Internet access, so you're only isolated from the world as you choose to be.

In addition to the grand pool and several smaller pools, the resort boasts a saltwater orkeling "aquarium" that allows guests to have close encounters with some of the native sea e, without the risk of a shark encounter. The highlight is a pair of spotted eagle rays that ll the pool home. There are daily interactive feedings of the rays that I cannot recommend ghly enough.

Dining at the resort is top notch, as you might expect at these rates, and won't disappoint. ome folks insist that Pauhui'a, which is the main dining room, is the finest restaurant on e island. It is certainly fantastic, but in this golfer's opinion, Alan Wong's Hualalai Grill on e top floor of the clubhouse is the spot. The food consistently represents the cutting edge of acific Rim cuisine prepared with a cornucopia of fresh Big Island ingredients. The service is eat and they aren't stingy with the rum in the Mai Tais.

BIG ISLAND HOTELS

HILTON WAIKOLOA VILLAGE
425 Waikoloa Beach Drive
Waikoloa, HI 96738
808-886-1234
www.HiltonWaikoloaVillage.com

ESSENTIALS
-62 oceanfront acres
-1,240 guest rooms and suites
-Nine restaurants, bars, and lounges
-Kohala Sports Club & Spa, with over 25,000 square feet of facilities for specialty massage scrubs and wraps, hydrotherapy treatment, salon, and unique sports enhancement training programs and classes
-Camp Menehune, for kids 5-12, with day and night camps offering activities such as fishing, cultural activities, luaus, and camping
-Two pools with slides, waterfalls, and whirlpools, plus a four-acre saltwater snorkeling lagoon with beach
-Putting course, wedding chapel, dolphin lagoon, banquet facilities, luau, shopping, extensive Asian art collection, business center

THE SCOOP
What may be hotel developer Chris Hemmeter's grandest vision, the Hilton Waikoloa Village is like a Hawaiian Disneyland. This sprawling resort is connected by your choice of tram or a boat, which wends unhurriedly through a mile-long river. Of course, the hotel also features classic Asian art and that Hemmeter look, as well as multiple pools and a snorkeling lagoon.

Of course, what really gets most visitors excited is the dolphin lagoon. Several Atlantic bottle-nosed dolphins (no local spinner dolphins!) call the Hilton home. Visitors can watch the goings on of the dolphin operations all day long as workers train, feed, and care for their intelligent friends. However, the ultimate engagement is an actual DolphinQuest experience with the dolphins, where you can get into the water with them and participate in their day!

Guest rooms at the Hilton are large, freshly renovated, and very comfortable. There are restaurants and food bars in nearly every corner of the resort, so you'll never go hungry. Of particular note, be sure to try Donatoni's, which serves authentic Italian cuisine in a faux Italian villa, and the phenomenal Kirin located directly above it that offers the best high-end Chinese food on the island.

The Hilton Waikoloa Village is located at Waikoloa Resort, adjacent to the Waikoloa Kings' Course and Waikoloa Beach Course, and is also situated for easy access to the other courses along the Kohala Coast.

IG ISLAND HOTELS

SHERATON KEAUHOU BAY RESORT & SPA

78-128 Ehukai Street
Kailua-Kona, HI 96740
808-930-4900; 866-716-8109
www.sheratonkeauhou.com

ESSENTIALS

2 oceanfront acres
521 guest rooms and suites
Four restaurants, bars, and lounges
Meandering pool with water slide, children's beach, and waterfalls
Ho'ola Spa with open-air treatment areas featuring exotic massages, facials, wraps, and treatments; 24-hour fitness center
Luau, wedding chapel, manta ray viewing area, tennis courts, basketball court, beach volleyball, banquet facilities

THE SCOOP

With its prime location on a rocky outcropping at the mouth of Keauhou Bay, the Sheraton Keauhou is the pearl of South Kona. The recently renovated resort features loads of cushy details that visitors will enjoy. The pool complex is extensive and fun, with the main pool and water slide on the ocean side of the hotel, which then spills into the heart of the resort.

Guest rooms are spacious and comfortable with all expected amenities, and rooms on the water have fantastic views. The beds are of the nouveau-comfy variety, and are difficult to part with in the morning.

For this ocean lover, one of the most compelling features of the resort is the lounge, which sits at the foot of the Pacific. At night, bright lights shine into the water to attract huge, graceful manta rays, which come to feed on the plankton attracted by the lights. It's possible to arrange trips to scuba dive or snorkel with the rays (an unforgettable experience), but that doesn't mean that watching them dance, flip, and swirl from the comfort of the lounge (with a cold Mai Tai in hand) isn't exhilarating.

Unlike most other high-end resorts on the Big Island, the Sheraton's location is ideal for dining and shopping in the town of Kailua-Kona. It is also situated right next door to the jumping-off point for most snorkel tours down to Kealakekua Bay and the southern coast. Most importantly, of course, the Sheraton is located adjacent to the two courses of the Kona Country Club.

FOUR SEASONS RESORT LANA'I
MANELE BAY

> 1 Manele Road
> Lana'i City, HI 96763
> 808-565-2000
> www.fourseasons.com/manelebay

ESSENTIALS

-Sprawling, oceanside layout
-236 guest rooms and suites
-Four restaurants (including the clubhouse), a poolside bar and a lounge
-The Spa offers massages and standard spa fare in **11** treatment rooms, plus exotic treatmen
such as ti-leaf wraps, and facilities that include rainforest showers and red cedar saunas
-Surf Shack Teen Center features wide-screen TV, video games, pool table, lounge, and pr
grams ranging from fishing to beach parties
-Beach, pool with two whirlpools, fitness center, tennis, business services

THE SCOOP

Like an image on a travel agency poster, the Four Seasons at Manele Bay is a sun-soaked luxu
resort on the edge of one of Hawaii's most exclusive locales. The hotel is perched on a scen
cliff above the white sandy beach at Manele Bay. The powdery arc of sand just down son
steps from the hotel would be glorious enough, but pods of spinner dolphins frequent the ba
regularly giving sunbathers the opportunity to snorkel and swim with them. You'd think th
would be enough!

Resorty-decadence abounds here, with a lovely pool complete with attentive service sta
to cater to your every need. A beautiful spa provides all the facials and treatments you cou
ever want (try the 19th Hole Golf Massage), and there are enough restaurants to keep your be
happily sated. Don't forget to check out the Hale Ahe Ahe Lounge, which is packed with ente
tainment options from billiards and shuffleboard to live music and specialty cocktails.

Guest rooms are large, well-appointed, and come equipped with flat panel LCD TVs :
you can tune into the Golf Channel at the end of the day. High speed Internet service is ava
able in all the rooms, the lanais are comfy and amply-sized, and the bed will make you wond
why you ever scheduled a 7 a.m. tee time. Even the sometimes lengthy walk to your room is
pleasure, as a network of waterfalls and koi ponds runs through the compound, which is rich
planted in fragrant tropical flowers and trees.

The Four Seasons Manele Bay and the Lodge at Koele are only a 25-minute shuttle rid
away, and many guests choose to hop back and forth for nightly stays, meals, or simply to exp
rience the widely diverse options at each venue.

LANA'I HOTELS

FOUR SEASONS RESORT LANA'I
THE LODGE AT KOELE

1 Keamoku Highway
Lana'i City, HI 96763
808-565-4000
www.fourseasons.com/koele

ESSENTIALS

Two wooded acres, with gardens and trails
104 guest rooms and eight suites
Three restaurants (including the club-
house), three bars and lounges
Massage and spa services available in-room
Fitness center, pool, two whirlpools, croquet, putting course, lawn bowling, business services
Skeet shooting, archery, horseback riding, four-wheel drive expeditions, mountain biking, and
helicopter tours are also available

THE SCOOP

Located in the interior of the island of Lana'i at over 1,600 feet, The Lodge at Koele seems more like a genteel hunting lodge hidden in the English countryside than a tropical-island resort in the middle of the Pacific Ocean, but therein lies its charm. Three grand structures comprise the lodge, and together amount to the largest wood structure in the state. Rich accents are every-where, including in the opulent lobby, the library, and the Trophy Room, where large fireplaces are lit nightly upon guest request and feed the English-manor vibe.

The grounds (yes, grounds) feature landscaped gardens, a pond, creek, huge banyan trees, gorgeous flowering ginger and heliconia, an orchid house, and a pagoda. These are adjacent to a massive lawn bowling green, two croquet courts (American and British), an 18-hole executive putting green, as well as a workout pavilion. To remind you that you are still in Hawaii, there's an understated pool, complete with two whirlpools, and the added decadence of Evian spritzes offered by the staff. Other amenities include archery, sporting clays, riding stables, mountain bik-ing, and hiking. Oh, and golf.

Guests are greeted at the door with fresh-squeezed pineapple juice and a hot towel (a nice offering in the cooler clime), then invited to sit at individual tables for check in with personal valets. After the sometimes harried check-ins at some of the major Hawaiian resorts, this is a welcome luxury. High tea is served in this same area each afternoon, and a beautiful bar, dining room, and dining terrace are just footsteps away.

The Lodge at Koele seamlessly blends a unique location and style with luxury and hospitality. The result is a lovely, peaceful experience that, while contrary to one's expectations for Hawaiian lodging, is an absolute pleasure.

COURSE LISTINGS

MAUI

The Dunes at Maui Lani
Type: Public
Holes: One 18-hole championship course
Kahului, HI
Phone: (808) 873-0422
www.dunesatmauilani.com

Elleair Maui Golf Club
Type: Public
Holes: One 18-hole championship course
Kihei, HI
Phone: (808) 874-0777
www.elleairmauigolfclub.com

Ka'anapali Golf Resort
Type: Resort
Holes: Two 18-hole championship courses
Lahaina, HI
Phone: (808) 661-3691
www.kaanapaligolfresort.com

Kahili Golf Course
Type: Public
Holes: One 18-hole championship course
Wailuku, HI
Phone: (808) 242-4653
www.kahiligolf.com

Kapalua Resort
Type: Resort
Holes: Two 18-hole championship courses
Lahaina, HI
Phone: (877)-KAPALUA
www.kapalua.com

King Kamehameha Golf Club
Type: Private

Holes: One 18-hole championship course
Wailuku, HI
Phone: (808) 243-1018

Makena Golf Courses
Type: Resort
Holes: Two 18-hole championship courses
Makena, HI
Phone: (808) 879-3344
www.makenagolf.com

Maui Country Club
Type: Private
Holes: One 9-hole course
Public play on Mondays
Paia, HI
Phone: (808) 877-0616

Pukalani Country Club
Type: Public
Holes: One 18-hole championship course
Pukalani, HI
Phone: (808) 572-1314
Web: www.pukalanigolf.com

Waiehu Municipal Golf Course
Type: Municipal
Holes: One 18-hole championship course
Wailuku, HI
Tee Times: (808) 270-7400
Pro Shop: (808) 244-5934

Wailea Golf Club
Type: Resort
Holes: Three 18-hole championship courses
Wailea, HI
Gold and Emerald Course
Phone: (808) 875-7450
Blue Course
Phone: (808) 879-2530
www.waileagolf.com

O'AHU

Ala Wai Golf Course
Type: Municipal
Holes: One 18-hole course
Honolulu, HI
Phone: (808) 733-7387

Barbers Point Golf Course
Type: Military
Holes: One 18-hole course
Honolulu, HI
Phone: (808) 682-1911

Bay View Golf Park
Type: Public
Holes: One 18-hole executive course
Kaneohe, HI
Phone: (808) 247-0451

Coral Creek Golf Club
Type: Public
Holes: One 18-hole championship course
Ewa Beach, HI
Phone: (808) 441-4653
www.coralcreekgolfhawaii.com

Ewa Beach Golf Club
Type: Public
Holes: One 18-hole championship course
Ewa Beach, HI
Phone: (808) 689-6565
www.ewabeachgc.com

Ewa Villages Golf Course
Type: Municipal
Holes: One 18-hole championship course
Ewa Beach, HI
Phone: (808) 681-0220

Hawaii Country Club
Type: Public
Holes: One 18-hole course
Wahiawa, HI
Phone: (808) 621-5654
www.hawaiicc.com

Hawaii Kai Golf Course
Type: Public
Holes: One 18-hole championship course and or
Robert Trent Jones, Sr. 18-hole executive course
Honolulu, HI
Phone: (808) 395-2358
www.hawaiikaigolf.com

Hawaii Prince Golf Club
Type: Resort
Holes: 27 holes
Ewa Beach, HI
Phone: (808) 944-4567
www.princeresortshawaii.com

Hickam Golf Course
Type: Military
Holes: One 18-hole golf course, and one 9-hole par-
course
Hickam AFB, HI
Phone: (808) 449-2300

Honolulu Country Club
Type: Private
Holes: One 18-hole course
Honolulu, HI
Phone: (808) 441-9400
www.honolulucountryclub.com

Kahuku Golf Course
Type: Municipal
Holes: One 9-hole course
Kahuku, HI
Phone: (808) 293-5842

Kaneohe Klipper Golf Course
Type: Military
Holes: One 18-hole championship course
Kaneohe, HI
Phone: (808) 254-1745
www.mccshawaii.com/golf.htm

Kapolei Golf Course
Type: Public
Holes: One 18-hole championship course
Kapolei, HI
Phone: (808) 674-2227
www.kapoleigolf.com

Ko'olau Golf Club
Type: Public
Holes: One 18-hole championship course
Kaneohe, HI
Phone: (808) 236-4653
www.koolaugolfclub.com

Ko Olina Golf Club
Type: Resort
Holes: One 18-hole championship course
Kapolei, HI
Phone: (808) 676-5300
www.koolinagolf.com

Luana Hills Country Club
Type: Public
Holes: One 18-hole championship course
Kailua, HI
Phone: (808) 262-2139
www.luanahills.com

Leilehua Golf Course
Type: Military
Holes: One 18-hole course
Schofield Barracks, HI
Phone: (808) 655-4653

Mid-Pacific Country Club
Type: Private
Holes: one 18-hole course
Lanikai, HI
Phone: (808) 262-8161
www.mpcchi.org

Makaha Resort Golf Club
Type: Resort
Holes: One 18-hole championship course
Waianae, HI
Phone: (808) 695-9544
www.makaharesortgolfclub.net

Makaha Valley Country Club
Type: Public
Holes: One 18-hole championship course
Waianae, HI
Phone: (808) 695-9578
www.makahavalleycc.com

Mililani Golf Club
Type: Semi-private
Holes: One 18-hole championship course
Mililani, HI
Phone: (808) 623-2222
www.mililanigolf.com

Moanalua Golf Club
Type: Semi-private
Holes: One 9-hole course
Public play weekends after 1 p.m.
Honolulu, HI
Phone: (808) 839-2311

Navy Marine Golf Course
Type: Military
Holes: One 18-hole course
Honolulu, HI
Phone: (808) 471-0142

Oahu Country Club
Type: Private
Holes: One 18-hole course
Honolulu, HI
Phone: (808) 595-6331
www.oahucountryclub.com

Olomana Golf Links
Type: Public
Holes: One 18-hole championship course
Waimanalo, HI
Phone: (808) 259-7926
www.olomanagolflinks.com

Pali Golf Course
Type: Municipal
Holes: One 18-hole championship course
Kaneohe, HI
Phone: (808) 266-7612

Pearl Country Club
Type: Public
Holes: One 18-hole championship course
Aiea, HI
Phone: (808) 487-3802
www.pearlcc.com

Turtle Bay Resort
Type: Resort
Holes: Two 18-hole championship courses
Kahuku, HI
Phone: (808) 293-8574
www.turtlebayresort.com

Royal Kunia Country Club
Type: Public
Holes: One 18-hole championship course
Waipahu, HI
Phone: (808) 688.9222
www.royalkuniacc.com

Ted Makalena Golf Course
Type: Municipal
Holes: One 18-hole course
Waipahu, HI
Phone: (808) 675-6052

Waialae Country Club
Type: Private
Holes: One 18-hole course
Honolulu, HI
Phone: (808) 734-2151
www.waialaecc.com

Walter J. Nagorski Golf Course
Type: Military
Schofield Barracks, HI
Holes: One 9-hole course
Phone (808) 438-9587

Waikele Golf Club
Type: Public
Holes: One 18-hole championship course
Waipahu, HI
Phone (808) 676-9000
www.golfwaikele.com

West Loch Golf Course
Type: Municipal
Holes: One 18-hole course
Ewa Beach, HI
Phone: (808) 675-6076

KAUAʻI

Kauai Lagoons Golf Club
Type: Resort
Holes: Two 18-hole championship courses
Lihue, HI
Phone: (800) 634-6400
www.kauailagoonsgolf.com

iahuna Golf Club
ype: Public
Ioles: One 18-hole championship course
oipu, HI
hone: (808) 742-9595
ww.kiahunagolf.com

ukuiolono Golf Course
ype: Public
alaheo, HI
Ioles: One 9-hole course
hone: (808) 332-9151

oipu Bay Golf Course
ype: Resort
Ioles: One 18-hole championship course
oloa, HI
hone: (800) 858-6300
ww.poipubaygolf.com

rinceville at Hanalei
ype: Resort
Ioles: One 27-hole course and one 18-championship
ourse
rinceville, HI
Iakai Course Phone: (808) 826-3581
rince Course Phone: (808) 826-5001
ww.princeville.com

uakea Golf Course
ype: Public
Ioles: One 18-hole championship course
hone: (866) 773-5554
ww.puakeagolf.com

Vailua Municipal Golf Course
ype: Municipal
Ioles: One 18-hole championship course
Vailua, HI
hone: (808) 241-6666
ww.kauai.gov/golf

MOLOKA'I

Ironwood Hills Golf Club
Type: Public
Kaulapuu, HI
Holes: One 9-hole course
Phone: (808) 567-6000

Kaluakoi Golf Course
Type: Resort
Holes: One 18-hole championship course
Kepuhi Beach, HI
Phone: (808) 552-0255
www.molokairanch.com
Status: Closed

LANA'I

The Challenge at Manele
Type: Resort
Holes: One 18-hole championship course
Manele, HI
Phone: (808) 565-2222
www.golfonlanai.com

The Experience at Koele
Type: Resort
Lanai City, HI
Holes: One 18-hole championship course
Phone: (808) 565-4653
www.golfonlanai.com

BIG ISLAND

Big Island Country Club
Type: Public
Holes: One 18-hole championship course
Kailua-Kona, HI
Phone: (808) 325-5044

Hamakua Country Club
Type: Public
Holes: One 9-hole course
Honokaa, HI
Phone: (808) 775-7244

Hapuna Golf Course
Type: Resort
Holes: One 18-hole championship course
Kohala Coast, HI
Phone: (808) 880-3000
www.princeresortshawaii.com

The Hualalai Club
Type: Private
Holes: One 18-hole championship course, plus access
to the Hualalai Golf Course at the Four Seasons
Kohala Coast, HI
Phone: (808) 896-9572
www.hualalairesort.com

Hualalai Golf Course
Type: Resort (guests only)
Holes: One 18-hole championship course
Kohala Coast, HI
Phone: (808) 325-8480
www.fourseasons.com/hualalai

The Club at Hokuli'a
Type: Private
Holes: One 18-hole championship course
Kohala Coast, HI
Phone: (866) 250-2582
www.hokulia.com

Hilo Municipal Golf Course
Type: Municipal
Holes: One 18-hole championship course
Hilo, HI
Phone: (808) 959-7711

Kona Country Club
Type: Public
Holes: Two 18-hole championship courses
Keauhou, HI
Phone: (808) 322-2595
www.konagolf.com

Kukio Golf Club
Type: Private
Holes: One 18-hole course and one 10-hole course
Kohala Coast, HI
Phone: (808) 325-4000
www.kukio.com

Makalei Golf Club
Type: Public
Holes: One 18-hole championship course
Kailua-Kona, HI
Phone: (808) 325-6625
www.makalei.com

Mauna Kea Golf Course
Type: Resort
Holes: One 18-hole championship course
Kohala Coast, HI
Phone: (808) 882-5400
www.maunakearesort.com

Mauna Lani Resort
Type: Resort
Holes: Two 18-hole championship courses
Kohala Coast, HI
Phone: (808) 885-6655
www.maunalani.com

Nanea Golf Club
Type: Private
Holes: One 18-hole championship course
Kohala Coast, HI
Phone: (808) 930-1300

aniloa Volcano Golf Club
ype: Public
loles: One 9-hole course
ilo, HI
hone: (808) 935-3000

ea Mountain Golf Course
ype: Resort
loles: One 18-hole championship course
unaluu, HI
hone: (808) 928-6222

olcano Golf and Country Club
ype: Public
loles: One 18-hole championship course
olcano, HI
hone: (808) 967-7331
ww.volcanogolfshop.com

Waikoloa Beach Resort
ype: Resort
loles: Two 18-hole championship courses
ohala Coast, HI
hone: (877) WAIKOLOA
ww.waikoloabeachresort.com

Waikoloa Village Golf Club
ype: Public
loles: One 18-hole championship course
Waikoloa Village, HI
hone: (808) 883-9621

Waimea Country Club
ype: Public
loles: One 18-hole championship course
amuela, HI
hone: (808) 885-8777
ww.waimeagolf.com

ACKNOWLEDGEMENTS

photos by Jen Reeder, with the following exceptions:
oto of the Bay Course at Kapalua, page 22, courtesy of Kapalua Resort. Photo of the Kapalua Golf Academy,
e 50, courtesy of Kapalua Resort. Photo of the Turtle Bay Palmer Course, page 76, courtesy of Turtle Bay Resort.
oto of The Makai Course at Princeville, page 138, courtesy of Princeville at Hanalei Resort. Photo of Hualalai Golf
urse, page 172, courtesy of Four Seasons Resorts. Photo of The Challenge at Manele , page 234, courtesy of Four
sons Resorts. Photo of the Hyatt Regency Maui, page 246, courtesy of Hyatt. Photo of the Grand Wailea Resort
tel and Spa, page 247, courtesy of the Grand Wailea Resort. Photo of the Kapalua Golf Villas, page, 248, courtesy
Kapalua Resort. Photos of the Makaha Resort & Golf Club, page 249, courtesy of Makaha Resort. Photo of Hyatt
aikiki Resort & Spa, page 250, courtesy of Hyatt. Photo of Grand Hyatt Kaua'i Resort & Spa, page 251, courtesy
Hyatt. Photo of Kaua'i Marriott Resort & Beach Club, page 252, courtesy of Marriott. Photo of Four Seasons
sort Hualalai, page 253, courtesy of Four Seasons Resorts. Photo of Hilton Waikoloa Village, page 254, courtesy of
ton. Photo of Sheraton Keauhou Bay Resort & Spa, page 255, courtesy of Sheraton. Photo of Four Seasons Resort
ua'i Manele Bay, page 256, courtesy of Four Seasons Resorts. Photo of Four Seasons Resort Lana'i Lodge at Koele,
ge 257, courtesy of Four Seasons Resorts.

e publisher wishes to thank the following people for their assistance with this project:
nie Els, Robert Trent Jones, Jr., Tadd Fujikawa, Rees Jones, Peter Jacobsen, Mike Kenny, Kevin Bell, Char Burke,
b Boyle, Tala'i Fuga, Fran Cipro, Sutee Nitakorn, Joe Niemeier, Leanne Pletcher, Noa Galdeira, Candy Aluli,
ott Kawasaki, Harmony Wady, Tiffany Benedict, Cindy Lawrence, Revell Newton, Dan O'Connor, Toni Max-
ll, Sanae Gathright, Brad Baptist, Steve Murphy, Peter Yamashita, Kevin Ginoza, Craig Duncan, Jeannie God-
y, Vicky Kometani, Rieko Takahashi, Kirk Nelson, Donna Kimura, Mike Yukon, Scott Head, Susan Bredo,
n Herrick, Jill Hamasaki, Rusty Hathaway, Sutee Nitakorn, Norma Andrade, Nettie Armitage-Lapilio, Scott
dges, Stacy Tamaye, Diann Hartman, Dan Honma, Cindy Lawrence, Ted McAneeley, Norman-Ganin Asao,
rdon Tsujimura, Brad Packer, Jennifer Sylvester, Brad Bowen, Dave Gleason, Yasuo Nishida, Melissa Ludwig, Ed
amoto, Craig Sasada, Ray Kachel, Matt Torry, Paul Ito, Dan O'Connor, Carolyn Comandini, Kenneth Kimura,
mithra Sumithra, Monica Davis, Carey Pickelsimer, Ken Terao, Guy Yamamoto, Robin Chang, Austin Kang,
rah Fust, Keoki Wallace, Lois Parker, Kevin Kashiwie, Mike Jennings, Caroline Witherspoon, Russell Hirata,
rin Sumimoto, Tracy Johnson, Kim Kessler, Mike Castillo, Chris Martello, Ron Kia'aina, Scott Ashworth, Ken-
c Kimizuka, Gary Planos, Arthur Rego, Barry Helle, Derek Claveran, Aileen Yamauchi, Tim Herek, Ken Terao,
ve Kowalczyk, Matthew Hall, Kevin Carll, Todd Stewart, Brendan Moynahan, Duane Otte, Tom Sursely, Dar-
Gee, Ken Yoshitomi, Brian Buechle, Doug Daguaui, Laura Purdy, Karen Saunders, Claude Brousseau, Booklines
waii, Dan Poynter, Pete Masterson, Jess Stephens, Eric Kampmann and the Midpoint team , Christina Jackson
her beautiful cover design, Les and Zora Charles, Colleen Dunn Bates, Lori Fryklund, Marcia Elvidge, Michelle
se. Special thanks to Tom and Sally Reeder.

anks to my playing partners during the research trip: Jim, Rick, Al, Stefan, Gilbert, Jason, Joe, Brendan, Bonnie,
, Crystal, Gary, Debbie, Karen, Rick, Paul, Vicky, Randy, Brian, Kyle, James, Patrick, and Nathan.

anks to my family foursome: George Fryklund, Chris Elvidge, and Tom Rose.

MAKE YOUR CORPORATE OUTING ONE FOR THE BOOKS!

Give customized prints of
The Golf Fanatic's Guide to Hawaii
to your employees!

Hot Tub Publishing offers customized print runs of Fanatic Guide titles to fit your function's needs. Add a corporate logo to the front of the book, and a letter from your CEO on the first page.

Go to www.hottubpublishing.com/customize for more details and a personalized quote.

Give them something special to remember your Aloha State gathering.